Florida A&M University, Tallahassee
Florida Atlantic University, Boca Raton
Florida Gulf Coast University, Ft. Myers
Florida International University, Miami
Florida State University, Tallahassee
University of Central Florida, Orlando
University of Florida, Gainesville
University of North Florida, Jacksonville
University of South Florida, Tampa
University of West Florida, Pensacola

Violence and Modernism

Ibsen, Joyce, and Woolf

William A. Johnsen

University Press of Florida
Gainesville/Tallahassee/Tampa/Boca Raton
Pensacola/Orlando/Miami/Jacksonville/Ft. Myers

08 07 06 05 04 03   6 5 4 3 2 1

Library of Congress Cataloging-in-Publication Data
Johnsen, William A.
Violence and modernism : Ibsen, Joyce, and Woolf / William A. Johnsen
p. cm.
Includes bibliographical references and index.
ISBN 0-8130-2665-2 (acid-free paper)
1. English fiction—20th century—History and criticism. 2. Modernism (Literature)—
Great Britain. 3. Woolf, Virginia, 1882–1941—Criticism and interpretation. 4. Ibsen,
Henrik, 1828–1906—Criticism and interpretation. 5. Joyce, James, 1882–1941—Criticism
and interpretation. 6. Modernism (Literature)—Ireland. 7. Modernism (Literature)—
Norway. 8. Sacrifice in literature. 9. Violence in literature. 10. Girard, René, 1923–.
11. Frye, Northrop, 1912–1991. I. Title.
PR888.M63J64 2003
823'.91209112—dc21   2003056424

The University Press of Florida is the scholarly publishing agency for the State University
System of Florida, comprising Florida A&M University, Florida Atlantic University, Florida
Gulf Coast University, Florida International University, Florida State University, University
of Central Florida, University of Florida, University of North Florida, University of South
Florida, and University of West Florida.

University Press of Florida
15 Northwest 15th Street
Gainesville, FL 32611–2079
http://www.upf.com

Contents

Preface vii

1. Myth, Ritual, and Modern Literature after Girard 1

2. Pillars of a Self-Sacrificial Society 34

3. Folkevenner og Folkefiender: Ibsen's Research
   in Modern Behavior 54

4. Joyce's Sisters 69

5. To Live, Not Die, for His Country: Stephen D(a)edalus
   and Ireland's Future 84

6. Finding the Father: Virginia Woolf, Feminism, and Modernism 108

Conclusion 139

Notes 143

Works Cited 157

Index 165

Preface

The fondest hope for one's writing is that it might need no introduction. The shortest introduction to *Violence and Modernism* would be that it spells out how three of our greatest modern writers corroborate and amplify René Girard's mimetic hypothesis for human behavior and Northrop Frye's conception of *literature as a whole* as they bear on modern life. But our fondest hopes in particular require longer proofs.

The year 1984 provoked millennialike reflections, few of them memorable. Most of the oxygen for Year 2000 was taken up with whether our computers could keep their time, but there is still enough millennial expectation available to welcome reflection on the last century's theories, which were prematurely outmoded by the competition that tinges all modern intellectual work.

It is time to write the history of modernism with a more confident and ambitious sense of finality. Theorists who were dismissed as too ambitious may now regain their provenance. Two of the most influential literary critics of our age were headed for just such a theory of modern literature when they were *sidetracked* by the prodigious opportunities their emerging hypotheses afforded for reading the Bible: Northrop Frye and René Girard. The most sustained work of Frye's last years was *The Great Code* (1982) and *Words with Power* (1990), and Girard's latest and perhaps definitive formulation of his mimetic hypothesis appears in *Je vois Satan tomber comme l'éclair* (1999) and *Celui par qui le scandale arrive* (2001), two books devoted to biblical inspiration.[1]

Central to both Frye's and Girard's work is the nearly constant but understated belief in a correspondence between secular and sacred writing, and following from this correspondence, a sense of a remarkable line of development or tradition in Western writing from its beginnings to the present, completing itself in the modern. Yet at an important moment in each of their careers, the consequences of this convergence becomes so prodigious that they change directions, away from a full theory of modern writing.

The Secular Scripture (1976) clarified Frye's understated position that secular and religious writing ran a parallel course, making explicit what had been present in his work since his groundbreaking book on Blake, Fearful Symmetry (1947). But Frye turned to the Bible directly, instead of using this remarkable supposition of parallel scriptures to redefine his theory of archetypes, and to redefine his central concept of literature as a whole and its history. He was never to rewrite Anatomy of Criticism (1957) from his new perspective.

Girard as well, in La violence et la sacré (1972) suggested that prophetic writing joined key Western texts written under cultural crisis in a common tradition of Judeo-Christian writing. Further, Girard suggested our history is a growing revelation of violence as of human, not divine, origin, leading us to a uniquely modern apocalypse: to choose a peace absolutely without violence or a violence without end.[2]

Although Girard has commented frequently on modern culture throughout his work, his next book after La violence, Des choses cachées depuis la fondation du monde (1978), inaugurated his primary interest in reading Christian theology and the Bible by means of the mimetic hypothesis. Je vois Satan tomber comme l'éclair (1999) and Celui par qui le scandale arrive (2001) formally rewrite the mimetic hypothesis, handing over copyright to scriptural authority. Although he speaks of modern culture frequently, including topics as disparate and compelling as anorexia and terrorism, in essays and interviews, he has not yet committed a book to rearticulate from his new perspective the secular insights of Deceit, Desire, and the Novel (1965) into early modern writing.

The work of Frye and Girard is exemplary in rigor, comprehensiveness, and unmodish clarity. Each writer has been able to absorb competing hypotheses into his own, and willing to be reductive in the name of a scientific rigor appropriate to the social sciences. For anyone who would follow out their ideas into the modern, there are two requirements to control quality and pertinence. First, of course, we must not attempt any facile correcting of their work that would cut us off from its power of synthesis. A theory of the modern which can profit from Frye and Girard must be developed out of work they left visible but undeveloped, and it must also be reconcilable with the rest of their work, amenable to their larger hypotheses. Secondly, it must include the emerging interest in secular literature as part of a tradition of Judeo-Christian writing which took them past a theory of the modern.

What unites Frye and Girard is their common and superior theorization of what others have seen as a "return" of myth in modern times. It is important to distinguish their ideas from the usual literary journalism which talks of a psychological or cultural neoprimitivism. Frye deliberately minimized his investment in psychological archetypes, and was always careful to keep the relation of the primitive to the modern schematic, saying that myth, classical and/or Christian, was the logical (not necessarily chronological) origin of literature. Girard argued that the "things hidden since the foundation of the world" were now revealed in modern times, yet fundamentally separated the primitive from the modern by his idea that the judicial system has replaced sacrificial religion as the final arbiter of violence and peace.

The efficiency of Girard's model is that he has *explained* at once both the similarities and differences among primitive cultures without recourse to some kind of collective unconscious or alternatively some impossible itinerary of tribal migration. According to Girard, the only historically successful solution to all the trouble that human violence causes humans has been to (collectively) blame it on someone else: the scapegoat. Communal rituals throughout the world resemble each other because they all derive from this scapegoat mechanism. The explanation for the contradictory symbolism of the sacred victim (at once holy and profane) resides in his dual and seemingly paradoxical responsibility for everything that goes wrong in human society, but also everything that goes right, once he is sacrificed. Rituals differ around the world because societies eventually "rationalize" the paradoxical quality of their central figure; some towards emphasizing his culpability at the expense of his value; some emphasize his value at the expense of his guilt. (Girard boldly derives the kingship system from the positive rationalization of the scapegoat.)

Girard makes a distinction between primitive and modern culture by the way each culture controls violence. The judicial system has replaced the primitive sacred (represented by taboo and ritual) by taking retributive violence into its own hands. Justice has the last word of violence, punishing transgression of law with such force that no reply, no outbreak of renewed violence is possible.

That the secular and sacred scripture converged for Frye and Girard was clearly a profound emotional and intellectual experience for them;

but, by itself, this sense of convergence is not remarkable. European writers have hardly written about anything else.

Although it would take a different kind of book to follow it out, this particularly modern sense of convergence is postanthropological: field reports as well as works of synthesis gave late-nineteenth- and early-twentieth-century writers the tantalizing parallels among primitive world cultures served up in the midst of their own. If Sir James Frazer was confident that modern society had outgrown scapegoats, outgrown this childish behavior of transferring guilt onto the backs of others as easily as giving over your luggage to the railway porter, modern writers were more interested in the essential continuity of the intertwined traditions of violence and peace delineated in myth and ritual.

We may underline their interest in these parallels between ancient myth and modern behavior by posing provocative questions which we will answer in due time. Why does Ibsen stage social crisis in the immemorial form of enemy twins fighting to refound the community? Why does Joyce make his hero Stephen Dedalus follow the steps of the Passion? Who does he think he is?

Like René Girard, modern writers are fascinated by primitive myth and ritual. Like Girard and Frye, Henrik Ibsen, James Joyce, and Virginia Woolf (to name only the writers discussed in this book)[3] became anthropologists early in their writing careers because they were struck by the recurring (even banal) patterns of primitive human conflict recognizable in modern culture. In the same way that Girard avoids positing a collective unconscious or tribal migration to account for similarities in ritual and taboo across human culture, both primitive and modern, we must avoid tying the similarities among these writers to the influence of a single preexisting anthropological theory or text.[4] The work of Ibsen, Joyce, and Woolf resembles each other because they are provoked by locally recurring signs of a sacrificial crisis, an outbreak of mimetic violence that cannot be resolved by blaming it on someone else.

In the modern period, we see the genetic mechanism for the origin of primitive ritual elaborated by Girard, starting itself up in all the places where the judicial system is inoperative or ineffective, where it doesn't "apply": private, domestic, or social interactions short of illegal behavior, and global relations where no transcendent judicial system has the last word (the empty place being kept warm by the United Nations). The generative mechanism can no longer deliver peace through a completed polarization on a single victim because it runs into or triggers the judicial system or, more alarmingly, it stalls in crisis, in the middle, because the scapegoat mechanism is so well understood in the modern period that we recognize what Girard calls the "stereotypes" of persecution, and side with the victim.

Until the modern period, the judicial mechanism (for the most part) kept us from seeing those it punishes as victims (that is, taking their side), and kept us from forcing others to be our scapegoats. But in the modern, things fall apart. The period identity of the modern is its passionate attention to victims. We will spend some of our time looking more carefully at this modern passion for victims. Although Girard has said repeatedly that what redeems our age is the unique and revolutionary idea that victims have rights, this peculiarly modern interest in victims is not inexorably moral. Often an intellectual curiosity discovers that the most revelatory sign of any social system in crisis is its victims. Apart from a positive ethics and a perhaps neutral intellectual concern, this preoccupation with victims can also degrade into the perverse belief that the status of victim itself guarantees superiority of being in comparison with those it accuses of persecution. Thus modern writers consider not only the remarkable reemergence of sacrifice as the focus of a community, but the curious willingness of its victims to embrace self-sacrifice.

The problem has always been violence, and the more or less covert and unstable mechanisms of collective violence to halt violence. These writers come to understand the sole way to peace in the modern period of limitless destructive power: a unilateral and certainly dangerous refusal to do violence, an awareness that earns the designation "millennial" not by the numbers but by its comprehensive understanding of the crisis of the modern: make peace or die. *Violence and Modernism: Ibsen, Joyce, and Woolf* has designs on several major areas: literary history as a whole, research and scholarship on canonical modern writers, theory, and the intersection of religious and cultural traditions. More precisely, my book contributes to the periodization of the modern, to the clarifying of the specific theoretical labor of three individual modern authors essential to any theory of modern literature, to the reforming of the customs of recent critical theory, which use these authors to corroborate, but never improve, what theory already knows. Finally, I want to contribute to the emerging research field shared by literary studies, anthropology, religious studies, and psychology.

My argument, briefly, is that discussions of modern literature have rarely been as self-critical as modern writers themselves about the dubious value of modernization itself assumed in the standard explanations of literary modernism; the more usual critical procedure is to identify an already established modernism as outmoded, in favor of some newer, rival modernism (or postmodernism).

The canonical writers who serve as examples of the modern, however, seem to have precisely the self-consciousness of the mimetic complicity between successive literary movements, and between literary and social modernization necessary to redefine modernism as a positive tradition with a positive understanding of the role of imitative conflict and violence in human behavior. These moderns serve as a countertradition to Western culture's sacrificial compulsion to "modernize," that is, confer value on whatever can *force* the past to pass for obsolete. These writers are the necessary fellow-theorists to accompany Frye's and Girard's remarkable suppositions of a tradition of Judeo-Christian writing: its development, and its goal of a peaceful society achieved by peaceful means.

From its beginnings in a reading of nineteenth-century European fiction, Girard developed his insights into mimetic behavior into a general theory of sacrifice and religion, and the origin of all social forms in rituals of violent unanimity. My first chapter offers a Girardian "mimeticization" of Frye's central concepts of identification, myth, and mode which underwrote Frye's global theory of literary history (the global theory which contains his implied theory of modern literature). This leads to a rewriting of the relation of modern literature to literature as a whole, and enables me to coordinate Frye's most powerful ideas about literature as a whole with Girard's "mimetic hypothesis," the shorthand term Girard uses to connect his early work on triangular or mimetic desire in modern society, to his later work on the origin of all cultural forms in scapegoat rituals. If Frye and Girard are right about modern culture, what ought modern literature to look like, if modern writers are taken as their fellow theorists?

I use Shakespeare's *King Lear* (as a self-consciously early modern play), from the period we have learned to call early modernism, and Orwell's *Nineteen Eighty-Four* as a *terminally* postmodern novel, to set the margins of the discussion of negative and positive reciprocity, peace and violence in the modern period. Shakespeare's characters are pre-Christian; they come before the revelation of violent origins. They cannot know what they do, and can only figuratively anticipate modern knowledge. Orwell's Oceania knows exactly what it is doing as it hijacks the

knowledge which Girard calls *"le souci des victimes"*: as I will show, it
"hypocritically" organizes resentment and hatred to unify the community in opposition, as it vaporizes any critical idiom which could include
any such revelatory terms as persecution and racism to thwart violent
unanimity.

This first chapter installs the principle of verifying ambitious theory
with close reading. More elaborate readings in subsequent chapters show
Henrik Ibsen, James Joyce, and Virginia Woolf preparing, each in their
own language and their own context, the redefinition of the modern away
from mimetic rivalry and violence, towards a tradition of peaceful identity
and reciprocity.

Ibsen's modernism is generally understood to have begun with his series of prose plays. I establish my reading of Ibsen's first prose play on the
small word *skyld*, which has developed, roughly, like *sake* in English: from
a specific legal connotation of strict accountability for wrongdoing, in the
medieval period, to a generalized, domesticated near-invisibility in modern idiom. Ibsen works the consequences of this word to illuminate the
contradictions of modern society. I argue that, beginning with *Pillars of
Society*, the characters in Ibsen's prose plays collectively demonstrate the
futility and hypocrisy of modern communal sacrifice (usually arranged
through and staged in the media), especially self-sacrifice, for the *sake* of
others.

In my next chapter I take up *Enemy of the People*, which pursues re-
lentlessly the consequences of the earlier play, especially Ibsen's interest
in modern crowd dynamics "mobilized" by the media. Ibsen represents
the turbulence of modern society by showing how a friend of the people
becomes "overnight" the enemy of the people, and how the process of
exalting and denigrating leaders in the modern period has become interminable and seemingly unresolvable.

Two chapters on James Joyce allow me to make more explicit a specific
cultural context of communal sacrifice and self-sacrifice, history, and
modernization. I revise current readings of Joyce by suggesting that he
discovered the nation he called "the most Catholic country in Europe" had
misappropriated the Passion as primitive ritual (instead of seeing the Passion as a critique of primitive ritual) by sacrificing itself through its leaders, by demanding that its citizens eat their own. Parnell's downfall is
Joyce's lifelong example of this Irish practice of scapegoating. Joyce's work
joins Frye and Girard in dis-covering the scapegoat mechanism, and in

proposing a postsacrificial version of the modern leader, in the figure of Stephen Dedalus, who refuses self-sacrifice for the sake of his community, choosing rather to live, not die, for his country.

My chapter on Virginia Woolf redefines feminism-as-modernism. Woolf began her work by extending and refining the feminist analysis of a patriarchal culture that made a consciousness like hers seem impossible, but she began as well to consider the incredible fact of her existence as irrefutable proof that she was possible (if barely allowable). Her remarkable and unique project became to research those hidden elements in a culture clearly patriarchal which "fathered" her as well as mothered her, and how these elements might be redefined and reallocated in a post-patriarchal/matriarchal tradition released from endless mutual recriminations across genders.

Ibsen, Joyce, and Woolf combine the exhilarating ambitiousness of their analytical power with the only note of peace now possible in a world divested of the violent mechanisms of achieving reconciliation at someone else's expense. This is the modest modern note of peaceful urgency caught so well in these exemplary moderns, in Frye, and at the end of Girard's *The Scapegoat:* "The time has come for us to forgive one another. If we wait any longer there will not be time enough" (212).

I would like to thank the American Council of Learned Societies and the National Endowment of the Humanities for travel grants to visit research collections in London and Dublin; the College of Arts and Letters, International Studies and Programs, and the Center for European Studies at Michigan State University for travel money to present early versions of this work in Paris, Antwerp, and Bergen; and the MSU English Department, for sabbatical leaves and other support, including travel, during the tenures of Victor Paananen, Philip McGuire, and Patrick O'Donnell.

I appreciate the permission given by the University of Illinois Press, Rodopi, and *Contagion* (the journal of the Colloquium on Violence and Religion—COV&R) to reprint from articles I have expanded for this book. As editors, Professors Joseph Natoli, Mary Power, and Andrew McKenna gave sympathetic readings and useful advice. Countless scholars like me who read René Girard have benefited from Andrew's advice and support.

The two readers of the manuscript for the University Press of Florida gave acute and helpful advice for improving the manuscript. Amy Gorelick has been an energetic and supportive editor throughout. Project editor Jacqueline Kinghorn Brown has been wonderfully efficient and helpful, and Eivind Allan Boe did a remarkable job of copyediting.

To my fellow Joyceans Bill McCormack, Alistair Stead and Tim Webb I am grateful for transatlantic amity and encouragement begun at Leeds University long ago.

Since 1995 the COV&R has organized my intellectual life. The continuing presence and contribution of René Girard and Raymund Schwager at the annual conferences inspires us. Whenever I write now I look forward to what this group will say: Sandy Goodhart (a friend since I began reading Girard), Wolfgang Palaver, and many others.

I want to thank two friends and colleagues at Michigan State University for introducing me to Girard and his work long ago: professors Michael Koppisch and A. C. Goodson. It is a pleasure also to thank Professor Girard himself for many kindnesses. In gratitude for his work I have written this book.

My daughters have waited for this book for a long time. I am grateful for Amanda, who never gave up asking (bless her); for Alyssa, who has kept her counsel.

To Lenna and Arnold, my children here at home, thank you. For their mother, who is my wife and companion, and my love, I give thanks.

1

Myth, Ritual, and
Modern Literature after Girard

The nineteenth-century dream that the comparative method would yield a global or total hypothesis to every research field, so spectacularly successful in natural science, economics, and linguistics, has remained for modern literary intellectuals tauntingly unfulfilled, backing up into provocative but unstable analogies derived from comparative structural analyses of myth, ritual, and literature. The chronological derivation of myth from ritual, or ritual from myth, and literature from both, in the early part of the twentieth century, especially by the Cambridge Ritualists (Frazer, Harrison, Murray, Cornford),[1] and in Freud's anthropological speculations, was prudently reduced to a merely *logical* derivation by the 1950s.

Who were the important midcentury figures in this prudent reduction? Lévi-Strauss chose synchronic linguistics, which had put aside the question of language's origin as unanswerable, as the model for structural anthropology.[2] The early fruits of this strategic retreat into structural linguistics, where language is a system of pure differences with no positive terms, where language's referential power is the wrong subject to pursue, was his groundbreaking work on elementary kinship structures.[3] By the sixties Lévi-Strauss could close the door on the ambitious attempts of previous anthropologists (and any future ones) to explain what the recurrence of totemism itself as a symbolic practice signified across primitive cultures.[4] Totems are merely signs in the local language of pure and empty differences, making distinctions between clans, not their individual characters or identities.

The intriguing parallels between the early stages of childhood and the early stages of primitive culture were merely schematized in favor of any strong genetic explanation of origins. Erich Neumann borrowed "sequence-dating" (ordering the stages of development where dating any of them is impossible) from the archaeologist Flinders Petrie to rule anachronism out of depth psychology's parallel development of individual and cultural consciousness.[5]

Universally recurring archetypes became, for Northrop Frye, the metahistorical building blocks for literature as a whole. What remained as the transcultural authority (in Frye as well as other system-makers) for these universally recurring archetypes, sequences, and structures was solely an appeal to a universally recurring mental structure. Edward Said's oppositional term for structuralism (in his review of Lévi-Strauss's *The Savage Mind*) was the "totalitarianism of mind."[6] Homologies followed from the common structuring principles of the human imagination of every time and place. But structure, as the key to all explanation, could not itself be further explained.

René Girard consciously positioned himself to follow through on the consequences of this research tradition of comparison aborted by structuralism. Beginning in the domain of myth, ritual, and literature, Girard intends nothing less than making good on the dream of a hypothesis that ultimately accounts for the generation of all cultural forms. One future for the systematic study of literature made possible by Girard becomes the comprehending of the relation of the modern to myth, ritual, and literature as a whole. In particular, Girard relieves us from the foolish idea of the neoprimitive modern as some atavistic return to origins.

This chapter will go "after Girard" in two related ways: "according to" his hypothesis, as well as estimating what "follows" from its explanatory power, especially for theorizing the relation between modernism and violence. I leave the contentious sense of "getting after" Girard to those captured by the contemporary myth that being critical in the human sciences means discarding without further consideration any hypothesis that claims by comparison to be superior to other hypotheses.

Girard's earliest work compared novels sharing the grand historical moment of comparison which culminated at the end of the nineteenth century. In Girard's brilliant reading, Cervantes, Stendahl, Dostoievski, and Proust proposed and confirmed a common model for human desire as mediated by the desires of others. Readers of French writing are now more likely to be ignorant of than obsessed by Jean Paul Sartre's promotion of the self's singularity and autonomy which became the signature of French and European intellectual culture after the war; Girard's insistence on recognizing all the ways in which the practices of desire, especially in advanced societies, give the lie to the sole self's autonomy, won back the opportunity to comprehend apparently obsessive or absurd human behavior as extensions of ordinary behavior. Girard, of course, has allowed for the existence of unmediated desire throughout his writing. Anyone certain that they have disproved the mimetic hypothesis by conjuring up an example of pure desire should be sent to their room.

Mensonge romantique et vérité romanesque (1961), translated as *Deceit, Desire, and the Novel* (1965),[7] is founded on the kind of historical threshold that is everywhere in Girard's work. Man once acknowledged his own incompleteness in deferring to the superior beings of the gods, kings, or nobility. Imitation was to properly follow their example, with no thought of equality. When the Enlightenment rationalized divinity for man's sake, there was no further excusing any deficiency of human autonomy.

Yet fictional texts show this promise of autonomy unfulfilled, to each alone; to mask this private shame, all pretend to possess the sufficiency each lacks. Each must copy the apparent originality of others, without giving himself away as a rank imitator. Such imitation among "equals" can only lead to rivalry, with the disciple reaching for whatever object the model has indicated as desirable, as the apparent source of the model's autonomy.

In early stages, the model can deny any coquetry, and the disciple can deny any rivalry; but in later stages of "deviated transcendency" the disciple will no longer find divinity (the promise of pure autonomy) in objects themselves, but only in those models who reject him. Modern desire is metaphysical, a fight over increasingly elusive and intangible goals. In Girard's thinking, sadism and narcissism are not autonomous instincts but related strategies of desire comprehensible as intensifications of "ordinary" desire (mimetic desire). Sadism and masochism become the decisively modern masks of autonomy, the expression of being desired while wanting (lacking) nothing, rejecting all.

Such a profound revolution in the way desire is understood could not but evolve as well into a theory of consciousness and the unconscious, instincts and their repression. Furthermore, the mimetic hypothesis led Girard to propose a radical revision, within the human sciences, of theories of prohibition, then ritual, then myth, and finally culture itself, the very process of hominization. If desire depends on a model for instruction, then the repression and prohibiting of desires cannot be understood as the restraining of instinctual drives, or the tabooing of instinctually indicated desirables.

If desire is imitative, then prohibition and taboo must be a restraint of imitation itself—in particular, restraining the mimesis of appropriation, but more generally, of all intersubjectivity. Religious ritual can no longer be (for believers and skeptics alike) the merely "symbolic" or imaginary exorcising of spiritual or instinctual agencies, a primitive form of metaphoric inoculation against real micro- and macrobic invasion. Instead, religious ritual is revealed as an effective if misunderstood rerouting of imitation away from potentially catastrophic behavior.

Girard's method has been appropriately comparative, appropriately initiated in nineteenth-century material, but distinctive in the seriousness that he allows literary as intellectual (ultimately, scientific) labor. Girard first developed this mimetic hypothesis on the authority of his comparative study of nineteenth-century European fiction, which proposes two rival traditions for the novel: the *romantic*, which reflects, without comprehending, the mediation of desire, and the *romanesque* (novelistic), which reveals it. The earlier romantic work of Stendhal, Proust, and Dostoievski discovers, first in others, finally in itself, the pretensions of romantic (autonomous) desire. This recognition enables a final, novelistic stage in these writers, singularly as well as collectively, which reveals the truth of desire.

How does Girard's next book, *La violence et le sacré* (1972; *Violence and the Sacred*, 1977),[8] make good on the scientific potential of his comparative analysis which centers on the novelistic tradition? The truth of the *romanesque* or novelistic tradition is that mediated desire among equals (internal mediation) produces the near-certain outcome of rivalry and conflict. Conflict gives Girard the strong constant needed for an effective comparison across cultures. Girard proposes *violence* as an intra- and transcultural constant that makes possible a comparative study of all cultural forms. Nothing more closely resembles a violent person than another one, from within or without the culture, and nothing better consolidates this resemblance than their mutual conflict. But if we learn, following Girard, to associate violence with the erasing of differences, what do we do with our modern enlightened presupposition that differences, not similarities, breed conflict?

Girard brilliantly turned this presupposition of peaceful equality back on itself to ask, in effect: What powerful modern institution could cultivate a presupposition so different from the primitive horror of the Same? The discrepancy between primitive and modern ideas about difference leads to a significant distinction between primitive and modern culture, based on their ratios of preventive to curative procedures for expelling violence from the community.

After some extremely suggestive paragraphs on the superior efficacy of the modern judicial system for incarnating divine vengeance, before which all are equal, Girard turned to the primitive world of preventive procedures. These suggestions, and other comments scattered throughout *Violence and the Sacred*, so pregnant with possibility for theorizing the modern, have remained somewhat essayistic in form, delayed, perhaps permanently, in deference to Girard's work on the Bible and Shakespeare. The return to modern myth and ritual has occurred mostly in the margins of something else, especially his readings of Freud.[9]

Our itinerary here will be to summarize Girard's hypothesis for cultural mimesis, as the key to primitive myth and ritual, and which also comprehends and consolidates the work of other major modern theorists. Next, we will observe his unique sense of the role of literature (especially novelistic fiction, Greek and Elizabethan drama, and the tradition he names *l'écriture judéo-chrétienne*) for *deconstructing* myth and ritual. As we proceed, we will relate Girard's theory to his midcentury contemporaries, especially Claude Lévi-Strauss, Walter Burkert, Jean-Pierre Vernant, and Northrop Frye.[10] Finally, we will begin developing the potential future of Girard's theory ("after Girard") for the myths and rituals of modern culture, especially in coordination with the most prominent and effective critical work of the end of the century: Edward Said's critique of the cultural myths and rituals of imperialism.

If violence travels so well, what keeps it from spreading like a contagion, enveloping and breaking down a whole community? Sometimes nothing works (any longer), as in the case of the Kaingang tribe in Brazil; their transplantation, which has deprived them of their hereditary enemy (everyone else), has left them to an internal blood feuding certain to wipe them out in a generation. Put another way, a community's survival, or even the very process of hominization itself, is sustainable only in the presence of some working solution to the contagion of spontaneous violence. All societies that have survived, or that have survived long enough to have left some historical record or trace, must have had some answer of varying effectiveness to the problem of breakaway violence.

If violence is a constant, what permissible variables effectively contain it? Prohibition and ritual. If one reverses the proliferation of modern theories of psychic complexes, agencies, and archetypes or atavistic returns (which resemble all too closely the primitive myths of the gods as sufficient cause) in favor of Girard's mimetic hypothesis, prohibition and ritual can be seen as the restraint of imitation itself. In particular, appropriation is the malignant form of mimesis which ritual and prohibition restrain: father, then son, reaching for the same object made irresistible by the indication of each other's rivalry. With that intellectual rigor and thoroughness that Lévi-Strauss taught us to admire, primitive prohibition also taboos all other indications of doubling as signs of incipient violence: mirrors, representations, twins.

If Girard is a more economical psychologist than Freud, he is a more down-to-earth anthropologist than Lévi-Strauss. Primitive rituals do not put twins to death as organizational crises, scandalous signs of two misfits vying for the structural position reserved for one. The reasoning that adults use for putting children to death is surely abominably mistaken, but hardly trivial or "philosophical." For Girard, primitives are not to be finally understood as protostructuralist intellectuals; behind the issues of structuralism there is always the more crucial issue of a social order threatened by, yet generated from, violence misunderstood as a divinity.[11]

If taboos prohibit imitation in order to foreclose violent rivalry, ritual legislates the effects of imitation. Ritual functions by imitating the progress of spontaneous violence. Because it is easy to imitate, violence spreads easily, uninterrupted until it has exhausted itself with the peace that follows the satisfaction of violence. In spontaneous violence, each is the other's enemy; as it ends, one is the enemy of all, everyone coming down on the last antagonist. Ritual mimics spontaneous violence in order to reach its grand finale of all united against (the last) one.

Ritual legislates this process of substitution: the ritual victim substitutes for each one's enemy. Because violence erases differences, one can stand as the enemy of all, their monstrous double. The double valence of the *pharmakos*, defiled as monstrous yet holy in his office, is *sacer*, sacred. Girard's mimetic hypothesis consolidates and comprehends those mid-century discussions of symbolic action that prematurely terminate themselves in the circular answers of ambivalence, human duplexity, and undecidability as the last word of human behavior and motivation.

Freud saw the father, as Hubert and Mauss saw ritual, as at once a potent source and unexplainable explanation of contradictory commands: "I am your progenitor; I am your enemy." Girard analyzes the Freudian father within the context of Freud's theoretical attempt to reconcile a mimetic with an instinctual model of desire (*Violence and the Sacred*, ch. 7). In the chapter of *Massenpsychologie und Ich-Analyse* (1921) on identification, Freud identified the father as the child's primary model, whose place he would take everywhere ("an allen seinen Stellen treten").[12] In the child's mental life, according to Freud, identification with the father (mimetic) and a cathexis towards the mother (instinctual) develop side by side, until he sees the father in his way towards the mother. His way blocked to the object by his father, who had helped to identify it as desirable, his identification now ("jetzt") takes on a hostile coloring: the son would take that place ("zu ersetzen") as well ("auch").

Girard brilliantly queries the offhandedness of Freud's *auch*: Does this mean that the child warily observed, up until now, the incest taboo meant to prohibit conflict? How can we account for the special category of the mother in the child's mental life, among the "everywheres" of the father, otherwise sufficiently comprehensible through the father's mimetic mediation of the son's mimetic desire?

Girard follows Freud's discussion of the Oedipus complex to *Das Ich und das Es* (1923), where a primary desire for the mother, originating in the son, now preempts the "nebeneinander" development of the father's mediation. Girard shows us that Freud has chosen an instinctual theory of desire over a mimetic theory. Furthermore, because the father no longer prepares the way he will later block, he (and/or patriarchal culture in general) is absolved of any responsibility for scandalously drawing the unsuspecting child into rivalry. He is absolved as well of responsibility for his own "ambivalence"; the instincts now serve the god-function, determining the fate of every modern Oedipus.

A coordination of feminist theory with Girard must begin here (we will take it up more fully with Virginia Woolf in chapter 6), by considering Freud's profoundly influential decision to blame the instincts (that is, the body, nature itself) for the regrettable ambivalence of the father for the child, and by considering how blaming the instincts in a patriarchy is the same as blaming women.[13] Such a beginning in a critique of Freudian myth could follow out Girard's provocative (but essayistic) suggestion for primitive culture, that the negative symbolization in myth and ritual of menstrual blood responds to "some half-repressed desire to place the blame for all forms of violence on women" (*Violence and the Sacred*, 36).[14]

To sketch out this future coordination of feminism and Girard's theory which we will draw up more fully with Woolf, let us follow Girard's reading over Freud's shoulder, to pay yet closer attention to Freud's development of his theory. In the *Massenpsychologie*, father-identification is at first a healthy, competitive, intimate, active sparring that prepares the son to assume in due time his manly prerogatives symbolized in the father ("Dies Verhalten hat nichts mit einer passiven oder femininum Einstellung zum Vater [und zum Manne überhaupt] zu tun, es ist viehlmehr exquisit männlich"). Once the father is seen as blocking the path to the mother, however—or once the mother refuses the "advances" of the son in the name of the prerogatives of (presumably) some absent adult male, who may or may not even exist—then father-identification becomes identical with the wish ("wird identisch mit dem Wunsch") to "take" ("zu ersetzen"), not to assume or inherit eventually, the father's place. We see that the language of father-identification now clearly voices violent rivalry, the son wishing to contest the Father-in-the-way, head-on, for the *same* place.

In the chapter of *Das Ich und das Es* on the "Über-Ich," Freud refers to his earlier discussion in *Massenpsychologie*. Although he repeats the phrase about father-identification taking on a hostile coloring, he no longer finds it identical to a previous father-identification *now* recklessly (that is, threateningly) exercised in a forbidden place. Rather, the intensification of sexual desire for the mother *precedes* the recognition of the father as an obstacle ("ein Hindernis," 37). Father-identification changes into a violent rivalry that had not before existed, "a wish to get rid of his father in order to take his place with his mother" ("wendet sich zum Wunsch, den Vater zu beseitigen, um ihn bei der Mutter zu ersetzen"). The universal logic behind the universally occurring prohibition of incest consequently identifies women *of every human society* as the source of violence to be legislated, isolated. Like violence, they are sacred (*Violence and the Sacred*, 219–20).

When we trace the customary history of the development of sacrificial substitution, given its most popular form by Robert Graves,[15] back toward its origins (totemic animal substitutes for *pharmakos*, who substitutes for *tyrannos*, who was once sacrificed for the queen), we must think past the premature termination of this sequence of substitutions in the cultic figure of the *magna mater* so dear to the romanticism of early-twentieth-century psychology, anthropology, and feminism. The sacred ambivalence of the Great Mother, definitively mapped as a structural principle of the collective unconscious in Neumann's work,[16] perhaps derives, like the king's, from a prior role as a sacrificial victim. Perhaps these cultic female figures even mean that women were the earliest sacrificial victims.

At this point we must bring ourselves back from the subtle but interminable deconstruction of other theories which, as Edward Said suggests,[17] easily confuses the power to critique cultural mythology with the ability to contest its influence with an alternative. Girard is no mere deconstructionist, leading us to the futility of all thought. Far from it. Girard is reading Freudian theory to recover the mimetic hypothesis which Freud discarded in favor of a theory of instincts, in order to place violent rivalry back within the domain of cultural, not natural, propagation, within the domain of pedagogy, not instinct, and for social reciprocity, not for repression.

How, then, does Girard's mimetic reading of father-identification differ from Freud's? First, the child who follows the familial and cultural indications of the father as a proper model is the last to learn that imitation is rivalry and that father-identification is appropriative, patricidal. Forbidden "this" place (the mother), the child can only assume that the father's ambivalence, his mercurial change of attitude from inviting the son's imitation, is a rejection justified by his son's failure; and the child can only conclude that such failure has been measured before an especially desirable object. Violence will thereafter indicate the desirable, an obstacle ("ein Hindernis") will indicate the surest sign of a new opportunity to retrieve the full being denied him previously. Subsequent identifications will take on the coloring of the ambivalent father-identification.

The consequences of such a reading have opened up a future for the practice of psychoanalysis apart from its own myths and rituals, and the possibility of situating psychoanalytic practice in a diachronic plan.[18] By recognizing the compelling yet also arbitrary nature of the distinction which society enforces between those places where imitation is required on the one hand or prohibited on the other, treatment can avoid the parallel fetishism of adjustment and perversion. It can comprehend at once the *function* of prohibition, and also the perspicacity of those unfortunate patients (*analysands*) who cannot blind themselves to its arbitrary nature (*Violence and the Sacred*, 172).

The ambivalence of the father as the primary model and obstacle who influences all subsequent identifications can only occur, Girard insists, in a patriarchal culture where the father's role is weakened but not yet effaced (*Violence and the Sacred*, 188). Freud tried to generate the incest taboo historically by arguing, in *Totem and Taboo*, that, because in Darwin's horde the king is father of all, it is by his "sons" that he is killed in sexual jealousy over "his" women. In remorse for this killing, or in "delayed obedience," the men prohibit themselves incest and commit themselves to exogamy. It is hard not to see this psychodrama of jealousy and remorse as fanciful. It is impossible to believe that this single patricide influenced every culture.

Girard's mimeticization of Freud's psychology depaternalizes it, and the mimeticization of Freud's anthropology depaternalizes it as well. Prohibition prevents rivalry: for the single murder of a single father, somewhere on the planet, Girard substitutes rite as the mimesis of spontaneous violence (which can happen anywhere, anytime), saving Freud's essential insight of collective violence as the origin of totem and taboo.

Thus the mimetic hypothesis explains the ambivalence of the sacred as well as the ambivalence of the father (or mother). Ritual prepares a sacrificeable victim by making him violate every taboo, by making him everyone's rival. Before such a rival all are united. He is the savior as well as the scourge because he is signed with the sacred, with the beneficial resources of sacrifice itself. Such awe can easily transform the enemy after his sacrifice, into the progenitor who allows his own sacrifice, who makes laws, who establishes prohibitions against (his own former) misbehavior and even requires sacrifice (of those required to imitate his former misbehavior) to earn the peace he alone can provide.

Walter Burkert's *Homo Necans,* which appeared in the same year as *La violence et le sacré* (1972), is a prodigious garnering of the literature of myth and ritual, under a hypothesis in many ways akin to Girard's reading of Freud.[19] Like Girard, Burkert is interested in relating classical studies to anthropology and psychology. He suggests the origin of the gods in the prohibition of some prior act of collective violence, but he derives prohibition from the *psychologisme* of paleolithic hunters who regret the killing of the animal they have hunted, because they belatedly identify with their victim. In reaction, they set this animal off-limits; eventually this difference becomes accepted by all, institutionalized, sacred.

The weak link in this analysis is the dynamic that Burkert's thinking shares with Freud in *Totem and Taboo*: the guilt or remorse for killing now seen as murder energizes a universally recurring system of prohibitions. How could one moment of remorse in a single horde (even putting aside for now the problem of where that moment of remorse comes from) extend and maintain its influence throughout human culture?

Girard's mimetic hypothesis has a superior *scientific* value that can account for the ritual of hunting societies, but it can function equally well for agricultural societies. A being who draws back from claiming an object, for the sake of another or in fear of another's desire, has acknowledged and limited the dangerous power of the mimesis of appropriation. Hunters circling their prey represent to each other, and reinforce mimetically, each other's reluctance to lay the first hand (which could provoke a second), to get too close to being on the other side with the victim. Prohibition and ritual legislate this prudence into protocols that ensure peace by making certain no one else gets mixed up with the victim's sacred difference.[20]

By showing the persistent influence of archaic ritual violence on the cultural forms of democratic Athens, Louis Gernet provided the historical scholarship required to evaluate the speculative profusion of the Cambridge Ritualists, who saw ritual sacrifice behind every king, every tragedy. Jean-Pierre Vernant, Pierre Vidal-Naquet, and Marcel Detienne followed out Gernet by structuralizing the observation of misrule becoming rule in ritual (as in literature) as a regulation of man's ambiguous nature: Oedipus is Everyman, *homo duplex, tyrannos-pharmakos.*[21]

To the persistent observation that Oedipus plays all the roles, father-brother, son-lover, savior-scourge, Vernant brought the structuralist hypothesis of binary opposition composing all symbolic forms. To play every role is nevertheless to play by the iron rules of structuration: the king must ultimately suffer reversal to the opposite pole of *anathema*. But what is the answer to binary opposition itself as a hypothesis? Mind? How can this *tyrannos* serve as both tyrant and king; how can this *pharmakos* be both the cure and the scourge of the city?[22] Girard's rethinking of structuralism, up to a certain point, parallels deconstructive thinking. Such orders can never be neutral, philosophical. Oppositions are privileged, interested, worldly; they make a difference for someone's sake.

Who benefits from each role that Oedipus plays? The proper opposition to watch is not that of scourge versus savior, but the opposition of each to the city, the one posed against all, which Girard insists is the primary sign of sacrificial reconciliation, the origin of all symbolic representation, of symbolicity itself, in the production of the sacred.[23] To see the play of the *pharmakos* as undecidable is, in one sense, true. (Here Girard follows Derrida.)[24] The identification of the victim is truly arbitrary—s/he is no more guilty of contagious violence than is anyone else. Yet to terminate analysis in ambiguity is to play along with the purification that tragedy comes to, to ignore the final decision (de-cidere) that always occurs at the moment purgation requires: the peripeteia of the hero.

In Girard's reading, Sophocles intolerably delays this expected moment of decisiveness as Oedipus tries to dodge his "fate." Girard's attention to such delays and reservations marks off his reading from those of Freud, Lévi-Strauss, Vernant, Burkert, the archetypalists, and Frye. What interests mythographers like Lévi-Strauss (or Robert Graves, for that matter) in Oedipus Tyrannos is a unidirectional, irresistible homology to another myth, leading as soon as possible to the myth of myth.[25] Myth, whether Classical or Freudian, never expresses any doubt about Oedipus's guilt. Audiences, whether in Athens or New York, consolidate themselves in impatient opposition to Oedipus's obstinate resistance. Why does it take Oedipus so long to admit what we already know?

But Girard suggests that certain literary works, especially in times of social crisis (modern fiction, Greek and Elizabethan tragedy, the long tradition of Judeo-Christian writing), deconstruct the myths that corroborate violent rituals of social cohesion. Sophocles goes part way, according to Girard, in calling the certitude of Oedipus's guilt into question. To follow out Sophocles, we must delay our accusation of hamartia against an Oedipus who is seen as the only intellect, temper or unconscious out of control.

Girard would have us see that Creon, Tiresias, even Jocasta give way to anger in their turn. Each becomes a mimetic rival to the other as each accuses the other of the same crimes, for the sake of the city's institutions. Sophocles rejoins the reciprocity between antagonists that myth decides. The play itself contains, as many have argued, uncertain evidence for Oedipus's guilt. As Sandor Goodhart demonstrates, the account of one or many murderers of Laios is never verified,[26] nor (one may add to Goodhart) is the context of that account, whether it was given before or after the Herdsman found Oedipus as king.

Even if the play more or less acquiesces to the myth's account of Oedipus's guilt, audiences, following Aristotle, agree rather on the all-too-human, all-too-common sin of pride, and the causal link of either sin to the plague is never verified by the play's conclusion. Vernant concludes as well that Sophocles locates an unstructurable ambiguity between Oedipus as Everyman and the social positions that would name him.

But Girard takes Vernant's discussion beyond ambiguity, arguing that Vernant's own observation of Oedipus as scapegoat ("bouc émissaire") as well as *pharmakos* critically identifies the structuring principle of the myth that Sophocles dis-covers: "The traces of religious anathema unearthed in tragedy should be regarded not as anachronistic survivals from a primitive past but as being in the nature of an archaeological find" (*Violence and the Sacred*, 84).

Violence and the Sacred openly acknowledges the priority of Gernet, Vernant, Benveniste, and Derrida. In each case Girard attempts a comprehension of their work. The mimetic hypothesis accounts for the ambiguity of the sacred in ritual (Gernet, Vernant) and in language (Benveniste, Derrida), but also for its partial demythologization in Sophocles.

If Girard is a brilliant reader of others, he is also particularly gifted in finding answers for the most stubborn misreadings of his own work. *Violence and the Sacred* first encountered in the early seventies an antireferential prejudice that prohibited any belief that myth (or more generally, religion) could refer to anything outside itself, and a pseudoscientific skepticism certain that all truth claims were now obsolete.

Almost immediately Girard began to answer this antireferential prejudice by discussing what he called the medieval "texts of persecution": poems, diaries, and other texts which blamed Jews, witches, or other available victims for everything that was going wrong in the community. These documents were composed of the same stereotypes as the myths he analyses in *Violence and the Sacred*.[27] Furthermore, he insisted that his reading of mythology and primitive religion, which scandalized contemporary antireferential notions of textuality, was the very method of reading that everyone used for these medieval texts, which describe how Jews and witches poisoned wells, caused stillbirths, and cast evil eyes until all problems were cured by their elimination.

Girard defied any reader to argue with a verifiable modern consensus for interpreting these texts which reveals the contemporary literary intellectual's version of textual practice as an anachronism of our age. Who would dare deny that (1) there are real persecutions of real Jews behind such texts, even when independent corroboration is difficult or impossible; (2) the intention of the authors of persecution, to find the single cause, to put the blame on one person, is knowable and explainable, whether the persecutors themselves know it or not; (3) we can, with certainty, replace the persecutors's mythical interpretation, which we comprehend, with our own (the *victims* are not guilty, and their *persecutors* know not what they do), with an interpretation that is theoretically (that is, scientifically) as well as morally superior?

Whether we consider Girard's hypothesis in relation to Lévi-Strauss, Burkert, Mary Douglas, or, more generally, to the fields of psychology, anthropology, and biblical scholarship which Girard's hypothesis addresses, to ask only who is the more competent specialist in each field is to foreclose all futures for the disciplines except departmental snobbery.[28] The only course, even in those cases where Girard is accused of having read lightly (or not at all), is to follow the theory that comprehends this work, even if it comes from one who has earned no credits in the field or the clinic, but who puts "the literature" to best use.

The most influential modern theorist for the relation of myth and ritual to literature has been Northrop Frye. In one of the most famous sentences of *Anatomy of Criticism* (1957), Frye argued that literary structure derives logically, if not chronologically, from myth and ritual.[29] This strategic retreat from the contested question of generative origins enabled Frye to consolidate F. M. Cornford on comedy, Aristotle on tragedy, Jung and Neumann on romance, and the best local authority on the pertinence of myth, ritual, and the primitive for modern literature.

Frye was outmoded by the journalists of critical theory because of the questions he strategically, but only momentarily, set aside: in particular, the question of *why* literary structure resembles the structure of myth and ritual. Such mythical lustrations as Lentricchia's *After the New Criticism* (1980),[30] which washed its hands of Frye after 1970 (because a decrease in Humanities Index citations marked Frye's loss of popularity) were necessarily *ignorant* of Frye's later work.[31]

Frye's anatomy presented the constituting literary structure as the story of a dying and resurrecting god. The ultimate motive of this story is to resolve the loss of identity between the human and natural world. Frye correlated the recurring narrative myths of comedy, romance, tragedy, and irony into a single monomyth, the story of one being who rises, sets, and returns like the sun: the spirit of comedy for the regeneration of society is reborn in a young man of mysterious birth, the knight of romance, who becomes the king of tragedy, who becomes the *pharmakos* of irony whose *sparagmos* feeds a new comedy.

Why does literature follow myth and ritual, according to Frye? Because it wants to. That is, the motive for literature is to articulate the desirable already comprehended most clearly in primitive myth and ritual, which are the structural building-blocks of the imagination. Myth narrates the adventures of beings empowered to do whatever they want.

However, Frye's "Theory of Modes" is very different from his "Theory of Myths." The "Theory of Modes" sees a descent or degradation in literary history from the classical to the modern period, in the hero's power of action, and a descent in narrative myths from the most powerful heroic actions to the least, ending in modern literature's preference for ironic myth and mode, stories of beings even less powerful than we are.

Why, then, is literature in history headed in the opposite direction from the desirable? Frye described this progress as displacement: accommodating the dream of literature to the increasing pressure of the reality principle at any subsequent historical moment. This gap between myth and mode, the relation between myth and history, and the corresponding underdetermination of the relation of secular to sacred scripture remained a vexed pressing issue to the end of Frye's work.

Yet a term like "displacement" suggests that Frye began by seeing literature measured against the norm embodied in primitive myth and ritual. Frye's earliest attempt to reconcile the historical descent of modes with the cyclical return of myth was to suggest that the modern interest in the ironic victim, the modern interest in primitive cult and ritual, signifies the *sparagmos* of myth, the performing of a successful sacrifice, which sacramentally fortifies the emerging spirit of a new comic society. This begins the monomyth anew.

What would a mimeticization of Frye look like? Like Girard, Frye defined desire comparatively, in the sense that he deferred plotting the intentions and desires of single authors whose only wish is to make a work, until such work accumulates a common and recurring pattern in the archetypal phase, where collectively recurrent desires and their prohibition articulate a dream of identification, all the world absorbed by one desiring human form. That is, human desires become legible collectively as the drive that cultural prohibitions imperfectly and variously restrain.

Thus Frye's theory of identification in *Anatomy of Criticism*, the "motive for metaphor" in *The Educated Imagination* (1964),[32] follows Freud: to identify is to absorb. In the *Massenpsychologie*, the ambivalence of father-identification, from which all future forms of identification take their coloring, behaves like a derivative of the oral phase, "in welcher man sich das begehrte und geschätzte Objekt durch Essen einverleibte und es dabei als solches vernichtete. Der Kannibale bleibt bekanntlich auf diesem Standpunkt stehen; er hat seine Feinde zum Fressen lieb, und er frisst nur die, die er lieb hat" (67) ("in which the object that we long for and prize is assimilated by eating and is in that way annihilated as such. The cannibal, as we know, has remained at this standpoint; he has a devouring affection for his enemies and only devours people of whom he is fond" [37]). But for Girard, such a desire for identification/absorption is, in the language of *Deceit, Desire, and the Novel,* "ontological sickness," an attempt to appropriate for one's own depleted resources the greater being of the Other.[33]

As we have seen, the mimetic hypothesis absolves the disciple of any instinctive, violent urge to appropriate, referring such accusations back to the anxieties of their mediator/accusers. If desire is mediated, if prohibitions control the consequences of mimesis, then archetypes can be understood rather as "articulating" *the desires that cultural prohibitions project onto the disciples.*

What is the opportunity opened up by this mimetic rereading of prohibitions and archetypes? The progressive displacement of desire in Frye's "Theory of Modes," read mimetically, becomes, adapting Raymond Williams's term for the modern, "the long de-volution,"[34] literature's progressive deconstruction of *mythic* desires, projected by prohibition and ritual as instinctive, as originating in nature, in the child, and persisting in those marginal (childlike) groups who never make the rite of passage into full being. This devolution culminates in the modern period. The modern interest in myth, ritual, the primitive is not a historical residue, not a sentimental or atavistic return, but (like Girard's claim for Sophocles) an archaeological dis-covery of the roots of all human societies in violent sacrificial resolution.

Frye identifies literary structure with the *pharmakos* (which Derrida quotes approvingly)[35] and, like Vernant, uses "scapegoat" as a synonym for *pharmakos.* Girard uses *pharmakos* and scapegoat, respectively, to *distinguish* between the reflection (*pharmakos*) and revelation (scapegoat) of victimization. When we see that Jews and witches are scapegoats, in the "texts of persecution," we see the dynamic invisible to the persecutor/author, the dynamic that structures the text. But a text that talks openly about victimization has articulated a scapegoat *theme,* whose structure, then, is postsacrificial.

For Girard, "scapegoat" is a term in the West's development of the precious critical vocabulary of social relations, generated by the modern comparative studies of cultures, religions, and languages. But comparison must not prematurely terminate itself by regarding all cultures as equally and irrecoverably ethnocentric, racist, sexist. Such collective, comparative labor in the West, on such an unprecedented scale, suggests an anthropological or even logological motive of our culture and the Judeo-Christian tradition. We have improved our comprehension of all cultural languages by minimizing our own; when the elaborate positive rules of kinship (such as those determining which cross-cousin one should marry) are deconstructed and discarded in the modern period, we are left with only the minimal prohibitions necessary to forestall violent rivalry.

Girard pursues the consequences of comparative religion in the nineteenth century beyond its premature termination in collecting homologies between the Bible and other stories of dying and resurrecting gods. If comparison left comparatists in the nineteenth century with the sole job of classifying variants of the Same, Girard goes on to ask, "What are the cultural conditions which make such global comparisons thinkable, possible?"

Girard's answer is the discourse of Judeo-Christian writing, an initially scriptural, but ultimately literary tradition. This discourse is founded in a motive discernible within the Bible, across the Old and New Testaments, to tell the story of the accused, even to identify with the victim. This discourse of the victim, as it develops within this tradition, increasingly emphasizes the innocence of the persecuted: Joseph in Egypt is not guilty of desiring to replace his "father" everywhere. The capacity to see those who are sacrificed as marked with the sign of the perfectly innocent victim makes possible, over time, the fundamental distinction between reflection and revelation of scapegoating.

Frye's positing of myth as the structural paradigm for literature, and his commitment to expel all value judgement as comparative class determination, dead-ends in the equivocal position of regarding any hero's *sparagmos* as good as any other, only arbitrarily authorized by a dominant interest. Dionysus would do just as well as Christ.

A mimetic rereading of Frye's heroic categories (myth and mode) would be less resigned to Zeus's criminal sexual practice as the articulation of the desirable (and closer, in fact, to the values that underwrote every word Frye has written). Zeus's desire is transgressive, mythologically attracted to obstacles, prohibitions, taboos. Myth rationalizes ritual as it tells its story. Zeus's sexual exploits are the story of the crimes for which a victim is ritually punished. All such "heroic" crimes are signs of the sacrificial origin of the divinity in a plague of rivalry resolved by his expulsion.[36]

If one theorizes the historical preference (or "privileging," to use the critical term of late-modern pseudoscientific skepticism) for the tradition of Judeo-Christian writing over other local Celtic and Norse "myths" in Western literature as something more than class privilege, "the long devolution" (the mimetic rereading of Frye's "Theory of Myths" and "Theory of Modes") is the contest of violence and nonviolence, the two logoi of Satan and the Paraclete, the accuser and the advocate, respectively, of the persecuted (*The Scapegoat*, chs. 14, 15). Following Frye according to Girard recovers the prematurely "outmoded" future of "literature as a whole," in relation to myth and ritual. That future becomes the revelation of violence generated from an emerging postsacrificial comprehension, whose critical moment (kairos) is achieved in modern literature.

For Frye, the scapegoat structure in modern literature must stand for the victory of the obstacle or reality principle over the solar hero of romance, who bears the dream of literature. A mimetic rereading of Frye's concept of mode suggests rather that modern literature finalizes Western literature's progressive *thematization* of the scapegoat mechanism. The sacred power of queens as well as kings was inherently unstable, was earned through victimization; they are victimized again when anything goes wrong because they are the sole cause of violence and/or peace.

The secularization of violent myth and ritual sustains, over time, the dissolution of violent difference between the turbulent audience and its heroes. An ironic hero who proves his power is less than ours is, in effect, our victim, our scapegoat. The vertiginous rise and fall of leadership in modern societies replays this devolution in a matter of years. The parallel deconstruction of social and literary forms forces us to consider that the crowd dynamic, served and magnified a thousandfold by the media, more than some reality principle, or some unique (tragic) character flaw in our leaders, is responsible for social crisis. We shall take up Ibsen's study of the media's magnifying power in mobilizing support or victimization for leaders in chapters 2 and 3.

Now it is time to follow Girard toward theorizing the modern by seconding the credit he gives to literature's own "quasi-theoretical potential,"[37] by considering two writers who consciously project their work before, and after, the postsacrificial revelation of violence. By using Shakespeare and Orwell we can indicate the *longue durée* of cultural historians of the modern. Shakespeare, in *King Lear*, deals with those who, because they do violence in the name of peace *before* scriptural revelation, cannot know what they do. Orwell, in *Nineteen Eighty-Four*, examines those of an anthropological, postcritical age who when they persecute know exactly what they are doing.[38]

Like all ambitious literary theorists, both Frye and Girard make Shakespeare central to their thinking. Frye referred repeatedly to a Shakespeare who returns to myth and ritual as the bedrock of drama. But for Girard, Shakespeare is equally important in a mimetic tradition: not as an imitator of universal forms, literary genres, or nature, but of the social play of imitation itself. For Girard, Shakespeare's reading of conflictive mimesis is not a structuring of the play by archetypes, but a revelation of how *stereotypes* (not archetypes) of persecution control the machinations of the characters (as well as the audience).

Even in England's prehistory, according to Shakespeare, desire is already advanced, modernized, metaphysical: to mimetically contend for the father's blessing is to fight over nothing, for nothing comes of nothing. How important are the material consequences of the father's love? After a somewhat perfunctory description of real estate ("plenteous rivers, and wide-skirted meads": I.i.65), *King Lear* nowhere pays any further attention to whatever wealth, privileges, and pleasures follow from taking the father's place everywhere.

The play begins in apparently arbitrary offers and withdrawals of paternal blessing which only the mimetic hypothesis can clarify. In the opening scene, Gloucester equalizes Edmund to Edgar on the one hand, but then mocks his getting on the other hand, and talks offhandedly about sending him off again. How is it that when Gloucester looks to Lear, he doesn't know what he is doing? Too late will he come to know, that when he had eyes, he could not see.

To be more precise, Gloucester and Kent don't know why Lear has made a contest to decide what everyone already knows. If Gloucester and Kent know that Lear prefers Albany to Cornwall, Cordelia before her "stepsisters," it can only mean that Lear has performed such "decisions" before. Why is it necessary to go through all this again? We cannot expect our answer from Gloucester, who does the same thing to Edmund, even though he is puzzled by Lear's behavior.

Lear requires this repetition because previous instances have been somehow unsatisfactory. Why hasn't Lear ever gotten what he wants, and why does this failure happen again and again? Girard explains the obsessive failures of metaphysical desire as having nothing to do with desiring defeat. A disciple drawn to insuperable obstacles is still interested in victory, but the only meaningful victory will be over the kind of obstacle that has defeated him previously.

Lear first asks Goneril which daughter loves him best. Goneril herself was once Lear's first and only daughter, in a time when such questions were inconceivable; but subsequent paternal blessings have been divided, first in half, then in thirds, as sister follows sister. Cordelia alone has never suffered this further diminution of being. Goneril says (as she always has, with increasingly strident insistence, for progressively diminishing returns) that she loves him best—she presents no obstacle to his desire. His dissatisfaction, signaled by his public reservation of a more ample third for another daughter, can only scandalize her anew. Regan is an even more violent contestant than Goneril. She forcibly removes all rivals to Lear's desire: she is enemy to her sister, as well as to all other "joys." Yet Regan's claim of superior difference is likewise annulled by her father.

Why is Cordelia loved best by all? The temptation (to which Kent, and audiences at large, usually succumb) is to take Cordelia's side against all these *other* snobs and hypocrites. But how then could such a daughter ever have become the favorite of such a father? The mimetic hypothesis offer the most lucid response and the simplest: this paternal ritual only repeats, in an exacerbated form, what has always happened. The father is unsatisfied by those daughters who love him without reserve, and he is drawn rather to that daughter who does as he does, reserving a portion of her love to some rival. And the more he asks, the less she gives.

It is to such rivals for Cordelia that Lear now turns, first by vanquishing Kent's paternal intercession for Cordelia, then by intervening between the competition of France and Burgundy. Burgundy, who would be the establishment suitor of Frye's comic archetype, obeys Lear's prohibition. Burgundy, like Cornwall and Albany, is vanquished as a rival for the daughter's love. But when Lear urges France, the comic suitor, away from loving where Lear hates, France, like Cordelia, opposes Lear's desire:

> Fairest Cordelia, that art most rich being poor,
> Most choice forsaken, and most loved despised,
> Thee and thy virtues here I seize upon.
> Be it lawful I take up what's cast away.
> Gods, gods! 'Tis strange that from their cold'st neglect
> My love should kindle to inflamed respect. (I.i.250–55)

"Most" modifies both "choice" and "forsaken," "loved" and "despised." That is, France's speech mimics the operation of mimetic desire. France is unerringly drawn by violence's cue that only the choicest parts are prohibited. Yet France is also blind; he can reflect, without revealing, the mimetic mechanism. That any action could make one the most worthless, but at the same time the most precious, is incomprehensible to France. Therefore he attributes such magic to the gods, not Lear. The Father's imperious obstacle inflames France's re-gard, re-spect. Paternal violence indicates the desirable. The prohibition against rivalry makes desire transgressive. We cannot help but confirm Girard's lucid explanation of Heracleitus's most scandalous apothegm: "Violence is the father of all."

Gloucester blames the "machinations" of Edgar's rivalry on the gods as well, but it is Edmund, and not a messenger from the oracle at Delphi, who tells him his son would replace him everywhere. Yet Gloucester is as ready to believe in the violent rivalry of the son as Laios was of his son, not yet born.

The quasi-theoretical power of *King Lear* is remarkable. Here are Frye's archetypes of tragic and comic action cooperating within the dynamic of a single stereotype of persecution—tragic from the point of view of the victim, comic to the society that profits by his expulsion. The symmetry of such a dynamic does not reflect the untranscendable structure of Mind. Symmetry is the ineluctable consequence of the mimetic rivalry of age and youth for increasingly elusive goals, ultimately being itself. With his report of Edgar's plot, Edmund consciously mimics the stereotype of Gloucester's anticipation of the other's violence, youth's comic agenda of replacing the aged everywhere.

It should be clear by now that to try to decide who gets the blame, to attempt to expel all the bastards, demonstrates the futility of all violent mythologies. All are guilty, yet none does offend. All (even Edmund) are applying preventive measures to forestall the violence they have come to suspect in others; all are one with Lear's intent that "future strife be prevented now."

Goneril at first seems ungrateful to us when we see her plotting against her father immediately after receiving his "blessing," but she is certain that Lear's riotous knights knowingly provoke her, to draw from her a sign of ingratitude that would require Lear's redress. Goneril and Regan have already exchanged suspicions that their mercurial father (like other retiring father figures in Shakespeare's plays) could arbitrarily take back what he has given. When Oswald faithfully follows the directive to breed an occasion of insult to Lear (to justify the preventive measures Goneril knows she must take), one of Lear's knights sees this initial insult as only the latest in a series.

KNIGHT. My lord, I know not what the matter is; but to my judgement your Highness is not entertained with that ceremonious affection as you were wont. There's a great abatement of kindness appears as well in the general dependents as in the Duke himself also and your daughter.

LEAR. Thou but rememb'rest me of mine own conception. I have perceived a most faint neglect of late, which I have rather blamed as mine own jealous curiosity than as a very pretense and purpose of unkindness. (I.iv.55–67)

Jealous curiosity fathers rivalry everywhere. That Albany would insult Lear is an especially incredible accusation. We are shown nothing in the play to suggest that he would ever insult the king, or even rival Cornwall (another rumor). If Cornwall is well known to be "fiery," sufficiently susceptible to retributive violence, what are we to think of our first glimpse of these two fraternal rivals, when Albany and Cornwall act in unison to restrain Lear's violence against Kent: "Dear sir, forbear!" (I.i.162). Violent reciprocity, once initiated, is a runaway mechanism whose cause is mythical, a plague for which everyone blames everyone else.

King Lear blames women; *King Lear* exonerates all the accused. The difference between the father and the play, the proper name and the play's title, distinguishes a difference, *a real difference*, between reflecting and revealing the scapegoat mechanism, revealing persecution. The voices of the fathers begin in coarse play on the place of Edmund's unlawful getting; Lear immediately associates Cordelia's independence to the barbarous, anthropophagous Scythians. The alacrity with which Lear curses each of his daughters in turn a beast, monster, rhymes with the servant who sums this fear of contagion: "If she live long, / And in the end meet the old course of death, / Women will all turn monsters" (III.vii.100–02). Women are monstrous doubles, pretenders to autonomy. They are contaminated by the sacred, which is to be plagued by all that threatens the social order.

O, how this mother swells up toward my heart!
Hysterica passio, down, thou climbing sorrow;
Thy element's below. Where is this daughter? (II.iv.54–56)

"Hysterica passio" connects "mother" to "daughter"; their element—like madness, misrule, lechery—is properly below, what violent rivalry leads Regan to name, perhaps by synecdoche, but perhaps not, "the forfended place" (V.i.11). Prohibition (forfending) fathers transgressive desires, fetishized desirables. The sacred is behind the play's mercurial veneration and fear of women, and violence is behind the sacred. Lear's madness is his raving fear of being contaminated by the infernal regions of the feminine: "There's hell, there's darkness, there is the sulphurous pit; burning, scalding, stench, consumption" (IV.vi.127–28).[39]

That future strife may be prevented now, sister contends with sister, brother and brother-in-law with brother, father with son, godson, daughter, bastards all. But the decisive blow can never be struck, and such "plays" of violence can only end for those who renounce their own stereotypes of persecution in humility before the abominable spectacle of breakaway violence.

> The weight of this sad time we must obey,
> Speak what we feel, not what we ought to say.
> The oldest hath born most: we that are young
> Shall never see so much, nor live so long. (V.iii.324–27)

Whether we follow the folio reading or the quarto, the speaker is a son, godson (Edgar), or son-in-law (Albany) who "ought to" stick up for his own side, the program of youth, the spirit of comedy, against this repressive paternal figure. Instead, in all humility, this choral voice defers to age. This same humble deference characterizes Lear and Cordelia's reconciliation to each other. Captured by their rivals, they renounce divine autonomy, prestige, all that violence promises for all the father's places. It is sufficient to be father of this daughter, daughter of this father.

But that is not all. Shakespeare has changed the ending of the Lear story as he received it. Why? When Shakespeare frustrates a narrative expectation uncertainly placed in Holinshed between pagan myth and a verifiable English dynastic history to rob Lear of Cordelia in the end, he reveals the "things hidden since the foundation of the world" (*Des choses cachées depuis la fondation du monde*). The play forecasts millennial modernism by enacting the last possible occasion when all in this society could still unilaterally renounce these scandalous repetitions of violent mimetic entanglements, for peace. They are *bastards* because they have distanced themselves from their Father since the foundation of the world. Because they live before Judeo-Christian revelation, they cannot know the day and the hour. It is futile to prosecute any sides, youth or age, to contest comic myth and tragic myth against each other, to put the blame anywhere. All are guilty, but none does offend. *King Lear* forgives all those who know not what they do.

But what of us, the modern beneficiaries of the precious critical terminology of a fundamental anthropology, interdividual psychology (Girard's term for the way individual psychology is shaped by the influence of others), and the long tradition of Judeo-Christian writing, the three major fields of knowledge which Girard commands in *Things Hidden since the Foundation of the World?* What forgiveness for those in the moment of millennial modernism who have eyes and cannot see?

For the centenary of its author's birth, let us re-gard, re-spect a text that we, as literary intellectuals, have twice modernized since midcentury (after its publication in 1949, and after its revival in 1984), each time putting it behind us with the same complacency with which Frank Lentricchia outmoded New Criticism and Northrop Frye: Orwell's *Nineteen Eighty-Four.* Further, let us test the future of Girard's work for theorizing the situation of millennial modernism against the work of Edward Said, a self-confessed opponent of "religious criticism" (although secular criticism, Said's alternative, is opposed solely to the title of Girard's work).[40]

The critic's job, according to Said, is not to serve wall-to-wall discourses that absorb any individual, resisting voice. Criticism must limit theory (rather than spread it) by localizing, circumscribing its itinerary from one site to another. A sanative interest in delimiting theory, however, faces its own challenge of premature limitation. Said unpersuasively restricted the travel of his widely influential reading of *Orientalism* in 1978 to other archival formations, and he resigned himself philosophically in that book, despite the example of his own passionate resistance, to culture as an exclusionary mechanism.[41] Yet in *Culture and Imperialism* (1993) he recognized and accepted the spread of his analysis to other archives within the globalized domain of imperialism. Further, he focused on the movements of liberation which resisted imperialism. Nevertheless Said still acknowledged that the culture which nationalism has produced in opposition to imperialism is likewise flawed by exclusionary processes,[42] requiring something more than nationalism for a just society.

Both Said and Girard agree on the cultural strength that the West derives from its anthropological interests in other societies, but Said has a more ominous vision of what these "interests" are. Balfour, he reminds us, defended England's imperium in Egypt, over a culture with an admittedly greater pedigree than England's, because it was European scholarship alone that could make such a comparison (*Orientalism* 32). Yet what makes the work of Girard and Said ultimately compatible is their common belief in the critical power of individual texts to reveal, as well as reflect, cultural mythology. For Girard, this critical position (Said's term is "strategic location") is achieved by the power of theory to be more scientific, more reductive than the dominant discourse; for Said, criticism *places* the worldliness of a dominant theory, influential texts, showing by inference where theory does not and cannot extend.

We have followed Shakespeare's work to demarcate the premodern as the critical absence of a theoretical comprehension of how the cultural order is founded and maintained in violence as the sacred, an absence or ignorance which makes a sacrificial society possible. Now we turn from Shakespeare's moment of early modernism to Orwell, to situate the "other" side of the modern or postmodern: the modus vivendi of the beneficiaries of a long tradition of demythifications, demystifications, deconstructions during the age of the triumph of critical theory: the period of the postmodern, extending from midcentury until now.

How well does Orwell represent this world of theory extending into the future which is ours? We will divide, then subdivide, two related considerations: the worldliness of theory and text in Orwell's novel *Nineteen Eighty-Four,* and the worldliness of the novel as theory, as text, from 1949 to now.

This second consideration can be further subdivided into three related categories: (1) the historical moment of the novel's composition—in general, the work of cultural historians, British Studies specialists, biographers such as Bernard Crick, as well as the personal reminiscences of family and friends; (2) the predictive value of the novel, over its first thirty-five years, for the year 1984, which made "Orwellian" a cliché of the signifying power of critical analysis; (3) most interestingly, the imagined world of its own composition. As a text, *Nineteen Eighty-Four* attributes itself to an anonymous, post-1984 scholiast who looks back complacently on 1984 from the twenty-first century, *as we do now,* with no sense of limits on his knowledge of Winston's limits, and no sense of responsibility for what he sees.

What is the place of a scapegoat hypothesis in a worldly text like *Nineteen Eighty-Four?* Winston, as the last man in a venerable European tradition, maintains personally a lingering historical animus against Jews, women, and Orientals, but Oceania has suppressed the modern public critical vocabulary of anti-Semitism, sexism, and racism, reserving the understanding of scapegoat effects to itself. Party propaganda efficiently applies some hidden theoretical model for violent unanimity, transferring enmity the way the "capitalists" transferred luggage and laundry onto someone else's back.

The Two-Minute Hate, which provokes Winston's diary, conforms to Girard's analysis of the scapegoat mechanism: (1) the characteristic preparation which qualifies a sacrificial victim; (2) the moment of oscillation, the crisis of difference, when violence apparently ranges at will, to choose its victims; (3) the technique of transference; (4) the order of polarization, where everyone is united in opposition to a single victim responsible for all their troubles; and finally, (5) the sacred peace attributed to the presiding divinity that follows the successful resolution of the sacrificial crisis.

The narrator places us so that we can see what Winston ought to see, a classic demonstration of the stereotypes of scapegoating as Girard diagrams them in *The Scapegoat:* (1) Sacrificial victims chosen outside the group to be unified must be rehabilitated, incorporated so that they can stand for the whole community; victims from inside must be estranged, to separate them from potential allies who might enter the conflict on their behalf. The double valence of familiar and stranger essential to the proper victim is well satisfied by Goldstein's qualifications: betrayer, parodist of Newspeak, Jew. (2) The moment of oscillation is when the ritual reenacts the crisis of degree, the moment when the whole community could fall into a violent, interminable conflict, into a loss of difference, because everyone has become everyone else's enemy. Not only does the contest of violent hatred oscillate back and forth between Big Brother and Goldstein (like the contest of violent mastery between Oedipus and Creon, or Bacchus and Pentheus), but Goldstein is also surcharged with the image of nondifferentiation: he bleats like a sheep (a classic sacrificial animal), he stands for the faceless Asiatic hordes. (3) Violent antagonism is channeled, transferred to Goldstein; everyone hates the same man, the Enemy of the People. Thus (4) the community is united in polar opposition to their single common enemy, who is responsible for all crimes, all treacheries. Finally, (5) there is the theophanic moment, when the god for whom the sacrifice is performed appears, to give his blessing. The sandy-haired woman sitting by Winston who offers her savior, Big Brother, a prayer is essential for blocking recognition of the real mechanism. The transcendent god is the misrepresentation of human violence successfully transferred, channeled to a single victim, which produces peace for everyone else.

Winston makes an important observation that could lead to a full critical understanding of the scapegoat mechanism: the arbitrariness of the victim. Winston sees that the collective animus against Goldstein is charged like an electric current, polarized, abstract, capable of being directed at Big Brother or Julia as well as at Goldstein. Characteristically, this observation doesn't make it into his diary, into *his* text, but it is clearly there in Orwell's novel as already understood by us.

Why? It will take the rest of this chapter to give an answer, but perhaps you are already anticipating that I will finally succumb to a theoretical snobbism that I have already attributed to all non-Girardian critics who minimize the quasi-theoretical potential of literary texts, who regard the term "hypothesis" as an admission of imaginary applications. You may suspect that I will show up Winston and/or Orwell before (me and) Girard.

The first answer is that we are all already accused of being theoretical snobs by Orwell himself. The text is structured so that reader and narrator are assumed to know full well what Winston at best suspects: the arbitrary nature of "the enemy of the people." This would remain true to Orwell's text even if, or when, we do exceed Orwell's acute understanding of totalitarianism.

As I hope to show, it is not the possession of superior theoretical knowledge alone that characterizes the strategic location of the reader of *Nineteen Eighty-Four* in whatever afteryear, especially in the present century. Rather, it is the scandal of such knowledge coexisting *hypocritically* (in the most literal sense) with violent mechanisms of social cohesion no longer misunderstood as divine.

If our interest is in the worldliness of text and theory, then surely the place to begin is with the Oceanic ambitions for the Eleventh Edition of the Newspeak Dictionary:

> We're getting the language into its final shape—the shape it's going to have when nobody speaks anything else. When we're finished with it, people like you will have to learn it all over again. You think, I dare say, that our chief job is inventing new words. But not a bit of it. We're destroying words—scores of them, hundreds of them, every day. We're cutting the language to the bone. The Eleventh Edition won't contain a single word that will become obsolete before the year 2050.[43]

The theoretical potential of *Nineteen Eighty-Four* is strikingly different from the postmoderning of new criticisms and new novels, in covert ideological harmony with the modernization of underdeveloped labor and nations. The novel shows us that modernization is only apparently the production of new forms; "ungood" is a linguistic device for setting aside the history in language that might resist a purification to perfect instrumentality.

> It's a beautiful thing, the destruction of words. . . . After all, what justification is there for a word which is simply the opposite of some other word? A word contains its opposite in itself. Take "good," for instance. If you have a word like "good," what sense is there in having a whole string of vague useless words like "excellent" and "splendid" and all the rest of them? "Plusgood" covers the meaning, or "doubleplusgood" if you want something stronger still. Of course we use those forms already, but in the final version of Newspeak there'll be nothing else. In the end the whole notion of goodness and badness will be covered by only six words—in reality, only one word. (45–46)

What does our attention to the worldliness of Orwell's text, and the worldliness of *our* privileged, strategic location of superior theory in relation to the year 1984, require us to see in the Eleventh Edition? Nothing less than a summary of our theoretical "advances" since midcentury. A postmodern or structuralist model of language, of course, a system of differences with no positive terms; but also a deconstruction of these oppositions as interested, anything but pure. Finally, the polarization of good/ungood as a violent structuration, the linguistic parallel to the scapegoat mechanism.

From a Girardian perspective, the oppositions that structuralists were so fond of collecting (and that poststructuralists were so fond of deconstructing) occur because there are ultimately only two sides to any violent resolution. We see not how language works by "itself" (we are too theoretically sophisticated to accept Syme's theory of how words contain their own opposites) but how it is to *be* worked, for ideological purposes, in the future. Structural oppositions are themselves deconstructed, to disable the language and the literature of the past that it renders obsolete.

This is the key to the work that Smith, as a literary intellectual, is asked to do with the public record, the social text, at the Ministry of Truth. His work with texts is not simply (as Winston seems to think) the legitimation of the Party's day-to-day interests, but involves the transformation of daily life into a system of pure oppositions with no positive terms—a network of pure intertextuality that renders the material reality of any opposition to the State obsolete, ungood, vaporized. We know, even better than Winston, how unworldly his manuscript evidence of Party misrepresentation is, against the Party's textual power, or even against O'Brien's offhand, specious, but unanswerable claim of authorship of *The Theory and Practice of Oligarchical Collectivism*.

How, then, is Winston's diary contained in the worldliness of *Nineteen Eighty-Four*? What happens to the potential value of what Winston has seen, for the necessary inventory of Oceania's traces on him? *Nineteen Eighty-Four* in fact begins with Winston coming home for lunch after the Two-Minute Hate, to begin his diary:

> For whom, it suddenly occurred to him to wonder, was he writing his diary? For the future, for the unborn. His mind hovered for a moment round the doubtful date on the page, and then fetched up with a bump against the Newspeak word *doublethink*. For the first time the magnitude of what he had undertaken came home to him. How could you communicate with the future? It was of its nature impossible. Either the future would resemble the present, in which case it would not listen to him, or it would be different from it, and his predicament would be meaningless. (7)

We are witness to the effect of an "instinct" produced by the Party. We see how well, in Winston's "Rezeptionstheorie," the structures of opposition embedded in social and linguistic forms erase the future, *by nature*, in advance.

Such structures dog Winston's view of Julia as well, as he desires her and hates her by turns. When she sends him something to read, he already knows she belongs to one of two oppositions, the Party or the Brotherhood. She becomes the sign of Winston's remedial education in Room 101 (the number reserved for the first course in an American collegiate educational system), where he learns to transfer the violence that threatens him: "Do it to Julia!"

How can we estimate what has happened to the potential for "critical elaboration" in Winston's recognition of the arbitrary sign of the victim, his knowledge that violence could have chosen another? Two aspects of Girard's theory will help us read the cultural order of Oceania. (1) Girard disagrees with Frazer and the Cambridge Ritualists, by insisting that primitives are not hypocrites. The social link missing from the victim, which allows collective violence against it to remain unanswered, is not a conscious criterion for choice. The scapegoat is not seen by primitive cultures as sacred because he is victimizable, but victimizable (an appropriate ritual subject) because he is seen as sacred. (2) Girard's mimetic model makes unnecessary Freudianism's proliferation of psychic agencies, especially an unconscious produced and repressed by a fleeting recognition of incestuous desires.

Doublethink, directed towards the recognition of violence's arbitrary signification of the Enemy of the People, unites all Oceania in a post-Frazerian *hypocritical* practice of sacrifice. Furthermore, each shares a post-Freudian unconscious produced not by a fleeting recognition of incestuous desires, but by doublethinking the arbitrary transfer of violence and then doublethinking itself, the trace of the trace. Doublethink, the technique of hypocrisy, becomes the primary psychic agency, solid enough for Winston's mind to bump into, in the passage above.

We watch Winston fail to understand the founding of the symbolic in unanimous violence, which allows only two sides to any question, in the clothes philosophy of Oceania. Forced to wear uniforms, Winston and Julia politicize taking them off. Winston dreams of Julia's gesture of throwing her clothes aside, which seems to "annihilate a whole culture, a whole system of thought, as though Big Brother and the Party and the Thought Police could all be swept into nothingness by a splendid movement of the arm" (29). Nothing could be further from the truth.

Similarly, Winston dutifully asks his prole-informant if the capitalists wore top hats. The yes-or-no answer format Winston's question allows cannot compare with what the prole offers him when he mentions that top hats could be hired for any occasion. We can see how radically this answer might shift the ground of understanding power, from the acquisition of property whose signified value is accepted, constant, natural (i.e., the capitalists are the bad guys in the top hats), to the market-regulated envy and obsolescence of arbitrated symbols of (violently, mimetically contested) being.[44] The capitalists "model" the top hats; others desire the privileges, the very being of the capitalists. The system accommodates their needs. It is hard not to sense Orwell's own justifiable pride in the acuteness of his own down-and-out journalistic fieldwork among the working class during the 1930s.

Although Winston's diary becomes more worldly, more interested in both circumstantial detail and theory, it never overcomes the influence of O'Brien, seen in the first chapter:

> Winston knew—yes, he *knew!*—that O'Brien was thinking the same thing as himself. An unmistakable message had passed. It was as though their two minds had opened and the thoughts were flow-

ing from one into the other through their eyes. "I am with you," O'Brien seemed to say to him. "I know precisely what you are feeling. I know all about your contempt, your hatred, your disgust. But don't worry. I am on your side!" And then the flash of intelligence was gone, and O'Brien's face was as inscrutable as everyone else's. (13)

Winston never followed out the consequences of his critical consciousness of the scapegoat mechanism in the Two-Minute Hate, even to the point of entering it in his diary, because O'Brien understands, *toujour dejà*, precisely what he feels, thinking exactly what Winston thinks. The diary remains only interpersonal communication written finally, for O'Brien, not analysis of the social text for some future. Like Winston's reductive formula for dismissing any future interest in his diary, the opposition of history and writing misplaces the real option of usable political analysis. Winston's "knowledge" of O'Brien is as dangerously totalized as the screen version of Goldstein.

But if O'Brien is Winston's future reader, so is the narrator of *Nineteen Eighty-Four*—and, following the narrator, so are we. If Winston is victimized by O'Brien's gaze of full comprehension, how are we to place the understanding that we have been assumed by Orwell to share with the narrator, as we look back to 1984? What are the sources of the narrator's information? Where did this narrator's knowledge of Winston's thought come from, and what is the context, the world of our own critical understanding? As modern readers we are accustomed to novels knowing the unconscious thoughts of others, but don't the pressing circumstances of the novel's political context compel us to think it more likely that limited omniscience of what Winston thinks comes from coercive interrogation rather than a sympathetic understanding?

We verify Orwell's worst-case scenario for the future by being unable or unwilling to secure theory from the fashion-dynamics of modernization. Can we deny that the proper name for the rise and fall of critical fame is *fama*? The real model behind the turbulence of the institution of criticism is the *turba*, which also requires a Girardian reading.[45] The appropriateness of these immemorial terms for primitive solidarity do not signify some atavistic return to origins. Conflictual mimesis persists in all those places not administered by the judicial system—in particular, the world of culture and consent. It would be hypocritical—*hypocriticism*, in fact—to blind ourselves to the *cyclothymia* into which the critical languages enter, with the perdurable violence of anti-Semitism/orientalism, racism, and sexism they pretend to cast out. The last scapegoat mechanism is to accuse *others* of scapegoating. The cultural strength of critical theory for the future is now decided by the mechanism of news: not just advertising, whose model is mimetic desire, but the turbulence and the modernizing of public attention itself.

What has our initial reinvoking and amalgamation of the strong hypotheses of Frye and Girard given us? Like their precursors, they were attracted by the prodigious comparing of cultures, languages, and literatures of the nineteenth century. Unlike their contemporaries, they have sought to provide the hypothesis which will account for these tantalizing similarities in myth, ritual, and literature.

If a Girardian mimeticization of Frye's concept of literature as a whole holds good, what should modern literature look like? First, we should think of the co-presence of myth and ritual with modern experience that everyone recognizes as symptomatic of the modern as something more than an atavistic return to origins. Modern writers, after all, are confronted with the same tantalizing material as Frye and Girard—they are their proper fellow theorists, a relationship that both theorists have welcomed. The best of the moderns recognize and speculate about the similarity of myth and ritual and modern behavior.

But that is not all. Frye and Girard together characterize what I've been calling millennial modernism as the moment when secular and sacred literature are seen to rejoin in a common tradition of Judeo-Christian writing, when we are empowered to recognize persecution. Yet even when we understand, there is still the possibility that this understanding can be "hijacked"[46] or derailed from its proper fulfillment in unanimous peace.

We have considered Shakespeare and Orwell as setting the boundaries of the modern. *King Lear* shows how close the revelation of violence and peace as human is, how it awaits a single redefinition. Lear tries to keep the peace by dividing up his patrimony before he dies, yet he wants to give most to her who loves him best. Jesus is quoted as saying that to do good for those certain to reciprocate is unremarkable. The revelation which must follow Lear will be that each must love all the others without waiting for reciprocity. It is not the day and the hour for Lear, but Shakespeare presses on his early modern audience a premodern example of a leader in crisis that nevertheless leads into the dynastic line of English kings and the crisis of degree and succession in Elizabethan England. In effect, Shakespeare writes an additional English book of the Old Testament (like

D. H. Lawrence's *The Rainbow*) to press home scriptural revelation in a time of violence. Orwell imagines the end of the modern in the ruthless hijacking of the comprehension of scapegoat practices in order to perfect them in perfect violence for its own sake.

We cannot afford to ignore the work of our greatest writers in thinking through this critical impasse. We will begin with Ibsen, who places the achieving of modern social standing or reputation (*fama*) squarely within the context of hypocriticism, the social world where everyone denies their investment in what the crowd believes, but everyone does what the crowd represented by the media wants.

Pillars of a Self-Sacrificial Society

Henrik Ibsen is a fundamental precursor of all subsequent modern literature. His development, which takes place over a lifetime of playwriting, is
nevertheless only obscurely recognized in theories of the modern. Critics
quarrel about *his* antecedents: Scribe, Feydeau, as well as Norwegian and
other Scandinavian dramatists and poets. Yet nothing in any of his prede-
cessors could prepare one for the great prose plays of the last twenty-five
years of his career. How did he modernize himself?

Ibsen said of this transition to prose, that he could no longer allow his
characters to speak in verse, the language of the gods.[1] It is tempting to
begin reading Girard in here, because Ibsen offers us an fascinating variation on the historical moment of crisis represented by Stendhal, Flaubert,
and Dostoievski elaborated in *Deceit, Desire, and the Novel,* the moment
of modernization itself, where the disintegration of an accepted political
and cultural aristocracy forced everyone to compete for prestige and for
unique being in a common marketplace.

In the case of Norway during Ibsen's time, it is the crisis caused by the
delegitimation of Dano-Norwegian as the uncontested literary language,
in favor of competing versions of an emerging national language for a
uniquely national literature that provokes a rivalry for atavistic or nativ-
ist preeminence: who is the most Norwegian of all?

Ibsen and Henry James do not choose chauvinist atavism,[2] yet they
also avoid becoming mere disciples to the dominant philosophical traditions which have marginalized them. They are more outspoken discus-
sants of the significant historical and cultural developments analyzed in
Deceit, Desire, and the Novel because they are from "new" countries, outsiders to European culture.

It is here we must avoid the occupational hazard of critical theory: we must not permit a resemblance between a literary and a theoretical text to degrade into a mere transcoding of the former into the latter,[3] without ever considering that their resemblance means that each proposes some contribution to a converging theory of human behavior. Girard has made the case for the quasi-theoretical potential of literary texts from the beginning. Only by staying as close to Ibsen as possible can we ever hope to add to the considerable work that Girard's hypothesis has already achieved.

If there is a general principle at stake in not prematurely transcoding the language of Ibsen's plays into theoretical language (not being prematurely theoretical for the sake of an already completed theory), there is also the specific risk of burying the peculiar diversity of his dramatic accomplishment. Ibsen is above all the playwright of complex characterization—no one before him was as subtle in motivating the *ordinary* characters of everyday life. Yet during his time, his plays were awaited for the intense discussions of ideas that they were certain to provoke. How is it that Ibsen is not considered the most theoretical and didactic of writers?

Partly, the sheer number of controversial ideas and positions dramatized in play after play kept him from being seen (for very long) as the propagator of any one of them. Michael Meyer reproduces in his biography of Ibsen a contemporary Norwegian political cartoon, which depicts Ibsen flailing first right, then left, then all.[4]

More importantly, Ibsen, beginning with *Samfundets støtter* (*Pillars of Society*—1877), created a drama of ensemble theorizing conducted through the characters themselves. Ibsen's work, beyond the creation of character, was to imagine the conditions and events that might make it possible for ordinary individuals to contribute discoveries about human behavior which, observed collectively, allow amplification and consolidation as a hypothesis.

The mimetic hypothesis first found itself explaining modern resentment as negative reciprocity. This means that each person experiences isolation resentfully ("they are together and I am alone") or resentment in isolation, as if no one else was feeling the same. As we have seen in the first chapter, Girard's hypothesis of conflictual mimesis goes a long way towards explaining the futile waves of successive modernisms, and the critical theories which attend them.

Having consolidated his grasp of mimetic dysfunction, it was logical that Girard would turn the mimetic hypothesis to consider positive as well as negative reciprocity and the latent positiveness of all reciprocity. If recent critical theory has often seemed a perfect expression of mimetic rivalry, its necessary intertextuality (as one form of human behavior) can also sustain more than a mere "conflict of interpretations."

Drama has something to offer theory besides soliloquy and theatricality. Drama has historically represented conflict, perhaps resolved. The spectacular quality of dramatic conflict need not prevent someone from the community of author, cast, and audience from imagining how to reassemble or reorder the results of representative human behavior in a sequence of positive, reciprocal nonviolence. The converging hypotheses of Ibsen's characters about collective human behavior will assist the reimagining of modernism as a positive tradition, the fulfillment of the tradition of Judeo-Christian writing.

If Ibsen's dramas present the potential for ensemble theorizing, what theoretical grasp of modern behavior is Ibsen's drama working on? Ibsen's groundwork in the sagas, which he first plundered to produce a Norwegian drama acceptable to his subscribers in Bergen in the 1850s, gave him, ultimately, an archaeological grasp of modern behavior. Ibsen discovered that the heroic rules which governed guilt and expiation for rivalry and blood feuds in the sagas,[5] apparently replaced by the modern judicial system, had survived under the guise of modern "psychological" behavior.

To begin to retrieve Ibsen's research on modern society, we might follow Ibsen's obvious interest in the remarkable omnipresence of the common word *skyld*. In the sagas, this word designates quantifiable and expiable guilt. Its degradation over time in the Scandinavian languages (and in Germanic: *Schuld*) to a common mark of courteous exculpation (Norwegian: *unskyld;* German: *entschuldigen*) is not unlike the gradual divestment of particular accountability in the English word *sake.* We will have to pay special attention to language in Ibsen; it is not simply because his plays are *about* the ordinary people of modern society that makes his significance to modernism strategic. After all, Ibsen had written about modern society while still writing dramatic verse: *Kjærlighedens komedie* (*Love's Comedy*), *De unges forbund* (*The League of Youth*), and *Brand.*

The first modern prose play is *Samfundets støtter,* where Ibsen portrays the turbulent dynamics of solidarity at work in family and society as exacerbated by modern media. There are a few words that reiterate the syntax of modern solidarity here, and throughout the prose plays: sacrifice (*offer*), especially self-sacrifice, for the sake (*skyld*) of someone else, or to earn the right to be ranked as the supreme support (to support, *å støtte*, supports or pillars, *støtter*) of the community (*samfunnet*), to bear their weight for their sake.

This looks like the syntax of primitive sacrificial rite, except that there are no gods addressed, who require this suffering and expiation. Sacrifice is secular and social, what others are reported to expect in one's own behavior. In modern life, the drama of sacrifice, especially the appearance of self-sacrifice, is carried out for others, and at a certain level of community, for and in the press, rather than at some predetermined public arena or altar.[6]

Further, it is possible to reduce this knowledge of the influence of self-sacrifice which Ibsen's characters carry to a schema—in part, because characters themselves discuss its operations more or less openly, as something well understood. What separates modern society from primitive rite is the secular, often even calculated and *hypocritical* nature of sacrifice. For the most part, modern sacrifice is psychological, which means it exacts its punishment in "private"—not in secret, but in all those "nonpublic" areas unregulated by the modern judicial system. Self-sacrifice is for prestige, for convincing others of one's superior being, through practices which others (not the gods) are said to be persuaded by. It is as if modern society alone has mastered the hypocrisy which turn-of-the-century anthropologists (notably Sir James Frazer) attributed to primitive ritual.

Aune, the foreman of Karsten Bernick's shipyard, initiates the rhetoric of the hypocritical solidarity of modern sacrifice in the play. When Krap, a senior employee who speaks in Bernick's name, accuses Aune of making speeches to the workers which make them "useless on the job," Aune claims with calculation that he did it "for å støtte samfunnet"—to serve as a support for society.[7] Krap contests Aune's exclusive claim on the authority vested in this language, by replying that Aune's "duty" ("*skyldighet*") is to the society of Bernick and Company, because it "supports" everyone who works there.

Meanwhile, in the next room, Rørlund incites his female audience to self-sacrificial service to society by reading to them from a gilt-edged book entitled *Kvinnen som samfunnets tjenerinne* (roughly, "Women as Society's Maidservants").[8] He cautiously and prudently courts the lowly Dina Dorf, who is treated by the other ladies as a case for pity. (Years before, her actress mother scandalized the village by permitting the young men of the town to be her admirers.) He excuses his timid and furtive lovemaking to her in the sacrificial syntax of the play:

> Når en mann er satt til å være en moralsk støtte for det samfunn han lever i, så—; man kann ikke være forsiktig nok. Dersom jeg blott var viss på at man ville forstå riktig å uttyde mine beveggrunne—(17)[9]

> When a man is singled out as a moral pillar of the society he lives in, why—he cannot be too careful. If I were only sure that people would not misinterpret my motives—(256)[10]

Rørlund's cautious ("forsiktig") lovemaking emphasizes the figure which characters develop throughout the play, that a pillar can be crushed by the same weight it supports to win prestige, should any person not interpret correctly his motivation ("beveggrunne") for being seen with Dina. Presumably, the politically correct interpretation for Rørlund's interest in Dina would be that he wants to uplift her—he doesn't want her for himself. In any case, Rørlund takes fright at a sound of some potential eavesdropper, and pleads with Dina "for his sake" ("for min skyld") to return to the group lest they be found out.

Samfundets støtter considers Karsten Bernick one of society's pillars. There is an uncertain mixture of self-deception and duplicity in all of the play's celebrators of self-sacrifice, varying between serving without question its compulsive force, and calculated manipulation of it. If Rørlund is of the former, Karsten Bernick is mostly one of the latter, a calculating manipulator.

Karsten is the only son of an influential shipbuilding family. When he returned home from extended European travel to take an active role in the family firm, he found it was insolvent. He turned his amorous attentions away from Lona Hessel to become engaged to Betty Tønnesen, Lona's half-sister, who had just been named as inheritor of their family's fortune. He was nearly caught in the hotel rooms of an actress (Mrs. Dorf, Dina's mother), but someone else took the blame for him: Johan, Karsten's future brother-in-law.

In addition to letting his future brother-in-law take the blame for his own amorous misadventure with Mrs. Dorf, he also let others believe that Johan had taken money from the firm that, in fact, the firm had never had. This is a mythical pattern we know well—rival brothers, one of whom is blamed for everything, and expelled, while the other becomes king and benefactor, responsible for all civic blessings that follow this founding difference. Although real public works are bestowed to the community which forms around Karsten Bernick, it is primarily in the psychologies of the public,[11] mediated by the press, that the ritual purification of the community takes place.

We get an immediate demonstration of modern psychological scapegoating from the conversation which develops within the Society for the Morally Disabled, which meets in the Bernick front parlor. Rørlund proposes a self-regarding comparison between the decadent societies of the greater world, and the stern moralism of the local community. His source of information is the newspaper. The pious way in which this community quotes "the news" is remarkable; yet, our own relation to the news is the same, so it is never noted in the commentaries on Ibsen.[12] Each character talks disparagingly of the newspapers, as a source of worldly contamination, yet surely this is the point of view proposed by the newspapers themselves to their readers, then and now, to ingratiate themselves. Each community learns from its newspapers how to piously disparage all these others, who reportedly commit acts of personal and public indecency.

But the force of Rørlund's comparisons do not stop at the edge of the community. Soon he is comparing the difference between the moral superiority of the Society for the Morally Disabled, the charity group sitting safely inside the Bernick's house, and whatever goes on in the street outside.

This group of women have very different interests, yet their gossiping is soon drawn to recite the founding event of the redeemed society to which they belong. Mrs. Bernick and Martha could have no wish to bring up the events of their own family's disgrace, yet their participation in disparaging others follows the dynamic of gossip, the contemporary arbiter of *fama* and *thumos*, which ultimately doubles back on them.

Several of the Society's members take this difference back to its source, by following up Mrs. Bernick's comment that this community itself was once like the outside: "everything ended in dissipation" (241; "da all ting gikk opp i forlystelser" [13]). The Norwegian "forlystelser" usually translates as "recreation" or "entertainment"; William Archer's translation, quoted above, presumably offers "dissipation" to catch the way values are polarized; every social event ended in ("resulted in" would better catch the formulaic quality of the idiom *gå opp i*) amusement *then,* but every social event must be for the good of society *now*—no parties or theatrical events are permitted.

Dina is asked to leave the room, on an excuse that fools no one, when events which involve her mother are hinted at. Mrs. Bernick and Martha, with excuses that fool no one, excuse themselves when it is time to talk about the black sheep of Betty's own family: her older stepsister Lona, and her younger brother Johan.

Mrs. Rummel remembers Lona: "det var en for seg selv! Vil De tenke Dem, hun klipte håret av seg, og så gikk hun med mannfolkstøvler i regnvær" (15; "a strange being! Would you believe it, she cut her hair short, and went about in rainy weather with men's shoes on!" [249]). The Norwegian gives a better sense of her motives than Archer's English. She is "one [of those who is] for herself." Mrs. Rummel sees that Lona boldly appropriates the greater autonomy and freedom of men, who wear short hair and sturdy boots.

Mrs. Rummel reports that when Karsten came forward with Betty Tønnessen on his arm, to announce their engagement to her aunt, "Lona Hessel rose from her chair, and gave the handsome, aristocratic Karsten Bernick a ringing box on the ear" (249; "—så reiser Lona Hessel seg opp fra den stol hun sitter på, og gir den fine dannede Karsten Bernick en ørefiken, så det sang i ham" [15]). This positive elaboration of the force of Lona's blow suggests that Mrs. Rummel, at least upon reflection, is not entirely on Karsten's side. What can this beautiful detail of her narrative mean but that Mrs. Rummel hears in Mrs. Holt's tone a potential sympathy for Lona's insurrectionary restiveness against male privilege, a buried resentment against the ascendancy of ("den fine dannede") Karsten Bernick.

Further, Mrs. Holt explains that Lona went to America after Johan, when the whole town was in an uproar over him ("hele byen naturligvis var opprørt over ham" [15]). Lona defiantly joined sides with the single antagonist of the whole community. The phrase "hele byen" ("the whole town"), invoked several times in the play as the supreme authority, the last word, carries the same register of mythological unanimity in English: they speak for an imaginary totality in just the way newspapers and other media do, only to remind each other of what everyone knows.

The whole episode is beautifully motivated by what everyone knows of the dynamics of modern gossip. Each interlocutor maliciously dares the other to break propriety by urging the other not to mention the single spots which mar an otherwise immaculate family ("å jo, Lona Hessel er nok også en av solplettene i den Bernickske familielykke" [15]). The common traits of transgressive reportage and retributive "justice" link free-form gossip to investigative or "deconstructive" journalism in the modern period.

We learn of Lona's antithetical practice both from the behindbacks chatter of the Society for the Morally Disabled, and from Lona herself, who suddenly returns with Johan after fifteen years. Lona immediately scandalizes her family in a way that they all remember. When they ask her why she says that "we" traveled second class, she answers "Jeg og barnet, naturligvis"(21); "Me and the boy, of course," daring them to misunderstand that she has a child and no adult male for a husband, or a young boy for a companion.

Then Lona asks if there has been a death in the family, because they are all sitting around sewing white things in the dark. Rørlund, falling for the trap, says impressively that they are the Society for the Morally Disabled. Lona replies ("half to herself"), "these nice-looking, well-behaved ladies, can they be—?" (271).

Lona fits herself beautifully into the expectations of insurrectionary behavior which have preceded her. Lona has a romantic ego. She has always sought the frisson of rubbing society the wrong way, certain of her singular preeminence if everyone is shocked. Ibsen, like Flaubert, Henry James, and James Joyce, is fascinated by the dynamics of modernism at work in the provinces of world culture. Lona, like Emma Bovary, seeks to scandalize the provincials, épater les bourgeoises. Emma and Lona belong to the portrait of "masochism" which Girard presents of the nineteenth century: the avante-gardist who seeks punishment from the crowd, to certify his/her unique virtue in single opposition to the vulgarity of those who reject them.[13] Romantics deify themselves as victims; they scandalously wrap themselves in the hermeneutic of the sign of Christ, the Lamb of God, the perfect victim.[14] This psychology accompanies and even perverts the growing comprehension of the sacrificial system which persecutes victims.

To plot the reappearance of the primitive scapegoat in modern culture is one way modern writers collectively theorize the social behavior of their own historical moment. Yet the theory that writers do must work within the research consensus of a common reading public's common (in Virginia Woolf's sense of "common") understanding. What might a recognizably human character believably do? The most pressing question, asked first by Rørlund, is why has Lona returned? Does she want more scandal? Revenge on all those who have rejected her, beginning with Bernick, and the community which has crystallized around him?

Ibsen gives Lona an incredible role to play, one that has never been adequately understood (except perhaps by Joyce). Like Christopher Newman in James's *The American*, she refuses revenge, having been refused in desire. Her difficulty is to articulate a postsacrificial nonviolence in a world where language is given over to hypocriticism. Her answer to Rørlund, which closes Act I, gave a young Irishman—James Joyce—a luminous alternative to that modern negative mutual reciprocity which Girard in *Deceit, Desire, and the Novel* characterizes as "resentment, rivalry, and impotent hatred."[15]

ADJUNKT RØRLUND. *De?* Med tillatelse, frøken, hva vil *De* gjøre i *vår* forening?

FRØKEN HESSEL. Jeg vil lufte ut, herr pastor. (22)

RÖRLUND. You? Allow me to ask, Miss Hessel, what you will do in our Society?

LONA. I will let in fresh air, Pastor. (273)

If Lona's scandalous effect on the community is the same as it always was, things have symmetrically reversed from festival to antifestival since her departure. Over fifteen years, Bernick's company, his personal standing in the community, and the community itself prosper from Johan's expulsion. The community as a whole gives up festival for one long antifestival, wary always of any disruptive force, any return to the gaiety of the past, for which playgoing is a recurrent emblem. The community forms around Bernick, under a program of never enjoying things, never doing anything for oneself. One must always appear to be doing for the sake of others.

Bernick is no Oedipus. He *knows* how the community was reconciled by a founding act of scapegoating, which made him its leader; the last thing he wants to do is to lead an inquiry into it, to deconstruct the founding myth.

Karsten knows that his own reputation must remain spotless, in order to continue his success in financial speculation. He clearly feels the necessity of approval from society as represented by the press. Throughout the play, he worries lest the whole society would come down on him, should he ever show any fault. Karsten's speeches are a litany of modern hypocriticism.

By Act II, Bernick's latent problems begin to converge on his household. He has secretly bought up land for an alternate rail route to the route he helped reject earlier, when he argued that the outside world would contaminate the community ("et hyppigere samkvem med en fordervet utenverden" [18]). In fact, the earlier route would have competed with shipping routes essential to his company's interests. If the town turns on him when it comes time to tell them that he bought all this land to benefit them, for their sake rather than his, he will lose everything.

He does not explain why he needs their approval. While we could rationalize that the town needs to approve the railroad, in order that Karsten's land-purchases will be valuable, Karsten never offers this explanation. The absence of such a rational explanation allows the impression that public opinion has some metaphysical, life-and-death authority over his being, his safety, as if their looks of approval could turn into a curse to destroy him.[16]

It is just at this delicate moment that Johan, his wife's brother, and Lona Hessel, her half-sister, have returned from America. Karsten is in danger of being contaminated by the false reputation he created to accompany Johan's departure, fifteen years before.

> At de også skulle komme hjem just nu,—nu, da jeg behøver en ublandet god stemning både i byen og i pressen. Der vil bli skrevet korrespondanser til avisene i nabobyene. Tar jeg *vel* imot dem, eller tar jeg slett imot dem, så vil det bli drøftet og uttydet. Der vil bli rørt opp i alt dette gamle—liksom *du* gjør. I et samfunn som vårt—. (kaster hanskene mot bordplaten.) Og ikke et menneske har jeg some jeg kan tale med og søke noen støtte hos. (23–24)

> To think of their coming home just at this time, when so much depends on unmixed good-feeling, both in the press and in the town! There will be paragraphs in the papers all over the country-side. Whether I receive them well or ill, my action will be discussed, my motives turned inside out. People will rip up all those old stories— just as you do. In a society like ours—[Tosses down his gloves upon the table.] And there isn't a soul here that I can confide in, or that can give me any support. (277)

Karsten asserts that his greater substance depends on his standing ("stemning"), the status of his being in the press—not simply the people who do business with him or who know him, but all who can read about him. In a way all too familiar to any modern public figure, Karsten knows that any stories about his scandalous relatives will damage him by contaminating him, no matter whether these stories tell of him welcoming or disowning these "Americans."

Karsten's anxiety first sounds like megalomania, that he even worries about newspapers in neighboring communities ("avisene i nabobyene"), but his good standing in his own community could be ruined by what other communities say about him (what is translated above as "paragraphs in the paper" would be translated more literally as correspondence or letters to the newspaper). Given the circulation within modern media, the whole world could turn against him.

Literally, Karsten worries about "the uproar" over this old trouble ("Der vil bli rørt opp i alt dette gamle. . . ."). The newspapers will bring attention back to problems that were overlooked at the time. The newspapers create in their unfortunate subject an agoraphobic sense of a crowd, a roaring mob that could materialize at any moment at his very door to denounce him for historic sins.[17]

Bernick sees threats everywhere. He complains to his wife about her relatives, then complains when she cries that the town will talk about how Mrs. Bernick was crying. Bernick's fears are augmented by the media's ability to enhance rumor's flight, to get stories out and around. Newspapers dig up old trouble with the same unerring and intimate accuracy as a domestic partner ("some du gjør").

In the end, Bernick fears, as Rørlund did, that they will be overheard: "anyone could come in here. You want them to see you with red eyes? A pretty business that would be if it got around that—Shh, somebody's in the hall."

The "somebody" in the hall is Aune. Bernick has pressed his shipyard to repair his own boat before those of other clients. But the *Indian Girl* has kept ashore American sailors whose carousing is scandalizing "the whole town" ("hele byen"). Bernick reads in the newspaper accounts an attempt to blame the American rowdy misbehavior on him, because his shipyard has worked on his own ship, not the *Indian Girl*. He must master these "ondskapsfulle og skumlende avisskriverier" (25).[18] "Enten å få pressen på halsen eller få den velvillig stemt for meg" (21)—"either these newspaper writers are on my neck, or they will serve as a willing support for me."

Aune's role in the sequence of Act II shows Ibsen's genius for imagining how individual "theorists" might come to conclusions in a sequence or context that allows them to be consolidated into a general hypothesis. Without knowing anything of what Johan will say to Karsten (and without being reduced to a mere mouthpiece for Ibsen or Girard), Aune's reply shows that he knows the nearest person, the one most likely to be sacrificed, will be the innocent, not the one responsible. Even Aune's family will blame him, not Bernick, for his dismissal ("ikke gi *Dem* skylden" [26]).

Unlike Johan, Aune is an unwilling and inappropriate victim, he argues, because he already bears enough responsibility for others. If Bernick argues that society must come before Aune himself, Aune argues that his family is itself a little society, for whom he serves as pillar.

> Dette lille samfunn har jeg kunnet støtte og holde oppe fordi min kone har trodd på meg, og fordi mine børn har trodd på meg. Og nu skal det hele falle sammen. (26)

> That little community I've been able to support and hold together because my wife believed in me, my children believed in me. And now the whole thing is to fall to pieces. (284)

Like Bernick, Aune could be crushed by the weight he carries of those who believe in his support.

Bernick, in reply, smoothly regains control of hypocriticism by identifying Aune as the minority that must be sacrificed to a majority greater than his family:

> så må det mindre falle for det større; det enkelte får i Guds navn ofres for det alminnelige. Annet vet jeg ikke å svare Dem, og annerledes går det heller ikke her i verden. (26)

> the less must fall before the greater; the part must, in heaven's name, be sacrificed to the whole. I can give you no other answer; and you'll find it is the way of the world. (284)

Bernick declares this formula of sacrificial offering to be immutable, in God's name, as the way things go in this world.

Hilmar, Betty's cousin, follows Aune into the room. Hilmar's narrative vividly contributes to the ensemble theorizing of sacrificial solidarity as well as Bernick's worst anxieties. When Lona and Johan walk in the street,

> Folk sto stille og så efter dem. Det lot til å være gått som en løpeild over byen—omtrent som en brann på de vestlige prærier. I alle hus

sto det mennesker ved vinduene og ventet på at toget skulle komme
forbi. (27)

people turned round and looked after them. It ran like wildfire over
the town—like a fire on the Western prairies. There were people at
the windows of all the houses, head to head behind the curtains,
waiting for the procession to pass. (286–87)

Public opinion, for better and for worse, is acutely contagious. Bernick is
especially alarmed when Hilmar warns that the papers will put a stop to
these "Americans," joined in the popular mind to Bernick's family. Hilmar
explains that a journalist at his club has questioned him, and knows the
story Bernick allowed to circulate about Johan embezzling the firm's
money.

As Karsten soon discovers, Lona Hessel has orchestrated this public
spectacle which so scandalizes Hilmar, as well as the entire community.
Lona and Johan are a remarkable couple at the center of the modern mob.
Each understands very well how public opinion is mobilized, yet Lona is
so avid, and Johan so indifferent to it. Johan's relative immunity to the
pleasures of avant-gardist posturing grants additional valuable insights
into modern hypocritical sacrificial practices.

Bernick fully admits to Johan that the founding event behind his success was the arbitrary designation of an innocent victim, who is blamed
for everything which went wrong.

BERNICK. "Mitt hus og hjem, min familielykke, min hele borger-
lige stilling i samfunnet,—alt skylder jeg det. . . . Ikke *en* blant ti
tusen hadde gjort hva du den gang gjorde for meg. . . . at du så
høymodig kunne vende skinnet imot deg selv og reise vekk—(30)

BERNICK. My house and home, my domestic happiness, my whole
position in society—all these I owe to you. . . . Not one in ten thousand would have done what you did for me then. . . .—that you
should have the generosity to turn appearances against yourself and
go away—(298–99)

While it is true that primitive sacrifice also tries to ensure the willingness
of the victim, which exonerates his beneficiaries from the charge of persecution and the danger of reciprocal, contagious violence (as explained by
the mimetic hypothesis), Johan's affable willingness to take the blame

strikes a modern, psychological note. Johan, fifteen years later, discusses his self-sacrifice with Karsten calmly, as an exercise in managing public opinion.

> JOHAN. . . . Var vi ikke begge to unge og lettlivede? En av oss måtte jo dog ta skylden på seg—

> BERNICK. Men hvem var nærmere til det enn den skyldige?

> JOHAN. Stopp! Den gang var den uskyldige nærmest til det. Jeg var frank og fri, foreldreløs. . . . Hvem ville ikke gjerne ha ofret seg for deg, især når det ikke gjaldt annet enn en måneds bysladder, og en så med det samme kunne løpe ut i den vide verden. (30–31)

> JOHAN. . . . Were we not both of us young and a bit reckless? One of us had to take the blame upon him—

> BERNICK: Yes, and the guilty one was the obvious person.

> JOHAN: Stop! Then the obvious person was the innocent one. I was alone, free, an orphan. . . . Who would not gladly have served as your scapegoat, especially when it only meant a month's town-talk, and an excuse for making a dash into the wide world. (298–99)

Johan insists that one of them had to take *skylden* on himself. We must restrain ourselves from simply transcoding these remarkable parallels to Girard into a comprehensive and already complete expression of the mimetic hypothesis, in order to see how the full articulation of modern sacrifice, across several characters, establishes itself in the play. Ibsen never seems didactic even when he is most insistently read for his ideas, because characters collectively work up the play's hypothesis of human sacrificial solidarity. Johan proposes the requisite singularity of the sacrificial victim by thinking that only one person, of all those men enamored of Mrs. Dorf, was caught in such a compromising situation.

Bernick does not disagree that only one person should take the guilt, but he argues that "the closer" ("nærmere") should have taken it. We know what Bernick means, but what does Johan mean when he counters that the "guiltless" one was the closest this time? (Archer translates "nærmeste"—literally, "closest"—as "most obvious," thus exchanging logic for proximity).

It is startling to hear Johan put aside so casually and knowingly Karsten's anxious commitment to the judicial determinism of guilt and punishment, in favor of a device that will pacify public opinion. Modern literature suggests again and again that within the world of justice, wherever no laws are clearly broken, the primitive world of sacrificial reconciliation reigns at the level of collective psychology.[19]

We must continue to honor Ibsen's commitment to credible characterization. There are local and specific reasons for what characters say, as their in(ter)dividual thinking excavates elements of the mimetic hypothesis. Johan works from the inside, as the play works toward the outside, to a greater comprehension of the system. Johan probably uses "nearest" first of all because he is certain that he is turning Bernick's argument (and thus his language) back on itself. He elaborates his appropriation of Karsten's use of "nearest" by recalling that he was free of any prior responsibilities for anyone else's sake. Johan has no children and no parents—he could choose for whose sake he would bear guilt and expulsion.

Karsten concludes his discussion with Johan by explaining how his sister Martha has taken responsibility for Dina Dorf. Karsten's glib explanation of how he has cared for his sister in answer to Johan's concern is quite damning. Karsten explains that he made himself a partner to his mother in the family business. "Her" share after accounting amounted to nothing, and thus Martha inherited nothing.

When Johan replies that in America women are not thought of as mere retainers in a male-dominated household, Karsten answers that "here, in our little circle, where, thank heaven, corruption has not as yet managed to creep in—here women are content with a modest and unobtrusive position" (304). "People ought not to think of themselves first; women least of all. We have each our community, great or small, to support and work for" (305).

Ironically, Martha's own explanation reveals that she has sacrificed herself for Johan, not Karsten, "to expiate where . . . [he] had sinned" (307).

FRØKEN BERNICK. Har du glemt at en kvinne døde i nød og skam for din skyld?

JOHAN. . . . har han aldri hatt så meget som et unnskyldende ord for meg? (33)

MARTHA. Have you forgotten that a woman died in shame and need for your sake?

JOHAN. . . . has [Karsten] never said so much as a word in my defense? (307)

Martha has sacrificed her life to pay for Johan's guilt. She has "stood in his place" (309) as his "substitute" ("vært din stedfortreder" [34])—raising Dina, waiting for the prodigal to return. Karsten has never uttered the "exonerating" word ("unnskyldende ord") for Johan, which would have also released Martha from her self-sacrifice.

Johan took the blame on himself because he admired Karsten, and only now mildly suspects that Karsten cultivated his friendship to win Betty. In any case, "exile" was preferable to grinding away in the office. At this point, he feels that he sacrificed very little of himself. In fact, the world beyond the community enhances the status of not only Karsten, but Betty as well; one returns glamorized.

Martha's sacrifice of taking Johan's place at home has cost her a good deal, yet it is perhaps solely in her analogy of the prodigal son that she expresses resentment against Johan, that she has dutifully, without credit, borne his burden at home ("her hjemme").

Karsten attempts to head off trouble with Lona as he had with Johan, but she is a more formidable interlocutor, undercutting his self-serving posturing. Karsten begs Lona's forgiveness, but Lona asks him not to get sentimental—it doesn't suit either one of them. He wants Lona to believe that he loved her, that his entanglement with Mrs. Dorf was a temporary aberration. Why should this matter fifteen years later?

The line of Karsten's comments makes it clear that he is trying to exonerate (excuse, "unskyld") himself: "jeg kan iallfall unnskylde meg" (35). He is listing off his guilty behavior, not preparing an argument. Lona stops him by asking, "What do you think has brought me home just now?" (313). It is an apt question—Betty has already accused Lona of returning for jealousy.

Karsten is like Burgundy in *King Lear*. He would not love what the community hates; if at first he appears to be different from the vulgar crowd, as Lona does, with his European sophistication, it soon becomes clear that he apes their desire. Lona accuses him of being unable to withstand the scorn the community directs towards her (which she has solicited). Lona reminds Karsten of the faintness of his love—how, when he returned, he was chastened by the community's attitude to Lona.

FRØKEN HESSEL. . . . da du hørte spotteglosene, som haglet ned over meg; da du fornam latteren over alt det som de her kalte mine forkjærtheter—

KONSUL BERNICK. Du *var* hensynsløs den gang.

FRØKEN HESSEL. Mest for å ergre disse skjørtekledde og buksekledde snerper, som sjokket om i byen. (35)

LONA. . . . when you saw the ridicule that poured down on me; when you heard the laughter at what were called my eccentricities—

BERNICK. You were inconsiderate in those days.

LONA. Mainly for the sake of annoying the prudes, both in trousers and petticoats, that infested the town. (314)

Lona believes that the first reason Karsten became infatuated with Betty was that she had the approval of the entire community: "young, beautiful, idolised by everyone" (314). Archer's translation doesn't let us see how Karsten's comment on Lona's obstinate contrariness ("forkjærtheter") corroborates Lona's analysis of him. Karsten doesn't sympathize with the people Lona "aggravates" ("egrer") by being "inconsiderate" of their sensibilities. Rather, he finds her reckless ("hensynlos") for deliberately setting the whole community against herself. She only adds as a second reason that it became known that Betty would inherit all her aunt's money, and Lona would inherit nothing.

Lona is shocked when Karsten tells her that he chose Betty "entirely for the sake of the money" (315; "for pengenes skyld likefrem" [35]). He claims that he had to find some way to save the family firm. "So you saved the house of Bernick at the expense of a woman" (316). Bernick excuses himself by saying blithely that Betty loves him (anyway), but Lona never lets him live in these lies. Lona's quick rejoinder "But I?" reminds Bernick that it has been at her expense.

The conversation between Bernick and Lona shows Ibsen's gift for representing how interdividuality makes research into human behavior possible. Lona doesn't already know the truth about Karsten, but she knows what the hypocrisy of a false, enforced unanimous resolution feels like, and resists it obstinately. Lona knows she is right if the whole community is against her. Karsten, on the other hand, compulsively works to get the whole community with him. He always tries to close an argument, to enforce agreement; Lona always wants to open one, or start one. Together, they force each other to learn what they don't already know.

Bernick answers Lona's reminder of what his desertion cost her, by saying she wouldn't have been happy with him (anyway). Then Lona asks him if that was why he rejected her—for her sake? Bernick replies with an answer that he has already given many times, that he does not act for his own sake, but for the sake of the community that depends on the Bernick family business.

FRØKEN HESSEL. Er det også for samfunnets skyld at du i disse femten år er blitt stående i løgnen? (36)

LONA. Is it for the sake of the community, then, that for these fifteen years you have stood upon a lie? (316)

Lona deflects Karsten's answer by asking why he has lied to Betty, what she later calls a triple lie—to her, Johan, and Betty. When Karsten answers that he wished to spare Betty's feelings, Lona can go no further, except to begin again, to ask him if he is happy. His answer is enough to organize any audience against him.

Rørlund tries to stop Dina Dorf from going off with Johan, by informing her that Johan was the cause of her mother's misfortune. Johan had remained indifferent to what the community accused him of, but demands that Karsten now "take the blame upon [his] own shoulders" (340; "ta skylden for"[44]). The verbal conflict between Karsten and Johan raises again the full spectacle of a hypocritical understanding of the sacrificial dynamics of society.

Karsten insists that his spotless reputation keeps him from being crushed by the community he supports. "All my opponents will join forces and overwhelm me. . . . They will crush me beneath the weight of rumours and slanders" (345). He is frightened enough to allow Johan to book passage to America on a ship he knows has been improperly recaulked in his own shipyard.

In Act IV, Rummel (one of Bernick's partners in the rail scheme) orchestrates a public show of unanimous support for Consul Bernick.

Our opponents must be crushed by an overwhelming utterance of
public opinion. The rumours are spreading over the town; . . . This
very evening, amid songs and speeches and the ring of brimming
goblets—in short, amid all the effervescent enthusiasm of the occasion—you must announce what you have ventured to do for the
good of the community. With the aid of effervescent enthusiasm, as
I said just now, it is astonishing what one can effect in this town. But
we must have the effervescence, or it won't do. . . . And especially
when such a ticklish point is to be dealt with. (367)

Rummel wants everyone to abandon themselves to "effervescent enthusiasm"[20] so that they can be easily mobilized under Bernick. Rummel
misses no point of unanimity. When a procession of townspeople arrives
at the Bernick household, their garden window curtains will be drawn to
face the "surging multitude" (371). Sandstad will address the crowd about
"harmony between the different classes of humanity"; Vigeland will "express the fervent hope that our new understanding may not disturb the
moral basis on which we stand"; and Rummel himself will call attention
to "the claims of Woman, whose more modest exertions are not without
their uses in the community" (368).

That evening, Rørlund introduces Bernick to his fellow citizens, hitting
all the themes of hypocritical solidarity, emphasizing Bernick's spotless
reputation, as well as the benefit to the community from the recent departure of Johan. When Bernick faces the crowd, he has been providentially
saved from being guilty of Johan's death, and the loss of his runaway son
in the same ship.

Bernick's speech begins by wishing to "bring home to ourselves the
truth—the truth which has, until this evening, been utterly and in all
things banished from our community" (399; "sannheten, som inntil i
aften gjennemgående og i alle forholde har vært husvill i dette samfunn"
[62]). Bernick begins by identifying himself as the person who has been
secretly buying up land for the proposed rail line, because he "knew and
feared the tendency of our society to suspect impure motives behind everything a man undertakes" (400; "fordi jeg kjente og fryktet vårt
samfunns tilbøyelighet til å skimte urene beveggrunne bakved alt det en
mann her foretar seg" [62–63]). Bernick is still defensive, of course, but
his disclaimer helps fill out the allomorphs of the mimetic paradigm, the
self in relation to Other and others in a hypocritical society. Success over

the Other and others only comes when one is seen as wanting nothing for oneself. Failure comes when one is found to want for oneself.

Finally, Bernick takes back the blame which Johan has carried onto himself. "Fifteen years ago I swung myself aloft by these rumours; whether I am now to fall with them is for you to decide" (403). "But do not decide this evening. I ask every one of you to go home—to collect himself—to look into himself. When your minds are calm again, it will be seen whether I have lost or gained by speaking out" (404).[21]

Bernick's sudden departure from his hypocritical self-presentation has temporarily broken the bond which keeps the crowd together. The play leaves its leader at the top of his influence—we do not know if the community will reorganize itself against him as their enemy.

When the crowd has dissipated, Bernick thanks his wife, sister, and Lona, calling them "the pillars of society." Lona once again serves as the reciprocal voice to Bernick, who tries to make women the new divine support of society. She refuses a new mystification of self-sacrifice by asserting rather that "the spirits of truth and freedom—these are the Pillars of Society" (409; "sannhetens og frihetens ånd—det er samfunnets støtter" [65]).

Ibsen's subsequent plays continue to theorize different aspects of the hypocrisy of modern sacrificial solidarity. Nowhere do they more powerfully share their understanding with an audience than in the exuberance of Nora's release from self-sacrifice for another's sake at the end of Et dukkehjem (A Doll House), or in the abominable scandal of Vildanden (The Wild Duck), that a child succumbs to the idea that she can win back her father's love by sacrificing herself for him. Now we will go forward to Enemy of the People, always regarded as a companion play to Pillars of Society, sharing characters as well as theme. There we will see the full pattern of adulation and persecution of the leader who is first the friend of the people and then their enemy.

Folkevenner og Folkefiender

Ibsen's Research in Modern Behavior

You would expect any discussion of literary modernism to have begun with Flaubert, whose friends shamed him into writing the ironic history of a sordid provincial adulteress, Emma Bovary, by accusing him of still being romantic, hopelessly passé for the 1850s. *Madame Bovary* re-presents, in the relation of the narrator to Emma, Flaubert's painful recognition of the double bind of mimetic modernization. The more modern the narrator tries to be, which is to say the more invulnerable he makes himself to the charge of being outmoded, the more like Homais he becomes.[1]

Yet it might be of equal value to continue to follow a writer whose cultural circumstances required him to assign *himself* the task of inventing his own research procedures into modern culture. To set yet another profitable relation between Girard's work and Ibsen's, let us begin by elaborating Girard's almost offhand comment in *La violence et la sacré* (1972) that modern culture persists in a state of sacrificial crisis. In Girard's model (as early as *Mensonge romantique et vérité romanesque* [1961]), modern crisis is caused by a loss of cultural difference and degree; the razing of degree comes from the competition inevitable to mimetic creatures, who copy each other's desires as well as other behaviors.

But why "sacrificial" crisis? In primitive culture an elaborate system of rules, prohibitions, taboos prevents rivalry, prevents desires focusing on an object common to members of the community. The incest taboo, perhaps a universal rule, prevents kin from rivaling over mother, son, daughter, father. Ritual complements rules. Ritual stages the loss of differences, forcing it to a state of crisis. Where all differences are lost, everyone is everyone else's enemy. Ritual sacrifice regains difference by appropriating this sameness in making one the enemy of all, the scapegoat of all united in opposition.

Girard distinguishes between primitive and modern culture on the basis of its control of violence. The judicial system has replaced the primitive sacred (represented by taboo and ritual) by taking retributive violence into its own hands, out of the hands of the aggrieved. Justice has the last word of violence, punishing transgression of rule with such force that no reply, no outbreak of renewed violence is possible. But wherever the judicial system loses its absolute authority, the human arrangements which move in to replace it, as well as the weakened system itself, increasingly resemble an aborted rite, a ritual *qui tourne mal.*

Ibsen's work is crucial for comprehending the modern state of sacrificial crisis. There are three interlocking preoccupations of *An Enemy of the People (En folkefiende)* I wish to discuss: (1) the "persistence" of myth and ritual in modern culture; (2) the odd inclination of some characters towards self-sacrifice and being persecuted as a source of social power and influence; (3) the co-presence of mythical practice and scientific practice, both "purgative."

Pillars of Society (Samfundets støtter), generally understood as the beginning of Ibsen's modern period, unmasked what looked to be residual forms of primitive ritual persisting in hypocritical acts of self-sacrifice used to gain the community's support for leadership. *An Enemy of the People* is part of Ibsen's lifelong project of theorizing human behavior, especially the places where individual and social behavior merge (Girard's "interdividual" behavior), at a particular historical moment.

My model here is Girard's remarkable book on Shakespeare, but I would like to emphasize again that I am not interested in transcoding all of Ibsen into what Girard already knows. We would learn nothing from Ibsen; for that alone we should be sent home. But we would learn nothing more than what we can already get from Girard, and we would in fact violate Girard's lifelong principle that the great literary texts have a quasi-theoretical potential that can accompany and contribute to and at times even anticipate the most rigorous theory-work.

In *Theatre of Envy* (1992), Girard credited Shakespeare with a nearly complete discovery of the scapegoat hypothesis as the sole solution to mimetic conflicts, and suggested as well a fascinating relation of Shakespeare's theoretical discoveries to his dramatic practice. Shakespeare discovered that both inside and outside the theatre, crowds (audiences) need scapegoats. The appetite for revenge tragedy is a compelling example of the audience's belief in "enemies of the people" or scapegoats. But Shakespeare did not make himself a victim of the mob by revealing to them their appetite for scapegoats, by thwarting their mechanism for solidarity. Shakespeare's dramas reveal the process of social unification which depends on blaming one person for everything that goes wrong, yet his plays retain their audience's favor by giving the popular imagination the victims they crave.

Ibsen eschews Shakespeare's caution, perhaps as a matter of temperament, but more importantly in favor of the frisson of scandal modern audiences desire. Instead of masking his discovery of the crowds' appetite for victims, Ibsen gains in prestige by rubbing their noses in it, whistling up a firestorm of controversy. One might consider Ibsen's agility in maintaining his preeminence by placing him between Shakespeare and Oscar Wilde. Shakespeare retired before the crowd could ever turn on him. Wilde's behavior became too risky: they were able to pull him down.

There are three propositions which I will discuss here. The first is that the play comes yet again to a subject which fascinates Ibsen and Girard as well as other modern writers throughout their work as they try to theorize it: the social process of polarization around a "friend" of the people, the dissolution of this order which restores itself by naming this same person as an enemy of the people. We have already glanced at this process represented in Orwell's *Nineteen Eighty-Four*. This social process has a particular relevance for Ibsen, since his audience had recently turned on him for the indecency of *Ghosts* (*Genganere*), accusing this play about the spread of pollution as itself polluting the community.

If this immemorial pattern from myth and ritual still persisting into the modern is one proposition, it leads to the second, which is that propositions prove themselves in the modern period through competitive modernization, meaning that they propose what the majority of the community cannot bear to accept as true, which scandalizes them. Whatever scandalizes must be true, and it is a sign of the modern intellectual's effectiveness that his word breaks up the community.

Finally, the third proposition is the remarkable parallel that exists between the emerging scientific truth of cellular behavior and "primitive" behavior, both understood as mimetic, turbulent, and purgative. Myth coexists with science, and Girard can help us here as well to recognize just how far Ibsen takes us.

Purgation is the key term here, for *An Enemy of the People* and for modern culture in general. Purgation is originally the sought-for consequence of sacrifice, to expel violence and disease from the community. The play wonderfully mixes mythological purgation with the verifiable benefits of purgation that scientific medicine proposes, which is the real significance behind the odd mixture of heroism and foolhardiness in Dr. Tomas Stockmann's character. For the last proposition, a more detailed and theorized understanding of Ibsen's successive vocations is crucial: *apoteker*, journalist, dramaturge, and dramatist.

Ibsen's knowledge of medical practice deserves separate and specialized treatment.[2] But drama itself offers a unique, quasi-scientific research lab for what is played out in the news—not just what happens (described in the newspaper), but the relation between the journalistic depiction of human behavior and the community's response to it, even the investigation done in their name, in the name of a community that never appears in person, "mobilized" as a group.

Ibsen discovered several additional features of modern sacrificial behavior not elaborated by Shakespeare or Girard: in the modern period, reports of crowds abstracted by politicians and journalists substitute for real crowds. Journalists and politicians speak for a crowd too large to gather, which perhaps only exists in the hypothetical form they give it.

In *Pillars of Society*, Karsten Bernick feared that every newspaper in Norway would talk about him. While it is true that a shipbuilder has global interests, Bernick feared the stories that can be told of him, not the appearance of a nationwide vengeful mob. In *An Enemy of the People* (like *Pillars of Society*), the imaginary crowd abstracted by journalism, which investigates, castigates, and pillories in the name of the public, shares the stage with the residual existence of noisy crowds (either parades or mobs) who cannot act decisively.

Like Karsten Bernick, Peter Stockmann identifies himself with the whole community to hide his own self-interest. Only his spotless reputation, his ostentatious self-denial, keeps the community from turning on him. Such leaders profess to have no personal desire which could compete with others—they only desire for everyone, the whole community. The modern term "self-sacrifice" aptly catches at once the private psychological note and the similarity to the function of the primitive kingship system.

As we have seen in the previous chapter, what makes modern leadership different is the co-presence of the public knowledge of crowd mobilization, that coexists together with its practice, as opposed to the efficacious misunderstanding in primitive culture, where the sacred governs and explains the rise and fall of peace and violence. The easiest way to mark this essential self-baffling element of modern culture is to consider, as Girard does, the presence and function of the term *scapegoat*, a word which has come to designate at once an age-old sacrificial practice as well as expose it, rendering its effects unstable.

Except for one final stage in the process of blaming others, the scape-goat process cannot coexist with the understanding of its arbitrary prac-tice encoded in the term *scapegoat*. This final paradoxical stage of scapegoating is to accuse others of scapegoating, to take the side of the (scapegoat) victim against his accusers. One element of this final stage of violent unanimity is to make an idol of the persecuted as uniquely inno-cent, to deify self-sacrifice, instead of recognizing the persecuted as being no guiltier than the rest.

Tomas Stockmann's daughter Petra makes a remarkable observation that helps tie together the relation of the abstracted crowd invoked by journalism and the media to modernism, and the modern unstable quality of social cohesion allowed by the preoccupation with expelling scapegoat-ing itself. Petra's idea about journalism is that it is on the side of the op-pressed and persecuted.

> PETRA. . . . Å, det er et herlig livskall De har valgt. Således å bane veien for miskjente sannheter og for nye modige synsmåter—; ja bare det å stå fryktløs frem og ta ordet for en forurettet mann—(185–86)

> PETRA. . . . It's a wonderful career that you've chosen: to pave the way for unpopular truths, and for daring new opinions. . . . Or sim-ply to stand up bravely on the side of a man who's been wronged.[3]

News is whatever no one knew or expected ("nye modige synsmåter"), which nevertheless turns out to be true. Anyone else (politicians, artists, writers) who depends on the mercurial attention of the crowd being formed by journalism and the media must do likewise. Truth comes from whatever was recently unpopular and currently daring, by which we must understand that it provokes dissent. We catch the instability of modern sympathy immediately when we try to match the persecuted minority championed by the press with the greater number of readers a newspaper needs to survive. The newspaper needs an ever-ready supply of innocent victims with which to identify its readers, as well as a new supply of perse-cutors *not* identified with its readers.

Ibsen's play shows the full pattern of the foundational myth of enemy brothers competing to be the leader of the community, but the conflict is not resolved decisively. At the end of the play, Tomas Stockmann envisions a new round of conflict and crisis to stir up the community yet again. Presumably, he aspires to regain the role of the friend of the people, this time alone, without his brother. As Girard suggests, the modern exists in a state of continuous sacrificial crisis.

In the beginning, it is easy to take Tomas's side. Like Cordelia, and countless others, he is the younger sibling, put upon by hypocritical elders. Tomas is a younger brother who has gone north, into exile, until he was able to return to his home village, by some dispensation that is never clearly explained but clearly depends on his brother's influence.

Why did he leave? If he was educated as a doctor, he initially had family support. No one would grasp this better than Ibsen himself, who lived out the difficulty of paying for an education in medicine without financial support from his family. In the middle of the play, we find out that Morten Kiil, Tomas's father-in-law, was "hounded" ("hundsvoterte"—170) off the City Council by Peter Stockmann and his associates. If Kiil was driven off after Tomas married his daughter, then a natural mentor and powerful ally of Tomas's was disenfranchised for the sake of Peter's interests.

In the beginning of the play, Tomas's open hospitality is stressed, even before he himself appears. Dinner guests keep arriving at his house; everyone is offered roast beef and hot toddies. Peter drops by, wearing the full mayoral insignia of hat and staff. His open disdain is in the classic tradition that Frye educated us in, of the comic denier of festivities: he refuses separately a dinner (as bad for his digestion) and drink (because he never joins in drinking parties).

Peter is very touchy about his preeminence and very disparaging about his brother, as if the two estimations were directly related. Hovstad, the editor, mentions to Peter that he has held over an article of Tomas's about the Baths; Peter guesses that it wasn't good enough to print. Mrs. Stockmann adds that Tomas works ceaselessly for the Baths; Peter replies that he is obliged to work as their employee. Hovstad's answer, that the Baths were Tomas's idea, especially rankles Peter.

> THE MAYOR. He? indeed? Yes, I have heard from time to time that there are certain people who hold that opinion. But I certainly imagined that I, too, had a modest share in the enterprise. (108–09)

Mrs. Stockmann tries to soothe Peter by sending Hovstad back to dinner, but Peter is inconsolable. When she asks "Can't you and Tomas share the honour? You *are* brothers" (109), Peter blames his resentment and their rivalry on Tomas.

We first hear Tomas before we see him outside his own door, laughing noisily ("ler og støyer der ute"—161). His boisterous hospitality compares favorably with Peter's abstemiousness. Later, when Peter has gone to Hovstad's office to dissuade him from publishing Tomas's exposé of the Baths' contaminated water supply, he leaves behind his mayoral hat and stick in his eagerness to hide from Tomas in another room, lest he be caught in the office of an opposition newspaper. Tomas discovers his hat and stick, and parades around the office wearing them, taunting and ridiculing his brother.[4] Tomas is a classic comic hero; the audience cannot but prefer him to his brother.

Peter does everything he can to thwart Tomas's attempt to purify the Baths. He persuades Hovstad not to publish Tomas's warning that the Baths are polluted, a pestilence, and hijacks the public meeting Tomas organizes to make the same announcement. Through parliamentary procedure, they silence Tomas and vote him an enemy of the people at his own lecture. When Peter delivers Tomas's termination notice as Doctor of the Baths the next day, he performs the same infuriatingly hypocritical lustration as the rest of the betrayers of Tomas and his family: they take no responsibility themselves for quitting his side, blaming all on the others whose wishes cannot be ignored.[5]

The most telling sign of Tomas's persecution is perhaps lapidation itself. The crowd from his lecture stoned his house, breaking the windows. Tomas promises his wife that he will "keep these stones as sacred relics. Eylif and Morten must look at them every day, and when they grow up they will inherit them from me" (197). Further, he complains that they have "pilloried me as a Public Enemy, branded me" (198). Modern Norwegian society no longer pilloried and branded its enemies, but Tomas has that unfair and barbaric practice at hand as a historical reference for characterizing his victimary status.[6]

Is there no justice in such treatment of someone who is first a folkevenn, a friend of the community? In fact, there is an edge to Tomas as well. Wonderful little details gives us second thoughts about Peter's early accusation to Tomas that he has

> inngrodd tilbøyelighet til å gå dine egne veie iallfall. Og det er i et vel ordnet samfunn omtrent likså utilstedelig. Den enkelte får sannelig

finne seg i å innordne seg under det hele, eller rettere sagt, under de myndigheter som har å våke over det heles vel. (163)

an ingrained tendency to go your own way, whatever the circumstances—and in a well-ordered community that is almost as reprehensible [as criminal behavior]. The individual must subordinate himself to Society as a whole—or rather, to those authorities whose duty it is to watch over the welfare of Society. (113–14)

Contained within Peter's criticism is the sharper observation that Tomas finds his own way to be against whatever direction the community is going.

When Tomas finally gets the lab report on the quality of the water at the Baths, he dashes for his study to read it: "I must go to my room at once and—I shall want a light, Katrina; I suppose, as usual, there's no lamp in my study!" (117–18). This is Ibsen's psychological observation at its very best. We hear the testy and unfair complaint against his wife as evidence of Tomas's sense of persecution everywhere.

One of Peter's early statements helps set the importance of the Baths to the community's welfare. When Peter first learns of his brother's article for Hovstad's paper (which identifies with political interests antithetical to Peter and the current Town Council), Hovstad expects trouble from him. But Peter is very carefully reconciliatory. Peter identifies the Baths as the source of the community's "tolerance": "I det hele tatt råder der en smukk fordragelighetens ånd i vår by; – en riktig god borgerånd. Og det kommer derav at vi har et stort felles anliggende å samle oss om,—et anliggende som i like høy grad vedkommer alle rettsindige medborgere—" (160; "Taken all in all, there's a splendid spirit of tolerance here in our town—a really good municipal spirit. And it all springs from our having a great common interest to unite us—an interest which is of equal concern to every right-minded citizen" [107]). Peter's speech is clearly political rhetoric, although it is mentioned only once in the play in passing that there is an impending election for the City Council. Ibsen is more interested in the production of unanimity or agreement which the election reads or registers or formalizes, but does not produce. Ibsen treats voting as the mere verification or tabulation of social practices normally invisible, more worthy of study.

As Tomas sets the stage for revealing the contents of the lab report to his family and friends, we see the modern version of the emergent leader who scandalizes the community, overthrowing their beliefs and their solidarity. Tomas makes all repeat back to him what everyone believes, that the Baths are a godsend to the town's economy, a therapeutic blessing to all visitors, so that he can deliver the news to them:

> DR. STOCKMANN. . . . But do you know what they really are—these splendid highly recommended Baths that have cost so much money? D'you know what they are?
>
> HOVSTAD. No, what?
>
> MRS. STOCKMANN. Well, what are they?
>
> DR. STOCKMANN. The whole Baths are a pesthouse! (121)

Interestingly, the first person he intends to tell the next day (beyond the report he has written to the Board of Governors) is "old Badger" (the town's uncomplimentary nickname for Tomas's father-in-law). He explains that his discovery will redress the opinion his father-in-law shares with others, that the doctor "is not quite right in the head," but we can't ignore what "old Badger" himself admits later, that he doesn't want his tannery to be identified as the polluter of the water source; he doesn't want his good name ruined. How can Tomas be so oblivious to what the effect of his discovery will be on his father-in-law as well as the rest of the community?

Tomas's certitude that the town will honor him as its *folkevenn* with parades when he reveals the pollution in its greatest source of income seems naive or at most somewhat disingenuous when we look to his character or psychology for an answer. It is better understood within the dynamics of mimetic interdividuality and modern public "mobilization." He will induce a crisis that he alone can solve, repeating in effect his greatest triumph, the installation of the Baths, but now they will be his alone, not shared with his brother (who successfully contravened Tomas's plans for installing the water pipes away from the source of pollution).[7]

As in all fraternal rivalries, there is some truth to the accusation of each resentful brother.

> Efter min formening viser det seg kun at du igjen trenger til et avløp for din stridslyst. Du vil dine foresatte til livs;—det er jo din gamle vane. Du kan ikke tåle noen autoritet over deg; du ser skjevt til

enhver der bekler en overordnet embedsstilling; du betrakter ham som en personlig fiende,—og straks er det ene angrepsvåpen deg likså godt som det annet. (177–78)

To my mind, it's perfectly obvious that you're looking for another outlet for your intransigence. You wish to attack your superiors— an old habit of yours. You can't bear to have anyone in authority over you: you look askance at anyone who has a higher post than yours, and you consider him a personal enemy . . . and immediately any stick's good enough to beat him with.[8]

Of course "anyone" superior to Tomas is first of all Peter, his brother.

But that is not all. Peter and Tomas are jealous of each other. Even Tomas's hospitality is polemical and rivalrous. Because Peter denies himself everything in social relations and food, to prove his immaculate absence of desire, Tomas engorges himself and becomes a missionary of the appetites. We need to restate their antagonism outside of our easy preference for Tomas, the character who pleases us and our comic expectations, a more advanced form of revenge on all those who oppress us.

Each brother claims to have proposed the Baths as the salvation of visitors and the economy of the town. By itself, of course, it is impossible to separate one brother's accusation from their interminable rivalry. They are enemy twins like Eteocles and Polynices, Romulus and Remus, signs of a social crisis.[9]

Perhaps now we are prepared to consider Peter's most aggravated and extreme accusation, that his brother Tomas has a persecution complex.

> Byfogeden. Ja, en gang må jeg dog tale likefrem med deg. Hittil har jeg søkt å unngå det, da jeg vet hvor irritabel du er; men nu må jeg si deg sannheten, Tomas. Du gjør deg ingen forestilling om hvor meget du skader deg selv ved din fremfusenhet. Du beklager deg over autoritetene, ja, over selv regjeringen,. . . påstår at du er blitt tilsidesatt, forfulgt. Men kan du vente deg annet,—en så besværlig som du er. (177)

THE MAYOR. Yes, for once, I must speak openly to you. So far, knowing how quick you are to take offense, I've tried to avoid it, but now, Tomas, I must tell you the truth. You have no conception what harm your impetuosity does you. You complain about the authorities—yes, about the Government. You revile them, insisting that

you've been slighted and passed over—but what else can you expect
when you're so intractable? (142–43)

Ibsen beautifully catches their mutual exasperation. Of course Peter does
nothing but "speak openly" of the truth of Tomas's impetuosity. But
Peter's criticism of Tomas's complaint that he has been passed over and
persecuted ("tilsidesatt, forfulgt"), while it demonstrates the interminable quality of mutual recrimination, is confirmed by Peter's censure of
it which, in effect, argues that he has been passed over and persecuted
because he resents it and complains about it. And neither denies that Peter
is in a position to grant or withhold preferment to Tomas.

We must restate our position that in the uncanny repetition of immemorial myth in the modern period, even the stoning of Tomas (he wants
to keep the stones as religious relics!), there is no need for atavism or a
collective unconscious to explain it. Characters feel or lean towards re-
sponses and strategies that seem to be working. We can imagine many
intuitive moves that would lose rather than gain power, just as there must
have been innumerable "societies" that never happened on any version of
a sacrificial process that could forestall mimetic violence, that never entered history because they couldn't sustain themselves long enough to
leave a record.

Drama is the kind of research project that (like history) focuses on con-
sequential cases. Ibsen, like many modern writers, is watching a generative mechanism of mimetic violence which unites the community by po-
larizing it against one sacrificial victim. This mechanism repeats itself in
places where it can survive, metabolically alter and metastasize like (very
like) some disease that resists global eradication.

The crowd and their leader, Peter Stockmann, is quasi-primitive, fear-
ing contamination. Peter's care in never seeming to do anything for himself, in always seeking the consent of the entire community, repeats the
strategy of primitive ritual, which enjoins everyone to agree by partici-
pating in the sacrificial expulsion of pollution. (Such caution ensures, at a
functional level, that there is no one left to join the victim's side.)

But if Peter Stockmann seems to reincarnate the solidarity of a sacrificial society in a leader who is perfect, Tomas Stockmann reincarnates the
sacrificial subject who polarizes the crowd against him. Both are metaphysical misunderstandings of mimetic relations and interdividuality. In
An Enemy of the People, we are given the error symmetrical to Peter's
excessive sense of virtue: Tomas's excessive sense of persecution, the one

whose sacrifice and persecution proves his innocence and virtue. Tomas Stockmann is the forerunner of the great subaltern texts of this century, which maintain their virtue by the measure of their (unjust) persecution.

In fact, the town is in a state of crisis; the amount of free-floating resentment and rivalry is remarkable. (Here is perhaps Ibsen's view of modern politics.) Morten Kiil, Tomas's father-in-law, resents the new city council of Peter and his cohorts. Anything which pays them back pleases him. Yet such potential allies as Tomas and his father-in-law go out of their way to upset each other. Tomas publicly names Morten Kiil's tannery as the greatest polluter of the water system, and Kiil provocatively invests a patrimony intended for Tomas's children in the devalued water spa stocks, intending to force Tomas to rescind his charge of pollution to recover the stock's value.

Hovstad and Billing are colleagues on *Folkebudet,* a liberal newspaper committed to social change. Yet they are rivals to each other, another set of enemy twins. Hovstad is scandalized when his printer Aslaksen reveals that Billing has applied for the position of Secretary to the Council. Billing suavely argues that he has done so only to be refused, to sharpen his antagonism against the establishment. Yet Aslaksen has already reminded Hovstad that Councillor Stensgård once sat in Hovstad's chair in the *Folkebudet* office. "Parties" are empty rivalries for power and prestige, for the support or service of the majority.

Of course the play enacts its interest in mobilization by putting the crowd itself on stage at Stockmann's meeting in Act IV. The great set piece of the play is the lecture where Tomas delivers his elitist and modernist principles, inspired in him through opposition, not conviction, through scandal, not belief. It is not impossible that Ibsen for a time believed what Tomas declares in his speech. We know that Ibsen himself seconded Tomas's lecture in a letter to his editor. Yet writers put more time and thought into their creative work than their correspondence, and it is more likely that the play will take us further in thinking these ideas through than arbitrarily terminating our thinking in deference to Ibsen's personal authority. Ibsen also was a public figure, and could never be indifferent to the public or dramatic quality of whatever he said. Dramas and fictions, unlike letters, essays, and speeches, reflect on their context and audience as well.

Let us begin our analysis of this provocative speech by remembering that throughout the play, Tomas speaks for disruption, teeming, outbreak, uproar. In their first exchange, Tomas directs Peter's attention approvingly (and indiscriminately) to Hovstad, Billing, Captain Horster, and his two sons as the new generation which will "stir things up and keep them on the move for the future" (110; "rote opp i det gjærende fremtids-stoff" [161]). Peter asks disapprovingly what requires "stirring up," and later castigates Tomas's "turbulent, aggressive, rebellious nature" (142; "uroligt, stridbart, opprørsk sinn" [177]). As long as Tomas is "our" comic hero, his turbulent temperament compares favorably with the personalities of Peter and Aslaksen, who speak for temperance, guiding flows. These metaphors apply to social, personal, and metabolic behavior, and such behavior is fundamentally mimetic. Individual elements copy each other's turbulence or peaceful flow, like sheep (or cells, or audiences) mimicking a quiet or an unruly leader.[10]

At the beginning of Act IV, it is clear that the audience forming on stage for Stockmann's lecture has come prepared to cause trouble. It is interesting that while Stockmann disregards it, Captain Horster speaks ominously about the crowd's potential for violence, next time if not this time. Crowds and parades in Ibsen's plays remind one of the Kaingang tribe so interesting to twentieth-century anthropologists, whose violent behavior made their "parties" notorious, indistinguishable from a brawl, a violent melee.

Stockmann caters to this crowd, up to a point. They roar approvingly while he makes fun of their elders, especially his own brother. He feeds their comic appetite for misrule, for a victim, but they react with fury when he turns on them.

Tomas leads the audience the way he led his domestic audience earlier to the scandal that only he knows about. As Northrop Frye taught us, all proposers of social change follow an immemorial comic model of redeeming society by taking it out of the hands of the hypocritical elders and turning it over (or returning it) to the great mass of society. Tomas has already suggested to Hovstad in Act II that he plans a series of articles which will expand his accusation of pollution to social contexts, but he has changed his target from the elders, the immemorial victims of comedy, to the audience of comedy itself, the supposed reservoir of all new redeemed societies. This is very dangerous work. Peter speaks for the whole community when he says "You cannot fling a gross accusation like that against a whole community!" (191).

Tomas proposes a position symmetrically opposed to the *Folkbudet's*, arguing that humans are like livestock, only the purebreds are capable of distinction and learning. Perhaps Tomas's greatest scandal is to set his position in relation to Christ himself:

DOKTOR STOCKMANN. Ingen bakveie, Katrine. (med hevet røst.) I skal få høre fra folkefienden før han ryster støvet av sine føtter! Jeg er ikke så godslig som en viss person; jeg sier ikke: jeg tilgir eder; ti I vet ikke hva I gjør. (203)

DR. STOCKMANN. No back way, Katrina. [Raising his voice]. You shall hear from your Public Enemy before he shakes the dust of this place off his feet! I'm not as forbearing as a certain person was. . . . I don't say "I forgive you, for you know not what you do." (195)

In both *Pillars of Society* and *An Enemy of the People* Ibsen has in mind the parallel of secular with sacred scripture. Both Karsten Bernick and Tomas Stockmann think of the Passion when they consider their vulnerable singularity before the mob. It is true that Ibsen edited out Bernick's quotation of the most powerful verbal formula ever uttered against scapegoat practices—"Let him who is without sin among you cast the first stone."[11] It was no doubt prudent that Bernick (or Ibsen) not inflame the crowd, but that is exactly Stockmann's intention.

But what of the secular scripture? When we recall yet again Henrik Jaeger's observation that alone of the major writers he knew, Ibsen had no working library, that he only read the newspapers and the Bible (only for style, he averred), then we may begin to grasp that for Ibsen the stories in the paper are themselves the secular scripture.

The very next day Tomas reverses both positions he fought for previously: he decides to remain rather than emigrate, and he declares he will start a school with the most lowly and disadvantaged children as pupils. Tomas is still assaying, probing the position of the outsider in his community, looking for whatever will provoke them.

Tomas, like Lona, loves the opposition of the crowd's "uproar." If Tomas is unmindful of Captain Horster's caution, that stirring the crowd can be dangerous, James Joyce was not. Now we are better prepared to understand Joyce's fear of suffering the same betrayal and persecution as Charles Stewart Parnell and Oscar Wilde. Joyce's fear has often been read as a harmless or mildly disabling psychological quirk, but it is perhaps his most valuable insight into modern collective behavior. We must credit

Joyce's faithfulness to a lifelong project first adumbrated in his early essay "A Portrait of the Artist," rejected for publication in 1904:

> To those multitudes not as yet in the wombs of humanity but surely engenderable there, he would give the word. Man and woman, out of you comes the nation that is to come, the lightning of your masses in travail; the competitive order is employed against itself, the aristocracies are supplanted; and amid the general paralysis of an insane society, the confederate will issues in action. (*A Portrait of the Artist as a Young Man*, 265–66)

Against everything which has already been said, beginning with the editors of *Dana* themselves, about the unsuitability of this early effort at publication, we might answer that already Joyce sees modern society in a state of continuous and contaminated crisis of competition.[12] Ontological superiority (aristocracy) is razed, a new confederate will, not competitive, is now possible.

"Who does the young Joyce think he is?" might be the way to formulate the usual reaction to the tone of this essay, but we must also acknowledge that the tone is astutely political, absolutely certain of its public resonance and effect, and who hasn't heard of Joyce now?

4

Joyce's Sisters

Here is the marvellous novel delivered upon you by my twenty-third sister.
"Stephen Dædalus" (James Joyce), 1904 letter

—What are you doing here, Stephen?
Dilly's high shoulders and shabby dress.
Shut the book quick. Don't let see.
—What are you doing? Stephen said.
A Stuart face of nonesuch Charles, lank locks falling at its sides. It glowed as
    she crouched feeding the fire with broken boots. I told her of Paris. Late
    lieabed under a quilt of old overcoats, fingering a pinchbeck bracelet, Dan
    Kelly's token. *Nebrakada femininum.*
—What have you there? Stephen asked.
—I bought it from the other cart for a penny, Dilly said, laughing nervously. Is
    it any good?
My eyes they say she has. Do others see me so? Quick, far and daring. Shadow
    of my mind.
He took the coverless book from her hand. Chardenal's French primer.
—What did you buy that for? he asked, To learn French?
She nodded, reddening and closing tight her lips.
Show no surprise. Quite natural.
—Here, Stephen said. It's all right. Mind Maggy doesn't pawn it on you. I sup-
    pose all my books are gone.
—Some, Dilly said. We had to.
She is drowning. Agenbite. Save her. Agenbite. All against us. She will drown
    me with her, eyes and hair. Lank coils of seaweed hair around me, my heart,
    my soul. Saltgreen death.
We.
Agenbite of inwit. Inwit's agenbite.
Misery! Misery!
Joyce, *Ulysses*

Meanwhile his extraordinarily gifted sister, let us suppose, remained at home.
She was as adventurous, as imaginative, as agog to see the world as he was. But
she was not sent to school. She had no chance of learning grammar and logic,
let alone of reading Horace and Virgil. She picked up a book now and then,
one of her brother's perhaps, and read a few pages. But then her parents came
in and told her to mend the stockings or mind the stew and not moon about
with books and papers.
Woolf, *A Room of One's Own*

"The Sisters" was the first work of fiction Joyce published. It is quite properly seen as a beginning for *Dubliners* and, in some ways, for all of Joyce's fiction,[1] and has received as much careful commentary as any other story. In particular, Hugh Kenner and Marvin Magalaner, early on, and then Therese Fischer and Florence Walzl, recognized the significance of the evolution of this story from the *Irish Homestead* to the "Yale" and "Cornell" manuscripts, to the final version, as an act of increasingly conscious self-criticism.[2] But where does "The Sisters" itself begin, and where does it ever end? And *why* do its revisions become increasingly self-critical?

It is true to say that revision makes "The Sisters" increasingly modern. But that is not all. If we develop the theoretical potential of Joyce's revisions, we will be on our way to considering Joyce's work together with Girard's work, to suggest an alternative theory of modernism. Further, we will understand how Joyce proposed to his country a nonviolent alternative tradition to what Conor Cruise O'Brien has recently described as *Ancestral Voices*, those voices of the dead (like Pearse) who ask for blood sacrifice, including self-sacrifice, voices that are more persuasive than the voices of the living who ask for peace.[3]

Against such ambitions we must yet again remind ourselves of Girard's own insistence on the theoretical power of literary texts to keep from simply transcoding Joyce into Girard at the beginning, a process that would teach us nothing more about either one of them. It will be time to introduce Girard once we have elaborated the theoretical potential of Joyce's many sisters.

Joyce first wrote "The Sisters" in July 1904. The story was an invited submission to the *Irish Homestead,* and its revision continued until July 1906, when it was revised yet again to serve as an introduction to a fourteen-story *Dubliners.*[4] "The Dead" would be written more than a year later.

To better understand the context of this compositional process for "The Sisters," we must begin with Stanislaus Joyce's invaluable commentaries, which explain that his brother had already tried out modes of short fiction entitled "Silhouettes," epiphanies of the sordidness of others, told by a first-person narrator. Stanislaus remembered the first story, which gave the series its title, as a young boy walking along the mean streets of Dublin, suddenly observing, in a window, a fight between husband and wife, which the husband ends with a blow. Then the shade is drawn. After a while, the profile of two figures reappears, cast by candlelight, this time a mother and child. The mother figure cautions the smaller not to "waken Pa."[5]

Stanislaus has clearly in the back of his mind, as he remembers "Sil-houettes," the entire progress of his brother's early work in prose. He consciously lines up "Silhouettes" as antecedent to *Dubliners* and threaded through the cruel dynamic of the intermediary "Epiphanies." As Stanislaus shrewdly explains them, the epiphanies expose precisely what the subject tries to conceal:[6] each draws the shade, each portrays itself in outline, revealed.

Stanislaus Joyce is our sole source for whatever we know of this mate-rial. Our gratitude to him should encourage us to work further the conse-quences of his associations, as well as his analysis. He thinks of his brother's epiphanic method as explanation for these early short silhou-ettes/narratives because he has just been describing in his own narrative how he discovered that other Dublin families, apparently more respect-able, hid the same sordid family life as the Joyces. This leads him to con-sider, with understandable preference, his brother's candor superior to the more general hypocrisy.

We could simply concur with Stanislaus that candor is superior to hy-pocrisy, but a much more interesting speculation opens up before us. If we remember that Stephen trumped the snobbism of Clongowes schoolboys by claiming one uncle a magistrate and another uncle a judge, we may see "Epiphanies" for the matriculated Joyce as a more advanced hand in the game of what Girard calls "mimetic rivalry."

Candor is not innocent of the pretensions which surround it; rather, candor characterizes, even accuses its fellows as hypocritical by compari-son, unless they can outperform it with a greater audacity. Later we will learn to ask, What identity does candor mask, when it mocks the hypoc-risy of its rival? How do "Epiphanies" themselves "epiphanize" their au-thor, revealing precisely the silhouette of what *he* would conceal?

The slender evidence of letters and manuscripts for whatever sequence Joyce intended for "Epiphanies" has made agreement difficult, but most critics accede to their division into two kinds:[7] confessions and observa-tions—the confessed ecstasy of seraphic life, and the observed meanness of others. In any combination or sequence, one kind tends to serve, vali-date the other. The writer has the authority to unmask others, having unmasked himself. The resentment of Oliver St. John Gogarty and other acquaintances of Joyce to being epiphanized is not answered by Stanislaus's disclaimer, pointed mainly at Gogarty, that friends were rarely the subject of his brother's writings. They had reasons to feel put down.

John Eglinton and Fred Ryan's refusal of Joyce's submission to their new journal *Dana*, and Joyce's response to their refusal, suggest that rivalry is the dynamic of "A Portrait of the Artist" (January 1904) as well as its subject. In the language of the rejected essay, the young artist, "divining of intrigue," composes "an enigma of a manner." He presents himself as indifferent to rivalry in order to vanquish rivalry, to reunite the children of the spirit, jealous and long-divided by a competitive order employed against itself. "But he saw between camps his ground of vantage, opportunities for the mocking devil."[8] The essay unmasks the artist in a manner too audacious for *Dana*, but what follows, in the covertly autobiographical *Stephen Hero* (the exponential expansion of this essay), according to Stanislaus, is the mockery of others.

Stanislaus's contemporaneous *Dublin Diary* insists on the satirical direction of *Stephen Hero*'s evolution after "A Portrait of the Artist" was rejected by *Dana*. Further, Stanislaus identifies satire, the mocking devil, as a family party piece, representatively Irish. Both of their parents, even Charlie, are credited as omnicompetent at mimickry. Finally, Stanislaus quotes Yeats with full approval, who said that Swift, the Dean of Satire, made a soul for Dubliners by teaching them to hate others as they hate themselves.

In the long run, *Dana*'s rejection of "A Portrait of the Artist" probably changed nothing. The common experience of Joyce's earlier editors, Longworth of the *Daily Express*, and Hugh Kennedy of *St. Stephen's*, or even Joyce's teachers, suggests that suffering, soliciting, or refusing Joyce's work could never blunt, could only sharpen "that little pen" "dipped in fermented ink" (*Selected Letters* [hereinafter abbreviated *SL*] 76).[9]

Granting Joyce what he himself called an "all-too-Irish" sensitivity, a reader could hardly imagine a more provocative invitation for a contribution than the oft-quoted letter of George W. Russell (Æ), especially if we consider it as issued sometime in July, after a certain discussion in the National Library which *Ulysses* dates as 16 June 1904.[10]

> Look at the story in this paper The Irish Homestead. Could you write anything simple, rural? livemaking?, pathos?, which could be inserted so as not to shock the readers. If you could furnish a short

story about 1800 words suitable for insertion the editor will pay £1. It is easily earned money if you can write fluently and don't mind playing to the common understanding and liking once in a way. You can sign it any name you like as a pseudonym. (*Letters of James Joyce* [hereinafter *Letters*] 2: 43)

Stories in the *Irish Homestead* were regularly published over pseudonyms as "Our Weekly Story," so although Russell would have been reading the early chapters of the *Stephen Hero* manuscript at this time (*SL* 22), it is not certain that he is referring disparagingly to their subject "Stephen Dædalus."[11] But Joyce had already perceived slights in much less ambiguous offers of assistance. Ellmann tells us that Skeffington, for example, when he became registrar of the college, offered Joyce, by letter, tutoring work in French. Joyce declined the offer, in person, going to the dean of studies himself, on the theory that the college authorities wished to silence him by putting him in their debt (Ellmann [hereinafter *JJ II*] 140).

No one before Hans Walter Gabler's edition of *Dubliners* for Garland Press ever identified *in print* Russell's model story for submission.[12] Because of a hiatus in story publishing at the *Irish Homestead*, the three published stories closest to hand (for the tone and construction of Russell's note suggest hastiness) would have been Louise Kenny's "Ryan Rascal" (11, 18, and 25 June 1904), Berkeley Campbell's "The Old Watchman" (2 July 1904), and Alice Milligan's "A Farmyard Tragedy" (16 and 30 July 1904). The late date of the last story, and the serial publication of both Kenny and Milligan (Russell writes of a single issue: "look at the story in *this* paper") make them less likely choices. Finally, H. F. Norman's letter of acceptance to Joyce for "The Sisters" is dated 23 July 1904 (*JJ II* 164).

On the other hand, "The Sisters" bears a striking resemblance to "Campbell's" story.[13] A narrator describes his interest as a twelve-year-old in an old watchman who took what he calls his "fancy. He was apparently about sixty-five, and his clean-shaved, wrinkled face had a sad and lonely expression." The narrator adds that he was "surprised to hear that he [the old man] spoke with a very nice accent and a cultivated voice." The boy becomes familiar with the old watchman, "my old man," as he calls him, from the boy's father's practice of walking home from the theatre, "as Dad said it was good for us to get a breath of fresh air after coming out of the stuffy theatre." Finally, the father talks to the watchman, who admits to serious illness: "sometimes my cough is too bad for me to go out, and James, that's the other workman, takes it for me. I have had a cough ever since I had pleurisy, and I'm afraid it won't leave me here much longer." On the way home, the narrator remembers "the many different conjectures we came to . . . as to what his story was. Then I got a very bad cold, and was not let out with Dad for about a fortnight" (Campbell 556).

Ultimately, the old man in Campbell's fiction confesses his story of opportunity ruined: he was the younger son of the dean of St. Patrick's, who was to have gone through Trinity and studied for the bar. But "I only stayed up to the small hours of the morning drinking and gambling, and losing more money than I could ever hope to pay." He ran away to Australia after his father offered him a new start in Canada. When he finally returned, he knew no one, and now waits to die. The boy's father gets him into a hospital: "I used to go and see him very often, but he only lived a few weeks, and I was awfully sorry when he died. But now I always look at the watchmen on the tramline and wonder if they have a story like 'my old man's!'" (Campbell 557).

This first-person attention of a young boy to the narrative of an old man gives a lot of material to Joyce's satirical mind for successive versions of "The Sisters" as well as later stories. Like Father Flynn, who is opposed to Old Cotter, the old watchman is opposed to a fresh-air advocate, his high education has come to nothing, and he is near death. Campbell's boy narrator is, as well, a curiously patient observer of his old man's decline: his interest is, like the interest of the narrator of "The Sisters" in Father Flynn, a "fancy"—"The fancy came to me" (*Irish Homestead* 677; *Dubliners* [hereinafter *D*] 14). The boy develops a "sympathetic" respiratory illness, an aspect of contamination Joyce would certainly have enjoyed trumping in "The Sisters" with a half-hidden prognosis of paralysis or paresis.[14]

The first version of "The Sisters" seems a pretty mean satire of unambiguous uplifting testimony characteristic of the fiction and verse published in the *Irish Homestead*. Most improper or sniggering readings of this story (like the suggestion that the "unassuming shop, registered under the vague name of *Drapery*" is meant to call up, to a Dublin cavalier, a locally known source for condoms)[15] or later stories,[16] have caught the spirit, if not always the letter, of *Dubliners*. Joyce has deviously violated every caution of Russell's, with stories that shock the *Homestead* readers, and later, Grant Richards's printer.

The early, Dublin Joyce, the Joyce of the university essays, reviews, and Dublin literary folklore, contentiously allied himself with the modern in drama and prose, suggesting everyone else, including Yeats, was already too old to be modernized. "The Sisters" modernizes "Our Weekly Story" according to the futile discipline perfected by Flaubert: the fashion-dynamics of modernization require that any text which aspires to virtue by breaking new ground must deconstruct a rival text as obsolete, but such a procedure must ultimately lead to self-modernization, self-rivalry, self-destruction. Such modernism can only end by rewinding Yeats's wonderful observation, that spiritual resentment of others begins in self-hatred. Having "modernized" the *Irish Homestead*, "The Sisters" must "progress," ineluctably, to modernizing itself.

However, as the beginning of *Dubliners*, it must modernize itself—as Hans Walter Gabler suggests—in the context of successive and strategic moments of reflection on *Dubliners* as a whole: in October 1905, just before writing out "Grace" as the end of a twelve-story collection, and in July 1906, when Richards sent the whole fourteen-story manuscript back to Joyce for major revision and recantation.

The "Yale" manuscript version of "The Sisters," which Gabler dates as October 1905 (*James Joyce Archives* [hereinafter *JJA*] 4: xxviii), remains very similar to the *Irish Homestead* version. First, Joyce improves accuracy: Father Flynn is given a real church (undoing an editorial revision of H. F. Norman), he is vested, not habited for burial, following Stanislaus's research (*Letters* 2: 114). But the narrator remains a stable, complacent if precocious agent of language and attitude. In the opening paragraphs, "providence" ("pro-videre") guides his attempts to *foresee* Flynn's demise, and he is a "prophet" to himself by *foretelling* his disappointment. (In contrast, the opening paragraph of the 1906 version will emphasize the powers vested in language which control the narrator.)

In 1905, he still speaks easily of how "people will blunder on what you have elaborately planned for" (*JJA* 4: 335), he dismissively refers to "three women of the people," to his aunt, "what they call good-hearted," and supposes that Father Flynn prefers his own intelligence to the sisters' lack of same. It is unsurprising that he tolerates Father Flynn's "egoistic contempt for all women-folk" (*JJA* 4: 341). His precocious scorn for others remains uncontested.

Most interestingly, in revision, the narrator grammatically removes himself from Dublin. The *Irish Homestead* version read "Now I find . . .

[Cotter] tedious," and his aunt "is a bit of a gossip." The present tense of
1904 makes "Stephen Dædalus," like "Berkeley Campbell" ("Now I always look at the watchmen") a Dubliner still, probably at the same address. "Afterwards he became tedious" (*JJA* 4: 334), and "she was a gossip"
(*JJA* 4: 345), like the signature to "The Boarding House" manuscript of
1 September 1905 ("Stephen Dædalus"/Via S. Nicolò, 30/"Trieste, Aus-
tria," *JJA* 4: 45), show how easy detachment and relocation seem in 1905,
in Trieste, before Joyce's elaborate conflict with Richards began.

It is only later, in the July 1906 ("Cornell" manuscript) revision, that
"The Sisters" will admit to the pros and cons of Dublin. The narrator will
still recall Cotter as tedious, but he will also remember puzzling his head
to extract meaning from his unfinished sentences, in a manner which suggests that he is *still* somewhat puzzled.

Critics have always been drawn to elaborate yet again the meanings of
simony in the Catechism, gnomon in Euclid's *Elements,* and paralysis in
The Principles and Practice of Medicine,[17] as important signs of revision
of "The Sisters." These revisions first occur in the 1906 version; the 1905
version retains the original first paragraph from the *Irish Homestead.* We
might add to this constant refinement in our understanding of these three
words that these improvements of 1906, as well as our refinements, are at
the boy's expense.

"Stephen Dædalus" in 1905 deals confidently with a material, a language, and an audience he has mastered. This narrator of 1906 is no master of his own words; rather, he has heard an adult voice give an elliptic
significance to simony and gnomon (probably in geometry and Catechism class), and paralysis (whenever Father Flynn is discussed), without
sufficient explanation. These adult voices are given more to denying than
granting him competence. Further, he cannot conclude his own imaginative attempt to extract meaning from the sentences Cotter uses to puzzle
him.

The series of notations of Cotter's tediousness, across successive versions of "The Sisters," mark nicely the narrator's "progress" of modernization as self-deconstruction. To the *Irish Homestead* version of 1904
("He used to be very interesting when I knew him first, talking about
'faints' and 'worms.' Now I find him tedious") the 1905 version "draws
the shade" in the way Stanislaus remembers "Silhouettes" ("afterwards
he became tedious"—*JJA* 4: 335). The narrator of 1905 removes himself in
a double sense: grammatically, as we have already seen, he is no longer

present, in time or place, to find Cotter tedious; secondly, Cotter *is* tedious, not found to be so by the narrator's subjectivity.

The 1906 version reads "When we knew him first he used to be rather interesting, talking of faints and worms; but I soon grew tired of him and his endless stories about the distillery" (*JJA* 4: 355). This sentence, by shifting pronouns from "we" to "I," shows how the boy modernized himself, alienating himself from them, rendering Old Cotter, his aunt and uncle, obsolete. Further, it strengthens the parallelism of Cotter and Flynn as rival pedagogues for the boy.

Here we see the local dynamics of futile resentment affiliated to cultural modernization. Irony is the technique of modern rivalry, artistic as well as sexual, and a defeated rival is necessary to the ironist's sense of superior being. To be defeated, in turn, is to think of oneself as a vanquished rival, to be exposed as a mere imitator or follower to that superior being. Joyce will name this ironic hero in 1907 the "loveless Irishman."

The new, comprehensive version of "The Sisters" in 1906 becomes the first story of *Dubliners* in a structural as well as a chronological sense. More than being the first story written, it introduces three narratives of self-defeat and self-hatred before going on, after "Araby," to the hatred of others. We might take up any of the subsequent stories, but perhaps "The Dead" is most important, because it ends the revisions of "The Sisters" as it ends the writing of *Dubliners* (and our reading of it). Joyce wrote two further stories during early 1906 before revising "The Sisters"—"A Little Cloud" and "Two Gallants"—but put them inside a series which still ended with "Grace." "The Dead" becomes the new and final ending. Only "The Dead" could end the revisions of "The Sisters" and complete *Dubliners*.

Girard is required reading on the subject of modern rivalry; and, as I have argued, his work implies a theory of the modern as well. In *Deceit, Desire, and the Novel*, Girard analyzes narcissism and coquetry as symptoms of the advances of modern emulation-as-rivalry. In the more advanced (modern) stages of mimetic or triangular desire, the *terzo incommodo* has become unnecessary, in fact outmoded. The coquette increases her self-esteem by inciting, then frustrating her lover's desire, produced by his imitating and unsuccessfully rivaling *her own self-love*. According to such a model of desire, if Gretta seemed to hold herself away, however lightly, from Michael Furey, then he emulated her apparent self-sufficiency with the ultimate narcissism of self-sacrifice, which makes him, in turn, an unattainable model of metaphysical desire, an external mediator without rival. One could at best follow him in self-sacrifice, but he would always be first.

But we cannot afford to make a scapegoat of Gretta, by making her the coquette responsible for instigating all this emulation. Like Isabel Archer in James's *Portrait of a Lady*, she was incapable at the time of resisting the interpretation put upon her by suitors representing an advanced system of disguised emulation which we ourselves still serve. Nor can we afford to completely exonerate her, to divinize her as the single being innocent of mimetic rivalry. We must not deny our identity to her, by exiling her below, or exalting her above our society.

If Gretta's letter to Michael Furey was written with design, similar in some way to the apparent coyness of Mangan's sister, or the practiced banter of the girl overheard at the Araby bazaar (although we must now, after Gabriel, warn ourselves that resentment perhaps makes our narrator a poor guide to what is on the mind of the women he meets), this woman we see is no coquette now. It takes (only) a snob to know one, to know the snobbism in others, as Girard argues, but it takes a revolutionary change of heart to renounce resentment and rivalry *unilaterally*.

—There were no words, said Gabriel moodily, only she wanted me to go for a trip to the west of Ireland and I said I wouldn't.

His wife clasped her hands excitedly and gave a little jump.

—O, do go, Gabriel, she cried. I'd love to see Galway again.

—You can go if you like, said Gabriel coldly.

She looked at him for a moment, then turned to Mrs. Malins and said:

—There's a nice husband for you, Mrs. Malins. (D 191)

Unlike the narrator (and most *sophisticated* readers), Gretta doesn't suspect Molly Ivors as a rival, and presents herself without guile as companion to both. Gretta Conroy is our sister as well, and we feel, without needing to see, that she nursed Mrs. Conroy through her last illness *unresentful* towards her primary rival for Gabriel's love. Like Christopher Newman, Lona Hessel, and especially Nora Helmer, Gretta has learned how to break the cycle of mimetic rivalry, by refusing to imitate an attempt to incarnate divinity through self-sacrifice, the last modernization of violence-as-the-sacred. It is from models like Gretta that we can learn what the heart is and what it feels.

In short, we need as readers to care more for Gretta's reading of Michael and Gabriel than the narrator's reading, who is Gabriel's spiritual brother. She wants Gabriel to live, with her. She is regretful, not proud, that Michael Furey died for her. Gretta is right about her husband: Gabriel *is* generous, although his generosity is crippled by irony and self-hatred. Gretta is greater than Gabriel's ironic reading, the narrator's, or the reader's, in such declarations as "I was great with him at the time" (*D* 220).

In the earlier stories of *Dubliners,* narrator and discerning reader mock the ignorance of simple Dubliners to the irony of what their words might be taken to mean. Here, in "The Dead," the skills of a scrupulously mean reading double back on themselves, shaming their practitioners. For critics to smirkingly suspect Gretta of conceiving with Michael Furey is not po-etry. Gretta Conroy and Nora Barnacle are sisters, Joyce's sisters, incipient signs (but without mitigating the necessary recognition of Joyce's sexism, which resists the fuller development of sorority) of the potential for Vir-ginia Woolf's enlightening *supposition* ("let us suppose"—*A Room of One's Own,* 49) of imagining the career of a great writer's sister. Virginia Woolf is herself Joyce's twin sister—they are the children of 1882, modernism's future, but that must be left for a later chapter.

"The Dead" *supposes* the remodernization of *Dubliners,* in part by a more generous portrayal of sisterhood than Mangan's, in "Araby," in "The Sisters" itself, or in "Clay." There is no clear family bond between the boy and the sisters in the first story. The sisters address the boy's aunt respectfully as "ma'm," and the narrator has no compunction in pointing up their commonness. The narrator's complicity in "The Dead," however, does not make inevitable or unalterable Gabriel's "modern" self-disparag-ing view that he has been orating to vulgarians, serving as a pennyboy for his aunts. Gabriel denigrates others whenever he has entered the zone of self-hatred. When we read as Gretta reads, we can see that these sisters love their sister's children, especially Gabriel, their favorite. We can learn as well to hear Gabriel's love for these aunts underneath his after-dinner speech (or perhaps even the narrator's love for Parnell, when he quotes Joe Hynes's poem, in "Ivy Day in the Committee Room"), now only par-tially muffled by the perverse devil of a literary conscience.

The perverse devil of satire which thwarts sympathy, only for it to return in a more sentimental, self-defeating form, like the suicidal narrative of *Madame Bovary,* continues to dominate Gabriel and the narrator. The failure of Gabriel's ironic treatment of Gretta (and himself) is exemplary of all Dubliners. When Gabriel, in his own mind, not Gretta's, fails to supersede Michael Furey, the rival he perceives, he sacrifices himself with his own irony. Better to pass boldly into that other region of superior influence, the dead. Better to maintain his precedence by killing himself before that "impalpable and vindictive being" (*D* 220), his sacred model, gets him first. In short, he becomes Michael Furey's disciple, in metaphysical rivalry.

The narrator of *Dubliners* remains, for the most part, a rival-disciple of the *Irish Homestead.* "The Dead" is written "in another sense" than the unfinished "Christmas Eve" (*JJA* 4: 5–11), which was clearly intended to mock the "Celtic Christines" (Joyce's mocking phrase for regular contributors to the annual "Celtic Christmas" issue of the *Irish Homestead;* see *Letters* 2: 77). The failure of Gabriel's irony, and Gabriel's self-sacrificial response (to the self-sacrifice of Michael Furey), incites an emulation of self-sacrifice by the narrator so complete that many readers find a single narrator deconstructed by ghostly mediators who speak through him.

But what does it mean for us to prefer to read as Gretta does, rather than the way Gabriel and the narrator (or narrators) do? When Gretta says of Michael Furey, "I think he died for me" (*D* 220), we hear an echo of the Passion, but surely Gretta must mean that Michael Furey made a terrible mistake that she would never see repeated for her *sake.* This allusion to the Passion is more properly the responsibility of its author, Michael Furey himself, as well as the reader. The narrator, like Gabriel, abandons himself to the glamorous self-destruction of Michael Furey, garnishing their suicide with the imagery of Calvary: crosses, spears, headstones, thorns.

The choice between Gretta's reading and Gabriel's reading (with which the narrator identifies), of Michael Furey's passion, is the choice between a sacrificial and postsacrificial unanimity of the living and the dead, fundamental to Joyce's analysis of what makes his country eat its young. "The most Catholic country in Europe" (Joyce's phrase) identifies with the Passion in Freud's hostile sense of "identifizierung"—identification-as-appropriation, rivalry. Ireland mimics, satirizes the Passion by sacrificing itself, and observes communion by eating its own—that is, the Irish in Joyce's understanding identify themselves with precisely the practices of collective violence the Passion exposes.

According to Girard's analysis, periodic human sacrifices in primitive culture are offered to totem, ancestor, the gods, to satisfy *their* insatiable appetite for blood victims, in the hope *they* will grant the peace they alone provide. In *Violence and the Sacred* Girard deconstructed this mythical explanation to expose a cultural mechanism for generating unanimity. Girard argued further that such an analysis as his is now possible in the modern period because the mechanisms of violent unanimity are themselves deconstructing, revealing their secular dynamic of human violence. Until his following book, Girard was mostly silent about what force it was that was accelerating this dissolution of sacrificial practice, which made his analysis possible.

Beginning with *Things Hidden since the Foundation of the World,* Girard proposed the hypothesis that the dominant agent in Western culture for the deconstruction of sacrificial practice, including the violent practices of a sacrificial Christianity, are the Gospels themselves. The Good News undermines, over time, the covertly violent mythology of historical Christianity, even the sacrificial reading of the Passion itself, by means of the absolute singularity of its innocent victim.

Jesus, according to Girard's postsacrificial reading, seized the historical opportunity to push forward the deconstruction of sacrificial unanimity already written into the history of the Hebrews as it developed in the Old Testament, away from neighboring sacrificial cults, towards an apocalyptic moment: the opportunity of unanimous peace without exclusions, the Kingdom of God now at hand.

In the Gospels, Jesus described the Father of this kingdom as one for whom sacrifice is an abomination, who loves all his children, hairy, smooth, dutiful, prodigal, and asks them to love their enemies, unilaterally if necessary, reconciling each to all through a common brother whose absolute commitment to peace shows him as a Son of God. In Girard's reading, Jesus does not masochistically or romantically seek self-sacrifice, divinity through violence, but he cannot moderate his commitment to the Kingdom of God when that commitment becomes personally dangerous.

The clarity of Jesus's analysis of violent unanimity, such as "let him who is without sin among you cast the first stone," provokes a crisis. The community of accusers is threatened with disintegration. If they are to remain a society, they must either follow his way of positive reciprocity, unanimously, without any exclusion, or they must expel this threat to the unanimity-minus-one of sacrificial violence. The community chooses negative reciprocity, uniting in opposition to this victim who serves the usual ritual function of enemy twin, enemy of the people. The Kingdom of God is delayed, but the crucifixion of an innocent victim introduces a destabilizing element into sacrificial societies that will now mark every outcast with the sign of Christ.

It is important not to follow one modern misreading (brilliantly half-stated by Nietzsche), which would masochistically heroize and identify with victims as superior to their accusers. This sign of Christ represents Jesus's analysis of victimization, not the divine being of the victim. The victims of unanimous violence are not perfectly innocent; rather, their accusers are guilty as well of what they charge. Thus, in 1909, in "Oscar Wilde, il poeta di «Salomè»," Joyce, following Wilde's own argument, calls Wilde a scapegoat, and insists that only those who are themselves guilty know enough to accuse him.[18]

Michael Furey is so potent an influence on Gabriel and the narrator because he sums Joyce's understanding, an all-too-Irish, all-too-suscep-tible motive to imitate self-immolation. For Michael to die for Gretta's sake is to make Gretta guilty for Michael's innocence. Self-sacrifice mim-ics, satirizes the singularity of Christ's innocence, his Passion, a negative discipleship of rivalry with divinity, a demonic *imitatio Christi*. In *Deceit, Desire, and the Novel* Girard calls this motive deviated transcendency.

What does Gabriel call it? "He had never felt like that himself towards any woman but he knew that such a feeling must be love" (D 223). Infi-nite are the resources of self-hatred: Gabriel knows that love is whatever he has never felt. All jealous rivals know that they alone are excluded from the true passion that others have. Michael Furey, Gabriel, and the narrator are what Joyce identified for his Triestine audience on 27 April 1907, a few months before completing "The Dead," as "the loveless Irishmen": these strange spirits, coldly enthusiastic, artistically and sen-sually uneducated, "pieni di idealismi ed incapaci di aderirvi, spiriti fan-ciulleschi, infedeli, ingenui e satirici" (*Scritti italiani* [hereinafter *SI*] 123). These Irishmen abort their enthusiasm with coldness, they are full of ide-alism but incapable of sticking to it ("aderire"/adhere), unfaithful, in-genuous, and satirical by turns.[19] This is the same self-defeating pattern Joyce admitted to Stanislaus in his remorse over *Dubliners*.

Will Gabriel not despise Gretta and himself the next morning, as faith-lessly as the "reluctant Indian" that narrates "An Encounter"? The narra-tor of "The Dead" is already breaking faith with generosity, by the callow, sly phallic humor of "one boot stood upright, its limp upper fallen down: the fellow of it lay upon its side" (D 222), and the possibility left open by cautious phrasing (unlike Gretta's forthrightness), that the generousness of Gabriel's tears describes their size more than their quality.

The possibility for choosing Gretta over the testimonies of Michael Furey, Gabriel, and the narrator makes the spiritual liberation of Ireland only a supposition for *Dubliners*, but the rewriting of *Stephen Hero* into *Portrait* calls forth a revolutionary change of heart, which constitutes Joyce's redefinition of modernism as a positive, postsacrificial tradition, adumbrated in "The Dead."

The ironic counterpointing of ecstasy and manure in the Agricultural Fair scene in *Madame Bovary* allows only one conclusion. Disciples of modern fiction know they are to read ironically, from the point of view of excrement. To know Emma's desire for a better life is manure is to have the last word of satiric violence on romance. Before such a unanimous judgement, which no one dares to contravene, narrator and reader betray, in both senses of the word, their identity (*c'est moi*) with Emma Bovary, their sister.

But the structurally similar juxtaposition of Stephen and his mocking school fellows at the end of chapter 4, potentially ironic, urges rather a choice for what Tom Paulin once called "Ireland's future" instead of irony, which has no future at all. By refusing to sacrifice himself for Ireland, Stephen chooses, in the same spirit that Gretta chooses Gabriel's generosity, the "great wish" Ireland, living and dead, has for *all* its children, despite its bafflement by the historically compromised forms in which they must express it: to live, not die, for them. Stephen must find, as he has *not* by the end of 16 June 1904, a companion very like Gretta, in order to be heartened to write a joyful novel like *Portrait*, for the spiritual liberation of his country from violent traditions.

To Live, Not Die, for His Country

Stephen D(a)edalus and Ireland's Future

Jusqu'à présent toute l'histoire humaine n'a été qu'une immolation perpétuelle et sanglante de millions de pauvres êtres humains en l'honneur d'une abstraction impitoyable quelconque: Dieu, Patrie, puissance de l'Etat, honneur national, droits historiques, droits juridiques, liberté politique, bien public. Tel fut jusqu'à ce jour le mouvement naturel, spontané et fatal des sociétés humaines. Nous ne pouvons rien y faire, nous devons le subir quant au passé, comme nous subissons toutes les fatalités actuelles. Il faut croire que là était la seule voie possible pour l'éducation de l'espèce humaine. Car il ne faut s'y tromper: même en faisant la plus large part aux artifices machiavéliques des classes gouvernantes, nous devons reconnaître qu'aucune minorité n'eût été assez puissante pour imposer tous ces horribles sacrifices aux masses, s'il n'y avait eu, dans celles-ci même, un mouvement vertigineux, spontané, qui les poussât à se sacrifier toujours, tantôt à l'autre des ces abstractions devorantes qui, vampires de l'histoire, se sont toujours nourries de sang humain.
Michel Bakounine, *Dieu et l'État*

He has an affection for the feudal machinery and desired nothing better than that it should crush him—a common wish of the human adorer whether he cast himself under Juggernaut or pray God with tears of affection to mortify him or swoon under the hand of his mistress.
Joyce, *Stephen Hero*

—No honourable and sincere man, said Stephen, has given up to you his life and his youth and his affections from the days of Tone to those of Parnell but you sold him to the enemy or failed him in need or reviled him and left him for another. And you invite me to be one of you. I'd see you damned first.
Joyce, *A Portrait of the Artist as a Young Man*

In fact, we do not meet an indifferent God in the Gospels. The God presented there wishes to make himself known, and can only make himself known if he secures from men what Jesus offers them. This is the essential theme, repeated time and time again, of Jesus's preaching: reconciliation with God can take place unreservedly and with no sacrificial intermediary through the rules of the kingdom. This reconciliation allows God to reveal himself as he is, for the first time in human history. Thus mankind no longer has to base harmonious relationships on bloody sacrifices, ridiculous fables of a violent deity, and the whole range of mythological cultural formations.
Girard, *Things Hidden since the Foundation of the World*

Joyce gave Ireland its epic, and its future.
Tom Paulin

The formidable challenge of trying to add to Joyce scholarship is to keep current with both research and critical theory, without losing the first-hand wonderment of Dedalus's fellows: "What kind of a name is that?" "Are you Irish at all?" (*Portrait of the Artist as a Young Man* [hereinafter *P*] 9; 202). It appears from Richard Ellmann's early access to Stanislaus Joyce's unpublished diary, that Joyce himself, prior to beginning the momentous re-creation of the balked *Stephen Hero* manuscript into *Portrait*, wondered whether to naturalize Stephen Dædalus as Stephen Daly (*JJ II* 264). Traces of such doubts against the Irishness of Stephen's surname surface and are answered in *Portrait* itself by Stephen, who stands on the authority of Giraldus Cambrensis and the Heraldry Office ("pernobilis et pervetusta familia," *P* 250). Ultimately, Joyce normalized the spelling of Dædalus to Dedalus, but the question remains fascinating: why was a name that served four years as the figurative, even literal signature of his early fiction rejected, then rehabilitated?

The growth of Stephen Dædalus's soul is compounded of *Dana's* patronizing rejection, in January 1904, of an essay ("A Portrait of the Artist") Joyce felt they had commissioned (*JJ II* 144–48) and, later that summer, of George W. Russell's patronizing advice to patronize the Irish public with short fiction "simple, rural? livemaking? pathos?, which could be inserted so as not to shock the readers" (*Letters* 2: 43). Stanislaus's Dublin diary asserts that Joyce adopted the name, and the autobiographical form, of *Stephen Hero*, as a satirical response to *Dana's* betrayal. The writings of "Stephen Dædalus" aroused so much resentment among both rural and urban readers of "Our Weekly Story" that the *Irish Homestead* was forced to refuse any more stories (*JJ II* 165).

After Joyce finished "The Sisters," to be published over "Stephen Dædalus," he sent his friend C. P. Curran, who was reading the early chapters of *Stephen Hero* at the time, an announcement, also over the Dædalus name: "I am writing a series of epicleti—ten—for a paper. I have written one. I call the series *Dubliners* to betray the soul of that hemiplegia or paralysis which many consider a city" (*Letters* 1: 55). "Dædalus's" use of the word "betrayal" foretells a revelation of the paralysis of others but allows, unintentionally, only a reflection of his own, unencumbered by any self-criticism. The "holy office" of Stephen Dædalus is to pay back satire for betrayal: "And though they spurn me from their door / My soul shall spurn them evermore" (*Critical Writings* [hereinafter *CW*] 152).

But the increasing violence of Joyce's transactions of satire and betrayal begin to include examples of victimage less alien than Dædalus to Irish Catholic culture. A year later, in a letter from Trieste to his brother, which begins in inquiries of fact for several *Dubliners* stories, Joyce notes with satisfaction the recent death and, hopefully, damnation, of a journalist who wrote patronizingly of Tolstoi. He detaches himself momentarily from willing such violent retribution ("By the Lord Christ I must get rid of some of these Jewish bowels I have in me yet"), but soon reenters this pleasant and vicious region: "by the crucified Jaysus, if I don't sharpen that little pen and dip it into fermented ink and write tiny little sentences about the people who betrayed me send me to hell. After all, there are many ways of betraying people. It wasn't only the Galilean suffered that" (*Letters* 2: 109–10). Joyce's letters often strike the mock-Irish note of familiarity ("Jaysus"), but he cannot here avoid recognizing an exemplary betrayal written into both popular and polite idioms. The example of the Passion, even as a "shout in the street," informs him at once of his instinct for sacrificing his adversaries, his Jewish bowels, and his own status as a victim. Joyce's barely concealed satisfaction in the violence and nobility of his own passion will ultimately transform into a revolutionary insight into Irish bowels: they betray each other as they betray themselves, perpetuating rather than breaking with a futile tradition of victimization born of metaphysical rivalry.

Betrayal is Joyce's great theme, the revealed structure of human relations in both his poetry and journalism, in *Exiles* as well as his fiction, from *Dubliners* to *Finnegans Wake*. Joyce's developing perspective on this all-too-Irish theme is the complicity of victims to those who betray them. He began in 1906 with an especially painful case: the complicity of the artist in the acts of betrayal he depicts.[1]

The prolonged debate with Grant Richards over the publication of the scrupulously mean, fourteen-story manuscript of *Dubliners*, forced Joyce, through a remarkable series of letters to Richards and Stanislaus, to examine more critically his intentions. The result of this itinerary from satire on the Irish as a race of betrayers, toward a self-critical awareness of the narrator's implication in the paralysis he depicts, can perhaps be summarized by comparing the note to Curran, already quoted above, with Joyce's later cautionary note on the proposed German title for *Dubliners*. Joyce preferred "Wie Wir Sind in Dublin" over "Wie Sie Sind in Dublin"

(*SL* 328): not how "they" (or perhaps a falsely polite "you"), but how "we" are in Dublin.

The most potent sign of this deepening self-reflection is the striking revision of "The Sisters" in July 1906, when Joyce gathered up the four-teen stories of *Dubliners* to resubmit them to an increasingly defensive Richards. The revisions, as many have suggested, improve the introduc-tory and expository relation of "The Sisters" to the rest of the series. In particular, revision makes explicit the bond of simony by which Father Flynn and the boy arrange to betray each other, forecasting the system of exchange depicted in the following stories, which unites each Dubliner to all the living and the dead. (Simony also unites Father Flynn to Simon Dedalus as betrayers of paternal authority).

Specifically, the increased emphasis on the narrator's own inner life, as educated by Father Flynn, incriminates the succeeding acts of observation which the following stories represent. The addition of the remarkable first paragraph, which ends "[paralysis] . . . filled me with fear, and yet I longed to be nearer to it and to look upon its deadly work" (*D* 19), implicates the apparently sincere rhythms of satire and remorse, found in both the "pro and con" vacillations of Joyce's letters, and the narrative attitude itself. The alternating of fear and longing is now better understood as the inter-nal rhythm of self-hatred, than as a response called out by the hospitality or meanness of Ireland itself. The rethinking of "Stephen Dædalus" im-plied by this radical revising of "his" story is revolutionary.

It is the ten years under the Dædalian spell, 1904–14, in which Ellmann establishes his diagnosis of incipient masochism for Joyce's courting of betrayal among family and friends. Critics who follow these masochistic traces properly emphasize those Dubliners who consent to immolation.[2] But if the revised version of "The Sisters" in 1906 leads more knowingly into a series that "betrays" the betrayers, the composition of "The Dead," in 1907, as the last of that series, presents a Dubliner with at least an opportunity to be released from masochism, and releases Joyce directly into the fundamental rethinking of *Stephen Hero* into *Portrait*, Dædalus into Dedalus.

Dominic Manganiello and Mary Reynolds followed out Ellmann's dis-cussion of Joyce's interest in Strauss's and Renan's "biographies" of Jesus at this time,[3] which served him as a constant authority for Stephen's tribulations in *Stephen Hero*, as well as his own suffering, expressed in the letters. But why does Joyce compare himself to Jesus Christ? Who does he think he is?

At least since the subtly ironic school essay of 1898, given the mislead-ing title "Force" by the editors of *The Critical Writings*,[4] Joyce sought to unmask the accommodation between Ireland's two masters, English and Italian, to whom he was subjugated. The modern historical method of Strauss and Renan, which supposedly deconstructed Christ's divinity, should have provided, led by its own logic, a secular explanation of Christ's influence, as well as explaining the historical moment of its own revelation into the global nature of victimization. As we shall see yet again, Girard completes the procedure of comparison so characteristic of the most ambitious nineteenth-century intellectual work.

The historical method of the nineteenth century, together with the anthropological typing of all such myths, including the Gospels, under the common heading of dying and resurrecting gods, numbers Christ as only another, perhaps belated scapegoat, one among many. Such uncritical and ahistorical thinking not only perpetuates the sacrificial reading of the Pas-sion, but more generally, perpetuates victimization as the universal and untranscendable bond of social cohesion.

The historical figure of Parnell depicted as uncrowned king, betrayed, denied, and awaiting resurrection, the mythology under which Stephen and Joyce are raised, is, in Girard's sense, a "religious" interpretation of violent unanimity, perfectly consistent with violence as the sacred. Joyce's interest in Strauss and Renan, especially during the years of D(a)edalus, lead not to another life of (another) Jesus, but a biography of his unique influence: directly on Dædalus, in *Stephen Hero*, as Mary Reynolds makes clear, then general all over Ireland, beginning with "The Dead."

Stanislaus's *Dublin Diary* and Joyce's letters to Stanislaus and Grant Richards are necessary auxiliary texts to *Stephen Hero* and the fourteen-story *Dubliners*. Once Stanislaus joined his brother in Trieste, their letters to each other became, for the most part, perfunctory; Stanislaus's impor-tant unpublished diary, except through Ellmann's reading, summarized in *James Joyce*, remains unavailable, and both Joyce and Richards, at this moment, had little more to say to each other. The works collected in *Scritti italiani* (1907–12) are the necessary theoretical accompaniments to the "seven lost years"[5] of Dedalus: they begin just before the composition of "The Dead," and follow its consequences as they counterpart the rewrit-ing of Dædalus into Dedalus.

The resubmission of the *Dubliners* manuscript to Richards just before he left Trieste in July 1906 gave Joyce no sense of completion: he thought of other stories, but was unable to write them, yet he was equally unable to turn back to *Stephen Hero*. Joyce wrote little in Rome other than a few additional pages for "A Painful Case" (*Letters* 2:151), perhaps never used.[6] "I have written quite enough and before I do any more in that line I must see some reason why—I am not a literary Jesus Christ" (*SL* 106). The invitation to lecture and publish on Ireland, in Italian, which greeted Joyce on his return to Trieste, helped encourage him to renew his analysis of the failed relationships in *Dubliners* and *Stephen Hero*.

The work for comparing the Hebrew and Irish races of such proposed additions to *Dubliners* as "Ulysses" and "The Last Supper" never got any "forrader" than their titles in Rome (*Letters* 2: 209). Because Joyce makes so much of the parallel between Celtic and Semitic in later years, it is important to note that he presents the *early* history of the island of saints and sages as very different from Renan's picture of the Semites, which gave Joyce the idea for what he called in his letter to Stanislaus "Jewish bowels." For Renan, "one of the principal defects of the Jewish race is its harshness in controversy, and the abusive tone which it always infuses in it. There never were in the world such bitter quarrels as those of the Jews among themselves."[7] If Renan's description of the Jews fits Joyce's own Irish case, as well as the painful cases around him, *ancient* Ireland, as Joyce argues in "L'Irlanda: Isola dei Santi e dei Savi," nurtured learning, and theology, invited discourse and speculation. Ireland was the sole country to have courteously welcomed the first missionaries and to have been converted "senza lo spargimento di una goccia di sangue," without shedding a drop of blood. Further, church history in Ireland lacked "il martirogio," a martyrology (*SI* 118).

Joyce clearly approves of the ingenuous spiritual hospitality of ancient Ireland, which makes it receptive to the new doctrine, and he approves as well the subsequent ecclesiastical history without martyrs, which makes it proof against mockery. "Shedding" a drop of blood would better translate "lo spargimento" than "spilling" (*CW* 169), because it catches up the sacrificial and Christian echoes latent in Italian and Latin cognate verbs (*spargere/aspergere*), which Joyce's itinerary to Italian via Latin, taught in Irish Catholic schools, would not have allowed him to miss.[8]

It would be preposterous to see ancient Ireland as a nonviolent post-sacrificial society without the need of purification through the sacrifice of a single victim, or Christianity's revèlation of victimization, but Joyce is deliberately preposterous to find a time before modern Ireland's present brood of mockers, before the present producers of a political martyrology through betrayal, denial, and sacrifice. What went wrong? How did Ireland become modern? The English "Seminò la discordia ·fra le varie razze"—sowed discord among the various races—persecuting the Church when it was rebellious and relenting when it became solely an instrument of subjugation ("strumento efficace di soggiogazione") (*SI* 114).

Joyce's Italian works his Triestine audience's common schoolboy immersion in Ovid to evoke Cadmus sowing ("seminò") dragon teeth in a field, which spring up as soldiers, each a race unto itself, yet fraternal enemies, locked·in mimetic conflict. The influence of England for setting in opposition those races that up until their arrival had made their peace in a common Irish identity is clear.[9] But how is the Church first rebellious, and how does it later become an effective instrument of subjugation?

We must not set Joyce aside, by putting our words in his mouth, or by saying what we think he can't say. Unless we believe Joyce knows something we don't already know, we are wasting our time. Although Joyce depicts the Irish Catholic Church as orthodox, faithful, and lacking a martyrology, he does not here, specifically, identify these Christian virtues as a threat to English rule. Are we then unable to comprehend this process of transformation, by what means, at what point, does the Church second subjugation?

The religious connotations carried by "persecution" (*perseguire*) suggest, by inference, the transplantation of English sacrificial violence into Ireland. "La verità è che il governo inglese innalzò il valore morale del cattolicismo quando lo mise sotto bando" (*SI* 117; "The truth is that the English government increased the moral value of Catholicism when they banished it" [*CW* 168]). For Ireland, the secular dynamics of mimetic strife determine that their master's enemy is their friend, the Catholic Church and Ireland on the same side, according to England's opposition. To place under ban ("lo mise sotto bando"), as in "Mammon places under ban / The uses of Leviathan" (*CW* 152), is a better translation than "they banished it" (*CW* 168), because "banish" suggests displacement and exile, whereas Joyce's "under ban" suggests an object still locally available but now tabooed, made attractive, like Lear's Cordelia, by the violence of the master's prohibition.[10] Finally, "innalzò" must be translated literally as "exalted," not "increased" (*CW* 168), because it describes the sacrificing (*sacré-fier*, making sacred) of the Church as the precise moment when the violent rivalry between England and Ireland became metaphysical.

Real and compelling issues between England and Ireland are carbonized as fuel for a fight over nothing. England perverts the Irish Catholic Church towards the only exaltation of moral virtue that negative reciprocity can provide: deviated transcendency. The Church is marked by England's persecution as the sole access to a being now defined as that which England doesn't want Ireland to have. The Church's central drama, the repeated celebration of the *singularity* of the Passion, is deviated to model a sacrificial resolution to the secular conflict England sows on Irish ground.

The sign of Christ becomes cultural masochism. What springs forth is a political martyrology, ostensibly made in the Church's image, but in fact a monstrous satire of the Passion. In Joyce's understanding, single leaders step forward, in quickening succession, in attitudes more openly self-destructive, each attempting to halt the crisis of rival races caused by the English plague. Ireland multiplies its victims as it moves closer to spontaneous violence, cultural crisis and suicide, civil war, where everyone is anyone's rival-mocker, counterpart, a paradise of pretenders, all king's sons.

Joyce begins "Il Fenianismo. L'Ultimo Feniano" struck by the irony of O'Leary's death on St. Patrick's Day to observe, sinisterly, that the Irish always betray their leaders "at just the right moment" (*CW* 190). Finally, he predicts the Irish will exalt O'Leary for ancestor-worship, "because the Irish, even though they break the hearts of those who sacrifice their lives for their native land, never fail to show respect for the dead" (*CW* 192). Joyce insists that Ireland follows the immemorial mechanics of sacrificial reconciliation.

Joyce clearly recognizes how self-sacrifice dominates religious and secular, public and personal motive, perhaps because he had already thought through how the Passion overshadowed Stephen Dædalus, ten years before Easter 1916. In "L'Irlanda: Isola dei Santi e dei Savi," and what we have of the following two proposed lectures, never delivered (see *JJ II* 255), Joyce gives this recognition its most comprehensive theoretical form: "Le nazioni hanno i loro egoismi come gli individui" (Nations have their egos, just like individuals)(*SI* 97). That is, Ireland's will to identity, its will to unanimity, rhymes with its victims, each achieving being at the expense of others exalted or despised for their *sake*.

Sacrifice exalts the community at the expense of the victim. But modern self-sacrifice exalts the being of the "victim," who is secure alone in the conviction of the incurable ignobility of those who persecute. ("Out of the material and spiritual battle which has gone so hardly with her Ireland has emerged with many memories of beliefs, and with one belief—a belief in the incurable ignobility of the forces that have overcome her" [*CW*

105].) The public becomes the last victim of scapegoating by being accused of scapegoating. As we saw in the previous chapters on Ibsen, modern leaders (and writers) prove at once their own worth and the crowd's venality by the witness of their stigmata.

Thus, the "anomaly" of the subjects of *Scritti italiani*: O'Leary, Mangan, Myles Joyce, Wilde, Parnell, each an Irish Oedipus, whose curious complicity in their own fall can only be understood as taking charge of, taking the credit for, their own victimization. Any attempt to describe this Irish "being" is, inevitably, to describe an ego modeled on a crisis of competing and irreconcilable factors: "quegli strani spiriti, entusiasti freddi, artisticamente e sessualmente ineducati, pieni di idealismi ed incapaci di aderirvi, spiriti fanciulleschi, infedeli, ingenui e satirici" (*SI* 123), "the loveless Irishmen."

According to Girard, ritual sacrifice in primitive culture, periodically performed, economizes violence, and promises, in the language of the divinity, a productive rhythm of sympathy and rejection, solidarity and exclusion. In the modern world, violence is mainly in the hands of the judicial mechanism, which has the last word. But violence can escape above and below the modern judicial system, at the micro and macro level, at the level of the interpersonal and the geopolitical, where being, ego, personal and national, are decided as of old. The present "heteroglossia" of judicial and primitive articulations of violent conflict in modern life help explain Girard's suggestion that the phrase "modern world" is synonymous with "sacrificial crisis."[11]

When these modern irregular and injudicious rites go wrong at the personal or international level, a catastrophic, inflationary cyclothymia takes place, ingenuous hospitality and satire contending for the same object, at the same time, drawing every being into the conflict. The passionate attention of the narrator of "The Sisters" to paralysis mimes perfectly the incurable appetite of modern media for social crisis: "It filled me with fear, and yet I longed to be nearer to it and to look upon its deadly work" (*D* 9). Joyce's parallel labors of literary and journalistic practice show that in the place of an ego, the Irish have a crisis of "contrasting tendencies."

In the second lecture, "Giacomo Clarenzio Mangan," incomplete and never delivered, Joyce makes clearer than in his 1902 essay on Mangan which serves as draft, why the Irish see Mangan "like one who does penance for some ancient sin" (*CW* 76). In effect, "it takes one to know one"—Mangan has an ego like his mob of accusers. "Vi sono certi poeti, i quali, oltre il merito di averci rivelato qualche fase della coscienza umana fino al loro epoca ignota, hanno pure il merito più discutibile di aver riassunto in sè stessi le mille tendenze contrastanti del tempo loro" (*SI* 125; "There are certain poets who, in addition to the virtue of revealing to us some phase of the human conscience unknown until their time, also have the more doubtful virtue of summing up in themselves the thousand contrasting tendencies of their era" [*CW* 175]).

Joyce devoted most of his lecture to the more "debatable" ("discutibile") merit of Mangan's "gathering up again" ("riassure") in himself "the thousand contrasting tendencies" of his race. "Reassuming," for "riassure," would be too strongly dubitative in English, a Norman legalistic nicety deferring from Saxon plainspokenness; the translation of *Critical Writings* "summing up" (*CW* 175), although lexically possible, carries a misleading suggestion, belied by Joyce's discussion, that Mangan somehow resolves these contrasting tendencies in his own person.

Essentially, Mangan is the poet of mimetic rivalry, and Joyce warns of the tyranny lying in wait for all who, following Mangan, fail to break with this "tradition loosened and divided against itself" (*CW* 184). Much of Irish poetry, Joyce argues, is full of injustice and tribulation, but none as full of "misfortune nobly suffered" (*CW* 184)—in other words, no one succeeds better than Mangan in drawing the ignobility of his persecutors. "Love of grief, despair, high-sounding threats—these are the great traditions of the race of James Clarence Mangan, and in that impoverished figure, thin and weakened, an hysterical nationalism receives its final justification" (*CW* 186).

Joyce's Mangan essay does not propose the idolatry of the artist-individual at the expense of the masses, the artist as enemy of the people, the ideology of modernism which postmodernism properly rejects. Joyce *does not argue* that Mangan's lyric poetry is worth the price of Ireland's troubles, just as Joyce does not *show* us (despite Stephen's disclaimers) Stephen thinking of Mulligan's offense to himself, not his mother, or later that evening, hoping that Ireland will die for him. These are the statements that Stephen is hurt into saying, but surely, these are masks for gaping heart-wounds that we (unlike Stephen's fellows) are allowed to see. If we follow out the consequences of Joyce's counterpointing of national and individual ego, we must see rather that Mangan "justifies" Ireland's hysteria by earning it for them, through his own victimization, transforming crisis into Ireland's being at the expense of one monstrous victim.

The implied structure of the lectures, together with several features of the Mangan essay, strongly suggest that Joyce's theoretical overview of Ireland was coming round to his own painful case. In Joyce's historical scheme, Mangan represented the fourth part of five stages in Irish literature, and the last example of the tradition of the triple order of the Celtic bards. It would hardly have been possible for Joyce to consider "the literary movement of today" (*CW* 177), his proposed third lecture, without considering Ireland's betrayal of the bard Stephen Dædalus.

The "Cornell 42" manuscript fragment added by the *James Joyce Archive* (3: 156) to Joyce's description of how Mangan, like other heroes and poets, above all, like Parnell, will be "honoured" by his countrymen clearly sets out the hero as scapegoat.

> molti altri poeti ed eroi, tanto più perchè egli, come pure il Parnell, peccò contro quella castità incorrigibile, la quale l'Irlanda pretende da qualunque Giovanni che vorrebbe battezarla o da qualunque Giovanna che vorrebbe liberarla, come la prima prova essenziale e divina dello loro idoneità a cotali alti uffici. (*JJA* 3: 140)

> many other poets and heroes, all the more so because, like Parnell, he sinned against that incorruptible chastity that Ireland would demand of any John that would baptize her or of any Joan who would liberate her, as being the first essential and divine test of their worthiness for such lofty offices. (*Occasional, Critical, and Political Writing* 130)

Conor Deane regretfully pastes from Joyce's 1902 Mangan essay wherever Joyce is translating his own previous essay into his 1907 essay in Italian, but misses here a passage from *Stephen Hero*:[12]

> [Lynch] had begun to suspect from Stephen's zeal and loftiness of discourse at least an assertion of that incorrigible virginity which the Irish race demands alike from any John who would baptise it or from any Joan who would set it free as the first heavenly proof of fitness for such high offices. (*Stephen Hero* 151–52)

After the rethinking of Mangan as Ireland's counterpart, within the fuller cultural context expressed in the Triestine lecture, Joyce would be even less willing to serve as scapegoat, to perform his holy "office of Katharsis. / My scarlet leaves them white as wool" "That they may dream their dreamy dreams / I carry off their filthy streams" (*CW* 151). Now Joyce is better able to see that spurning others because they have spurned him, or proactively, before they have the opportunity, would be to enslave himself to that figure Mangan adores, that "regina abietta," the goddess of mimetic rivalry, goddess of the "vendetta" (*SI* 137), to whom "la pazzia è venuta" (*SI* 139), but a madness (pazzia) spread by metaphysical, not syphilitic contagion.

Despite Mangan's justification of Irish violence, there is a zone in his ego that resists complicity, that preserves, like certain exemplary artists and heroes, the potential for revealing "qualche fase della coscienza umana fino al loro epoca ignota" (*SI* 125), a real future for Ireland. Somehow, despite the degree to which he is all-too-Irish, he kept his

> anima poetica pura da ogni macchia. Benchè scrivesse un inglese così mirabile ricusò di collaborare per le riviste od i giornali inglesi, benchè fosse il foco spirituale dei suoi tempi ricusò di prostituirsi al popolaccio o di farsi il portavoce dei politicanti. Era uno di quegli strani aberrati spiriti i quali credono che la loro vita artistica non deve essere che la continua e vera rivelazione della loro vita spirituale, i quali credono che la loro vita interna vale tanto da non aver bisogno alcuno di appoggio popolare e quindi si astengono di proferire confessioni di fede, i quale credono, insomma, che il poeta è sufficiente a sè stesso, erede e detentore di un retaggio secolare, e quindi non ha alcun bisogno urgente di farsi strillone, predicatore o profumiere. (*SI* 137)

> poetic soul spotless. Although he wrote such a wonderful English style, he refused to collaborate with the English newspapers or reviews; although he was the spiritual focus of his time, he refused to prostitute himself to the rabble or to make himself the loud-speaker of politicians. He was one of those strange abnormal spirits who believe that their artistic life should be nothing more than a true and continual revelation of their spiritual life, who believe that their inner life is so valuable that they have no need of popular support, and thus abstain from proffering confessions of faith, who believe, in sum, that the poet is sufficient to himself, the heir and preserver of a secular patrimony, who therefore has no urgent need to become a shouter, or a preacher, or a performer. (*CW* 184)

Grammatically ("Benchè . . . , benchè . . ."), Joyce faces the apparent contradiction of Mangan mastering English prose and Irish resentment without serving the English or the Irish mob, but how is the poet sufficient to himself? Unlike the *Critical Writings* "patrimony" (*CW* 184), Joyce clearly avoided "patrimonio" for "retaggio" to make the poet heir and "holder" ("detentore," in the sense of "title-holder") of a secular *heritage*—as if there existed the form *(e)retaggio*—independent of religion and family, two nets of complicity in Ireland's great tradition. Joyce will be able in 1909 to regret Wilde's vanity for each of his all-too-Irish names, each of which symbolizes victimization, because by that time he will have reconsidered in his own fiction the patrimony of any son whose given name is Stephen, whose father's name is Dædalus, whose father is a Simon.

The subsequent journalism of 1907 follows the Università del Popolo lectures, and continues the thinking provoked by O'Leary's death. Like "L'Ultimo Feniano," "L'Home Rule Maggiorene" ends in a sacrifice, by bringing up again the endlessly repeated trope of contemporaneous Irish political journalism, the referring of Parnell's betrayal to Christ's betrayal. The Irish "diedero prova del loro altruismo soltanto nel 1891, quando vendettero Parnell, loro maestro, all coscienza farisaica di nonconformisti inglesi senza esigere i trenta scudi" (*SI* 54; "have given proof of their altruism only in 1891, when they sold their leader, Parnell, to the pharasaical conscience of the English Dissenters without exacting the thirty pieces of silver" [*CW* 196]).

We can perhaps remind ourselves of how close Joyce is coming to *Dubliners* and "The Dead" by first noting the publication dates of the two remaining articles on Home Rule and criminal violence for *Il Piccolo della Sera*, 19 May and 16 September 1907, then by considering that pharisaic hypocrisy is, in effect, the social practice of Swiftian satire, accusing everyone but themselves of breaking codes whose primary purpose is to justify the being of the accusers. (After two more years work on *Portrait*, where Stephen's fate is shadowed by Parnell's, Joyce as journalist identified Oscar Wilde as a scapegoat lapidated by those who could not even have accused him if they themselves weren't already as guilty of their own accusations.)

The nicely polished looking-glass for Joyce to get a good look at himself is probably "L'Irlanda alla Sbarra," which characterizes Irish justice by a journey westward to County Galway, "Joyce Country," to consider the example of the only-Irish-speaking Myles Joyce, incapable of defending himself in an English judicial system, unjustly accused of killing a family of Joyces, and executed in 1882 (Joyce's birth-year). When the judicial system practices genocide, and cultural masochism is blessed with the sign of the cross, the Irish show themselves capable of what Christ said was impossible, serving two masters.

But how does the analytical process we have followed in Joyce's Italian journalism lead to "The Dead," completed, according to Ellmann's reading of Stanislaus's unpublished diary (*JJ II* 264), a month after publication of "L'Irlanda alla Sbarra"? And how will *Portrait* follow "The Dead"? "Nations have their egos, just like individuals."

Girard's model of triangular desire as a hypothesis has a power superior to "human nature," or the "instincts," for explaining the contradictions of desire. In *Deceit, Desire, and the Novel* Girard develops his model by focusing on the portrait of snobbery in Cervantes, Stendahl, Proust, and Dostoievski. What is a snob? One who understands the secondariness and the snobbery of others, without ever admitting his own snobbism which makes such recognition possible. In other words, snobbism is a powerful analytic glass wherein the beholder does see everyone but himself. It takes a snob to know one, but it takes self-blindness to accuse anyone else, to recognize rivalry in others, but not in himself.

When the ego copies his desire from a model, they become rivals. If this disciple successfully appropriates the model's desirable objects, they mysteriously lose their desirability. When Gabriel thinks of how Michael Furey's beloved is now his wife, "He did not like to say even to himself that her face was no longer beautiful but he knew that it was no longer the face for which Michael Furey had braved death" (*D* 222). As long as the ego refers his disillusion to the object, not the structure of mimetic desire, he is effectively fated to failure.

Girard finds in the masochism of modern lovers (belated knights, complaisant husbands, and underground men) not an instinctual desire for pain, but a more lucid understanding of the goals of mimetic desire, which attempts to place itself more securely in direct relation to a being greater than its own. These modern lovers do not seek pain as such, but they no longer believe, like more innocent disciples, that possessing certain objects indicated by models can ever grant the being each alone seems to lack.

Each seeks directly a relation with a model whose decisive rejection of him as an equal has already indicated him as a divinity, a permanent model. Thus the most powerful instigator of desire to a masochist is the narcissist or coquette because one must rival, unsuccessfully, their self-love, which intensifies at once their desire, and desirability, each time it vanquishes its challengers. The narcissist and coquette are by self-definition, self-sufficient.

Finally, the traces of gender determination in "narcissism" and "coquetry" must yield to a recognition of a single structural position within an ensemble of relations. There is no future in falling back into the curious history of interpretation of the women in Joyce that Suzette Henke and Elaine Unkeless proposed to leave behind, that "all girls were not so good as they seemed to be if one only knew"[13] (D 26).

Thus Michael Furey can redirect or reengender, without loss of meaning, the lament of the lass of Aughrim which *she* had addressed to Lord Gregory, to Gretta, because he has, like the lass, trumped his beloved's desertion (to a Dublin convent) with a greater one. The lass, and Michael Furey, become external, inimitable mediators, chastening the mortality of their rivals from the land of the gods, the dead.

Gretta does not reply in kind with what Christopher Newman calls "a sacrifice more sterile than [her/his] own," but struggles still against Ireland's great traditions, especially in her husband. Gabriel, despite Gretta's unambiguous encouraging of his generosity, and his new feeling of unresentful, friendly pity for her pain, tragically misinterprets this experience at the end of the story. He mistakes Michael Furey as a superior rival for Gretta's affection, and becomes a disciple to that passion which finds it easier to die rather than live for Gretta. The last swooning paragraph of the story allows no escape from complicity with Gabriel's self-sacrifice for "Stephen Dædalus," this narrator, or the reader. Each is what each longed to be nearer to, a Dubliner, *hibernes hiberniores*.

In hindsight, it must seem inevitable that Girard would bring his model of triangular desire (developed in *Deceit, Desire, and the Novel*) to Freud's talismanic example, to reread Oedipus's "instincts" in a radically mimetic fashion (in *Violence and the Sacred*). "Stephen Dædalus" has the same talismanic significance for Joyce's thinking on the fate of Irish artists and heroes. (And, as we shall see later, Joyce's family romance from the beginning of *Portrait* has the same revisionary power for Freud's Oedipal triangle.)

As we have seen, the "Stephen Dædalus" pseudonym, and the *Stephen Hero* manuscript, were put aside in the early summer of 1905, as *Dubliners* progressed. Although the Italian writings are journalism in the progressive sense that Guglielmo Ferrero was a journalist, Joyce must have realized that "dilettante sociology" (*CW* 173) and Gabriel Conroy could not fulfill the promise of an "engenderable" future for Ireland made in "A Portrait of the Artist" in early 1904. The occasional phrases of self-criticism in *Stephen Hero*, perhaps to be attributed to Stephen Dædalus himself as author,[14] required a radical rereading to advance the more fundamental understanding of satire as self-victimization in *Dubliners*.

"What's in a name?" To know, from *James Joyce's Schooldays*,[15] that Book VIII of Ovid's *Metamorphoses* was a set-piece for the 1896 Latin exhibition Joyce sat, only partially explains why an islander under foreign occupation would give himself a new surname that, in effect, makes every son in his family a potential Icarus. Stephen, an equally treacherous precedent, was equally ripe for mimickry by Stanislaus according to what he calls variously the satiric or onomatopoeic principle: "Stuckup Stephen," "Sighing Simon, etc."[16]

Joyce could have chosen "Dædalus" innocently, as no more than a necessarily non-Irish augury of escape. Renan says of the naming of Jesus that "it is thus that more than one great vocation in history has been caused by a name given to a child without premeditation. Ardent natures never bring themselves to see aught of chance in what concerns them."[17] An equally ardent nature of a more suspicious kind than Renan's may come to see how insufficient premeditation yields nothing fortuitous. That the traces of victimization reemerge in the alternative histories each has chosen for himself is the common career of the Dubliners, of Irish artists and heroes.

> Oscarre Fingal O'Flahertie Wills Wilde. Tali furono i titali altisonanti ch'egli, con alterigia giovanile, volle far stampare sul frontispizio della sua prima raccolta di versi e con quel medesimo gesto altiero con cui credeva nobilitarsi scolpiva, forse in modo simbolico, i segni delle sue pretese vane e la sorte che già l'attendeva. (*SI* 60)

> Oscar Fingal O'Flahertie Wills Wilde. These were the highsounding titles that with youthful haughtiness he had printed on his title-page of his first collection of poems, and in this proud gesture, by which he tried to achieve nobility, are the signs of his vain pretenses and the fate which already awaited him. (*CW* 201)

The names by which Wilde would ennoble himself are, of course, already netted by family, race, language. To translate the above as "in this proud gesture . . . are the signs" (*CW* 201) omits Joyce's fundamental observation that this "same (medesimo) proud gesture" (of self-ennoblement) "sculpts, perhaps in a symbolic mode" the signs of vanity and the fate of victimization. What is at issue here is the power of Ireland's "great traditions" latent in the family names, and the power of the poet as maker. If the signs of vanity and victimization are already in the gesture, fate is carried irrevocably in the names themselves. But if the gesture "sculpts" such signs, "perhaps in a symbolic mode" (like "medesimo," these words are omitted altogether from the CW translation), then the poet consents to his own immolation in a mode where his complicity was required to complete it, where, by implication, resistance, also perhaps in a symbolic mode, was also possible, even for one so named and netted.

In the same way, at least temporarily, in 1907, "Daly" would seem a more apt surname than the strange-sounding "Dædalus" for the common everydayness of the artist's self-betrayal. ("Daly" remains in the text as one of the Dedalus pseudonyms for the pawnshop—P 174.) But, ultimately, Daly cannot account for Stephen's Irishness without denying the beginning of the itinerary that led to such a realization, without denying the self-ennobled young Dædalus, author of the *Irish Homestead's* weekly story ("The Sisters") who, in 1904, escaped the island.

Thus, to the first question, why go back to the name Dædalus? Joyce's answer would be, remembering 1904, "because that *was* his name." The simplified spelling perhaps renders the name in Anglophone Irish, but certainly admits that Ireland made him what he is. More interesting, of course, is the question, "what future follows from Ireland having made a Stephen Dedalus?" *A Portrait of the Artist as a Young Man.*

This short answer requires a somewhat longer proof. The only way for a son of Dedalus to survive is to survive as a future Dedalus. That is, a future father. To avoid becoming an Icarus, a son of Dedalus must be able to see himself as a father would see. When Stephen comes down to the parlour dressed for mass, "his father had cried. That was because he was thinking of his own father. And uncle Charles had said so too" (P 30).

First, we must recognize that Mr. Dedalus, in seeing his son, thinks of his father, not himself. He was not present at his own father's first Christmas dinner, and it is unlikely that he is thinking of some photographic resemblance between Stephen and his father at the same age. Rather, Simon now knows, belatedly, as a father himself, what *his* father felt when *he* came downstairs to go to mass, dressed for *his* first Christmas dinner. It is hard not to imagine Simon's father crying also, with his son only partially understanding why.[18] This touching moment shared by Simon, Stephen, even Uncle Charles, where paternal love is passed on by repeating an act of religious faith, shows there was a great deal more than Simon's dinner which was spoilt by the sacrifice of Parnell.

Simon tries to tell Stephen, when they travel to Cork, that no Dedalus wants his son to be an Icarus. Simon's father treated him more as a fellow Dedalus, and Simon would do the same. Simon loves his own father, perhaps now more than ever, because he has discovered, as a father himself, how a father loves his son. He remembers "standing . . . with some maneens like myself and sure we thought we were grand fellows because we had pipes stuck in the corners of our mouths" (P 92). Simon now sees himself as his father saw him then, a young boy attempting to ennoble the diminished being of maneens with the mystified (tabooed) possessions of adult models. Simon's father avoided the trap of exalting tobacco by making it a gift, not an obstacle.

Simon, in *his* turn as father, is trying here in Cork to recover for Stephen, in the face of growing impoverishment and subjugation, the sense of inheritable plenitude he felt able to offer Stephen in the beginning as *Portrait* opened, by once again telling him a story, as he did then. "He was baby tuckoo. . . . That was his song" (P 7) repeats what the father had just assured the son and anyone else who cared to listen moments before, in the delighted voice of the child recognizing the good gifts of the father. This initial sense of plenitude empowered Stephen to imitate his father and mother without desiring *their* possessions, *their* places, as tokens of a being he alone lacks, without rivaling them as model-obstacles. "When they were grown up he was going to marry Eileen" (P 8). The Oedipal conflict does not arise at the beginning of the novel because *identification* (in Joyce's thinking, unlike Freud's) is not inherently, by nature, in advance, a desire to take the place of the other. Identification expresses the great wish to *be with*, to *be like* (mitsein), the great wish for positive reciprocity behind all pedagogical practices, all rites of passage, all cultural forms, even the most violent.

When Stephen is punished for his wish to marry Eileen, the potential reconciliation of rival races, Catholic and Protestant, into "united Irishmen" is thwarted by sacrificial Christianity, the perfect instrument of Ireland's subjugation. Stephen is thereafter driven across *Portrait* into what he will later call in *Ulysses*, following Aquinas rather than Freud, *incest*, defined as "avarice of the emotions," the withholding of affection from the outsider (*Ulysses* [hereinafter U] 203).[19] Further, what might be called narcissism in Stephen according to orthodox Freudianism is the perfection of transgressive desire, the internalizing of incest by internalizing the external model.

Already by the time of the trip to Cork, when Simon sobs with affection for his father, Stephen suffers because he cannot understand at all the great wish the father has for him. Instead, he feels monstrous, fading out in the sun, Icarus-like, beyond the limits of reality. He retrieves himself by telling a story about a boy who is taught geography as if he is alien to himself.

First the son wanders away from the father, then begins to break up. Stephen's answer to suffering the fate of Icarus, fading out in the sun, is to imagine himself, like certain other self-composed Dubliners, composing "in his mind from time to time a short sentence about himself containing a subject in the third person and a predicate in the past tense" (D 108). The son still suffers the fate of Icarus (Stephen dates his dissolution from the victimization of Parnell), but now in his own image, a narrative that the son himself has fathered.

In this narrative, which he himself composes, he consents to his own immolation, consents to being Icarus in order to become his own father, an estranged Dedalus looking strangely at Icarus. To be able to view the failure of the son to fly like a Dedalus is to reconfirm the viewer's own Dedalian being, at the expense of another. Then the reconstituted Stephen appears again for a moment, a little boy in a grey-belted suit.

Stephen's metaphysical fatherhood is indifferent to the warmth of Simon's, or Dædalus's in Ovid, for that matter, resembling rather the narcissistic project of becoming one's own father.[20] He takes command of his own immolation by sacrificing the son for the father's sake, thus prolonging the abominable version of the Father who requires victims. He makes proof against needing a father or son, rather than a Dedalus among fellow Dedaluses.

Stephen's artifices of eternity throughout Portrait are, like Yeats's, unstable. Finally, Stephen feels less of a son than his father was: "he had never felt like that himself . . . but he knew that such a feeling must be love" (D 223). Like Gabriel Conroy, Stephen imitates a rivalry that was never intended, because he cannot feel love as he has been led to believe in it, arising spontaneously within himself. He must learn what the heart is and what it feels.

Stephen is likewise excluded from the "simple fact" of his Father's love; he finds, in the imagery of the Trinity, the Father in self-contemplation begetting the Son, easier of acceptance by reason of its "august incomprehensibility" (P 149). This image of the Father begetting the Son as in a mirror, and the Word proceeding out of this transaction, rhymes with Stephen's narcissistic project of self-sufficiency. This is, in effect, the intellectual masochism taught by Father Flynn, the preference of a masterly ("august") obstacle, divine precisely because the self can never understand it, over a "simple fact." Once again, both secular and religious models teach subjugation. "Simple fact" is to be heard by the reader as what Stephen is told by someone who pretends to autonomy, who needs no lessons in what Stephen can't feel at all. But such a fact as the Father's love can be simple only for those able to see as a father sees, feel as a father feels.

> Ask, and it shall be given you; seek, and ye shall find; knock, and it shall be opened unto you: For everyone that asketh receiveth; and he that seeketh findeth; and to him that knocketh it shall be opened. Or what man is there of you, whom if his son ask bread, will he give him a stone? Or if he ask a fish, will he give him a serpent? If ye then, being evil, know how to give good gifts unto your children, how much more shall your Father which is in heaven give good things to them that ask him? (Matt. 7:7–11)

The social consequences of prohibition are legion, especially in advanced societies, where rivalry is sacred, and given total license in all domains not specifically protected by the laws of property. Maturity can become the arbitrarily designated being adults prove by the dependency of children, each adult pretending to have received the patrimony, the father's blessing of being all youth is promised in the future, but which each alone seems to have been denied in adulthood.

Yet the social mythology which derives from human institutions is also human, imperfect, and imperfectly applied, leaving zones of possible resistance. This passage according to Matthew addresses itself to such a zone, asking parents if they really want to scandalize their children, become an obstacle to them. Even "being evil" ("πονηροι οντεσ," the workers of violent contention), they can manage positive reciprocity, preventing real need from becoming the sign of diminished being.

Because Stephen (like Icarus, in spite of Dædalus's good intentions behind his prohibitions) sees his father as an obstacle, he cannot see himself as his father sees, and therefore cannot follow this love through to reach the loving Father of the Gospels. Rather, the Father of the Trinity that Stephen accepts gives him the authority for the God-like artist of his aesthetic theory. Once begotten by self-brooding, his creations have no recourse to their indifferent Father, who is "refined out of existence." "The esthetic image in the dramatic form is life purified in and reprojected from the human imagination. The mystery of esthetic like that of material creation is accomplished. The artist, like the God of the Creation, remains within or behind or beyond or above his handiwork, invisible, refined out of existence, indifferent, paring his fingernails" (*P* 214–15).

Such a fathering, as in the episode at Cork, narcissistically contemplates its perfections as it resigns from their fate. The father is so external to his handiwork that internal mediation of his "good things" (fishes, loaves, blessings) for his children is impossible. Yet this apparently irrevocable, inimitable refusal of reciprocity, for self-sufficient, indifferent nailpairing, betrays an affinity for the handiwork of Tusker Boyle and Simon Moonan, disciples who arrange their own punishment by their models' hands.

But we must be careful, in exercising our modern gift for satiric, deconstructive understanding, not to describe Stephen in a way that ignores or forfeits what Ireland has born: its first hero of a "fase della coscienza umana fino al . . . [sua] epoca ignota" (*SI* 125), "from the days of Tone to those of Parnell" (*P* 203), who refuses to be sacrificed.

Where can we learn to see as the father sees, as *Portrait* sees Stephen, what Ireland has born? Ellmann's reading of Stanislaus's unpublished diary suggested to him that the revision of *Stephen Hero* into *Portrait* "bogged down" at chapter 3 by 7 April 1908 (*JJ II* 264). At least, Ettore Schmitz (Italo Svevo) saw only three chapters and a later "sample" of Stephen's development "to a strong religion felt strongly and vigorously or better lived in all its particulars" (*Letters* 2: 226), when he commented on the manuscript on 8 February 1909.

The "sample" must be from the first section of chapter 4, which most modern readers, benefiting from a completed manuscript, and collective, cumulative critical labor, interpret ironically, as the passage on the Trinity discussed above. In fact, Kenner inaugurated the ironic reading of Stephen on such material, the beginning of each subsequent chapter ironizing the heroic program of the previous one, each promising flight ending in bogland: football field, dairy cowpen, a bowl of greasy stew, a dark pool of yellow dripping.

Yet what modern reader wouldn't wish for himself the on-site wondering intimacy of Schmitz's partial reading? This is the endlessly encountered modern contention between the romantic and ironic mode, Flaubert as Emma or Dieu, Pound as troubador or Mauberley, Stephen as hero or alazon, the problem of *Dubliners* (especially "Araby"), the problem of modernism itself. From the rival point of the future, any modern hero is already obsolete, romantic, adolescent.

The Dublin 1904/Trieste 1914 dateline which ends *Portrait* insists that its artist escaped the fate of Icarus, just as its last two chapters insist that Joyce got beyond the place where he bogged down. How? Gabler dates chapter 4, and the first thirteen pages of chapter 5, of the Dublin holograph manuscript (*JJA* 9: 739–893; *P* 147–80) as inscriptionally the earliest, perhaps dating back to the 1911 manuscript saved from burning.[21] To say this section is the earliest to achieve final form is perhaps to say as well, looking back to where Joyce "bogged down" in 1908, that it represents the breakthrough to the final form of all of *Portrait.*

The work on chapter 4 and the beginning of chapter 5 is chronologically parallel to Joyce's essay on Oscar Wilde (29 March 1909), whose first paragraph considers the fateful consequences for the artist who confirms himself in his given and Christian names. In the last episode of chapter 4, Stephen confirms himself by taking the calling of both his names as a prophecy of the end he was born to serve, as his friends mock him for it, calling him a sacrificial victim ("Bous Stephanoumenos! Bous Stephaneforos!"—*P* 163), probably with the same voice he hears "from beyond the world." The juxtaposition of Stephen's ecstasy of flight and Irish satire passes through more intense levels of contention.

Kenner remains the most influential reader of this episode: "the interjecting voices of course are those of bathers, but their ironic appropriateness to Stephen's Icarian "soaring sunward" is not meant to escape us: divers have their own "ecstasy of flight," and Icarus was "drownded."[22] The gaps and ellipses of ironic juxtaposition suppress the explanations which "others" need; we ought to know that Stephen's flights will always "bog down." Kenner is invoking the protocols of irony, the dominant mode of modernism, which insists that the most debilitating interpretation is the strongest. (Deconstruction is a late phase of modernism.) If it comes to a choice between Emma and animal waste, in Flaubert's Agricultural Fair scene, we all know where we stand.

Wayne Booth's midcentury intervention in Joyce criticism, in *The Rhetoric of Fiction* (1961), sprang from his observation that the finely nuanced irony of the narrator towards the protagonist of *Stephen Hero* was refined out of existence in *Portrait*, so that Joyce critics were uncertain how to take Stephen, ironic and heroic readings taking place side by side.[23] How do we know that Stephen is a snob, and how do we account for the conflict of interpretations?

Joyce and Girard seem to have the same answer to the first question. To call Stephen (or Oscar Wilde) guilty is to incriminate oneself. To call him innocent is to encourage the subject's masochistic project of gaining innocence by self-victimization, at the expense of the "persecutor's" guilt.

What is present in Stephen's situation, and Kenner's persuasive rhetoric, is the powerful predisposition of the modern, and especially the Irish, towards irony and mockery. Stephen is ripe for the mockery of his "friends," but under modern conditions, who is not? We can be Irish, that is to say, in Joyce's uncompromising analysis, false to Stephen, but an ironic reading alone will never comprehend what Ireland has born.

Joyce was not free of history, free to choose between irony or sympathy. Rather, what Joyce has accomplished here, as a breakthrough to the final version of *Portrait*, is the partial detotalization of preexisting irony, and the further opening of a potential zone of resistance in a characteristically ironic situation. We are able, if we dare to resist the dominant mode of modernism-as-ironic-modernization, to feel for Stephen, under duress, what a father would feel, a great wish for him.

The difference between the ending of "L'ombra di Parnell" (16 May 1912) and the end Stephen was born to serve is fundamental.

> La tristezza che devastò la sua anima era forse la profonda convinzione che nell'ora del bisogno uno dei discepoli che intengeva la mano con lui nel catino stava per tradirlo. L'aver combattuto fino all fine con questa desolante certezza nell'anima è il suo primo e il più grande titolo di nobiltà. Nel suo ultimo fiero appello al popolo suo implorò i suoi connazionali di non gettarlo in pasto ai lupi inglesi che gli urlavano attorno. Ridondi ad onore dei suoi connazionali che non mancarono a quel disperato appello. Non lo gettarono ai lupi inglesi: lo dilaniarono essi stessi. (*SI* 83)

> The melancholy which invaded his mind was perhaps the profound conviction that, in his hour of need, one of the disciples who dipped his hand in the same bowl with him would betray him. That he fought to the very end with this desolate certainty in mind is his greatest claim to nobility. In his final desperate appeal to his countrymen, he begged them not to throw him as a sop to the English wolves howling around them. It redounds to their honour that they did not fail this appeal. They did not throw him to the English wolves; they tore him to pieces themselves. (*CW* 229)

Joyce follows the popular tradition of seeing Christ's betrayal behind Parnell's betrayal, with the remarkable improvement that "il re senza corona" (*SI* 83) himself understands what end is served by this "symbolic mode." When Parnell asks the Irish not to betray him to English mob violence, the Irish honor his request in a way that shows how well England has subjugated Ireland. Each pack of animals suggests that the sacrificial resources of each country are nearly exhausted; there is no difference between English and Irish wolves, except that the Irish have taken the last step into cultural suicide by tearing apart one of their own.

Joyce's suggestion in 1912 that Parnell himself knew that he was marked for betrayal perhaps indicates how carefully he was reconsidering whose ends his novel's symbolism served. C. G. Anderson's "The Sacrificial Butter," of the same period as Kenner's early work on Joyce, taught us to read Stephen in a symbolic mode as Christ, and to unify the symbols of Dædalus, God the Father, and the betrayal-crucifixion. Others, following Kenner, found it easier to refer the symbolic identification with Christ to Stephen's egomania, but perhaps Stephen observes the formation of such symbolism not to glorify himself, but to mark warily, even gaily, preparations being made by others for yet another Irish crucifixion, "forse in modo simbolico," which he finds it inconvenient to attend.[24]

To accept, even provisionally, at the end of the novel and his diary, the prayer of his mother that he learn "what the heart is and what it feels" (a prayer on the way to being answered on 16 June 1904, as Stephen suffers "pain, that was not yet the pain of love"—*U* 5), to ask for the help of his old father, perhaps (*pace* Anderson) all of them, is to know in some way the great wish they all have for this boy, behind the augustly incomprehensible roles of dolorous mother and artificing, simoniacal father, that he *live*, not sacrifice himself for them. Hopefully, in 1904, away from home and friends, in the company of someone very like Gretta Conroy, he can begin learning how to write a joyful novel like *Portrait*, which sees so powerfully as the father and mother see, one future conscience of their race.

Finding the Father

Virginia Woolf, Feminism, and Modernism

Mirrors are essential to all violent and heroic action.
Woolf, *A Room Of One's Own*

When you light the lamp you will see him. He sits there behind the door . . . the
eyebrows so heavy, the forehead so light . . . lonely in his whole body, waiting
for you.
Robert Bly, "Finding the Father"

The new millennium ought to be a great time to study Woolf. Diaries,
letters, essays, recovered and edited; continuous biographical and critical
attention; and all her work in print. We have opportunities to improve our
comprehension through a global reading that wasn't possible in Woolf's
own lifetime. Yet too many critics, whether supporting or limiting her
reputation, forfeit this opportunity to learn more by restricting her to
anticipating our (fuller) knowledge, by telling Woolf, in effect, what she
ought to know.

In reading about Woolf, we encounter the recurring problem of contemporary criticism, which thinks of itself, oddly, as obsessed with theory,
and thinks of theory-obsession as its credential for participation in the
human sciences which profess knowledge. What, according to any theory
applied so far, do we learn from reading Woolf? Why do so many people
bother to write books about Woolf, if they are always explaining her
through someone else's ideas? And, if we are so concerned with theory,
why is it that theorists so rarely find out from the writers they discuss,
anything they don't already know about their own theory? We ought to
know that knowledge of Woolf and knowledge of theory is never enlarged
or advanced by making Woolf the secondary file of some merge docu-
ment, that could as easily accommodate Jean Rhys, Dorothy Richardson,
or Djuna Barnes.

We should ask of a reading of Woolf what we ask from any serious piece of research: what do we find out that we don't already know? Thomas C. Caramagno's simple formula is exemplary: "we must let her instruct us."[1] Woolf's potential contribution to our existing knowledge is in her attempt to theorize an origin for what others find it easier to call feminism, in the observed behavior of women, before finding analogies in other liberationist enterprises. Although she seems constantly aware of the analogies, Woolf's feminism does not originate in Marx or Freud, and does not begin in the conflict of race or class. (This is why Woolf's comments on class and race are enlightening—because she is not recycling insights already contained in the racism/classism archive.)

Over her career as a woman literary intellectual, the question of women's liberty became for Woolf a matter of historical moment, of strategic possibility. Quentin Bell's biography suggests how early Woolf first thought of feminism—at about the age of fifteen, she projected a history of women.[2]

The social and psychological theory of Woolf's time encouraged only one kind of women's history, over and over again: how the patriarchy represses women. For Woolf, existing theories of race, class, and the unconscious were insufficient because such theories of repression as they could provide to feminism could not properly answer one essential question, the question of origins: how is someone like Virginia Woolf possible now? Where did she come from? Why wasn't Julia Stephen or Stella Duckworth born a Virginia?

Woolf seriously proposes that we try to comprehend modern human behavior, by characterizing the inequalities *peculiar* to sexism, and by characterizing feminism's historical moment of crisis and opportunity in the modern period. In Woolf's research, sex (and sexism) are both more intimate and more formalized than race or class: men and women live legally with (that is, legated to) each other, as siblings, spouses, parents, children. Cultural prejudices are most intensely structured, but also most at risk in the intimacy of the family.[3]

It is perhaps because of the intimate, familial circumstances of gender that English feminism as a systematic practice has been lost and found, again and again, in the mixed living arrangements of the sexes. "Almost the same daughters ask almost the same brothers for almost the same privileges. Almost the same gentlemen intone almost the same refusals for almost the same reasons. It seems as if there were no progress in the human race, but only repetition."[4] To find progress, it is clear that modern feminism must historicize itself, to characterize how successive, critical historical moments allowed it to be found, permitted it to be "almost" lost.

How? If the daughters ask for the same privileges, they are first of all asking for what they see the sons already have. They are cast, historically and structurally, in a position of rivalry and belatedness. If "same" indicates identical to male privilege, it also indicates that daughter after daughter's desire is identical, through its discipleship to male refusal. Each generation's consciousness is founded on the same "no" uttered by paternal authority.

"Almost" measures difference as well as repetition; more importantly, it expresses the moment of critical consciousness finding itself. Woolf's fiction is devoted to representing the sources of modern feminist critical consciousness. How does the sense of a lack of progress which Woolf expresses above become possible in a patriarchy?

Woolf's theoretical feminism is better studied *alongside* work like Lukács's theory of class consciousness (not reduced to Lukács) as the work of a fellow researcher in human behavior.[5] For Lukács, capitalism reduces workers to things, to separated and alienated isolates. Class consciousness becomes possible whenever workers recognize they share with others an isolation and alienation from what they produce and create.

Woolf brings the special power of fictional representation to characterize the moment of recognition, which is also a moment of resistance, when a woman recognizes isolation and alienation as a common thing for women, but often for others also.[6] Yet for Woolf, consciousness (and human work) is often bound up less in commodities than in the reflection of common but not therefore negligible social exchanges: gestures, faces, advertisements.

One cannot think of English feminism without *A Room of One's Own*. The tone of the lectures given in 1928 that are rewritten to produce the book in 1929 reflects Woolf's consolidation, over her exemplary career as England's preeminent woman writer, of a public voice which speaks for a commonweal of those who read.[7] The voice of these talks is lucid, sane, sure of its audience's support. Can you imagine anyone able to disagree, from some superior theoretical standpoint, when Woolf remarks, "you know, I often like women."

Three Guineas (1938) is the great companion piece to *A Room* in Woolf's work, but the differences are remarkable, and sobering. *A Room* imagines itself as speaking to a small group of women, but with the whole world able to hear. (Woolf was not wrong—it is hard to find any undergraduate who doesn't know her book.) *Three Guineas* is imagined as a series of postal correspondence, three belated replies to requests for support received by mail. Woolf is not asked to come to speak, she is asked to send money.

The conditions addressed in *Three Guineas* have undermined the very premise of *A Room of One's Own:* give a woman her own room, and five hundred pounds a year, and nothing can touch her. *Three Guineas* considers the circumstances that can touch her, even there: the regimes of Germany and Italy annul the safety of bank accounts and rooms everywhere.

The differences between these two books show us Woolf's acuteness in addressing the opportunities and limits of her own historical moment, as she imagines the literary intellectual's role of work. In 1928–29, the possibilities for feminism seem limited only by the failure to imagine them, to call them collectively into being. Why shouldn't we free ourselves of unfreedom so completely that we may return to the more rewarding task of thinking of things "in themselves"?[8] Woolf's wonderfully common phrase for ordinary sanity contrasts with the obsessive lunacy of inequality of race, class, and gender. Prejudice is seen as a lingering anomaly, unnecessary, an anachronism susceptible to being put aside.

In 1938, Woolf does not represent her voice as the focus of a community where feminist values are common. This is a matter of *her* three guineas, requested separately: she may give them, without heroizing the consequence, but keeping them won't change much either.

Yet what is common to both books is the point Woolf makes of declaring that she is making up a story, without ever giving up her credibility for proposing theories about historical events and human behavior. It is not mere habit that brings Woolf to tell stories. Fictional representation is at the center of Woolf's practice of research into what people want. Any attempt at a global reading of Woolf must start here.

A Room of One's Own and *Three Guineas* work in concert with her novels. Woolf works up a story for her audience to show them how they can think about what people do and what they want. That is, stories do not simply report the results of her consideration of human behavior. Stories repeat the steps of the research process, inviting the audience to follow her thinking from its origins. Woolf teaches her audience how to do her own kind of research. Ultimately, her stories verify the research potential of fictional representation. "In this case, fiction will have more truth than fact."[9]

Yet it is precisely this relation between the novels "Mary Beton" calls for that have not yet been written, and the novels Woolf had just written, and would write afterwards, which has always troubled readers. Why didn't Woolf write into being the confident modern professional woman Mary Beton wants?[10]

The connection between the novels and A Room is at once more basic, and personal: Woolf's fiction researches the origins of her own possibility to speak out, in the antecedent (and largely anonymous) protofeminist researchers who make the knowledgeable voice of A Room possible (utterable, audible, comprehensible).[11]

If we look at the novels first, we would follow the chronology of publication but not the order of research. Writing the novels did not permit Woolf to say what she says in A Room—she could always have said that (at least, the part which we always summarize). Rather, the research in human behavior which her novels embody helped her understand *how* she was always able to say that women needed rooms and income, from the beginning. We will see how Woolf's fiction written directly prior to A Room of One's Own serves as part of her lifelong project of a history of women, now understood as including the question of origins: what makes feminist consciousness possible? Once its possibility is understood, it can become progressively and positively modern, freed from the cycle of futile competitive and vengeful modernizations.

To attune herself, and her audience, to the possibilities of feminism's historical moment in 1928, Woolf first renegotiates the unpromising conditions of her invitation to speak. She has been asked (as a famous woman writer) to give the women students of Girton and Newnham a lecture on women and fiction. That is, the students forfeit the promise of research by posing Woolf a question to which they already know the answer.[12]

To give them what they don't already know, Woolf rewrites her assignment, her form, and her identity. She asks her audience to think of her as Mary Beton or Mary Seton (not Virginia Woolf). Instead of a finished lecture, a form she mocks throughout, she tells them a story about what happened to her while she tried to write her lecture. "Fiction here is likely to contain more truth than fact."

What she gives her audience, in effect, is both a representation of the conditions of intellectual labor for women (she retells the kind of common worksite insult they are accustomed to as women students at Oxbridge) and a demonstration of the research potential of fiction. We can do no better than to turn to the famous example of Mary Beton innocently transgressing the male turf at Oxbridge, while thinking of her upcoming lecture.

> Instantly a man's figure rose to intercept me. Nor did I at first under-
> stand that the gesticulations of a curious-looking object, in a cut-
> away coat and evening shirt, were aimed at me. His face expressed
> horror and indignation. Instinct rather than reason came to my help;
> he was a Beadle; I was a woman. This was the turf; there was the path.
> Only the Fellows and Scholars are allowed here; the gravel is the
> place for me. Such thoughts were the work of a moment. As I re-
> gained the path the arms of the Beadle sank, his face assumed its
> usual repose, and though turf is better walking than gravel, no very
> great harm was done. The only charge I could bring against the Fel-
> lows and Scholars of whatever the college might happen to be was
> that in protection of their turf, which has been rolled for 300 years in
> succession, they had sent my little fish into hiding. (A Room 6)

The advantage of fictional re-presentation ensures that her audience will in time see how to see for themselves (and not need to be lectured about) how Mary Beton sees herself. Once they get the hang of imagining fic-tion, they can analyze and re-present for others the "facts" which sur-round them, perhaps teaching them the art of representation as well. What we first hear as the voice of the Beadle, a perfect mimicry of the masculine sentence that Woolf devastates at the end of A Room, was never spoken aloud by the Beadle. Mary hears it in her imagination; she reprimands herself, speaking in his voice. The Beadle only looks angry, and waits. Mary does the rest on her own: she assumes responsibility for assuaging his anger. How? "Instinct" comes to her aid.

Woolf is certainly aware of the notoriety of this term.[13] It is clear that she does not mean "instinct" to remain intact in the received sense of the word, as a force of human nature that can at best be repressed or deferred. As we shall see in its next instance in A Room, "instinct" is a "fact" (an-other word that Woolf refurbishes). That is, this "instinct" is a pedagogical fiction learned so perfectly that it works better than nature, by getting itself accepted as a fact—not in the proper sense of fact as something made through human work, but accepted in the demotic and mystified sense of "fact" as a given whose origin is occluded, a thing forever done.

Another fictional situation in the next chapter releases this recognition of the learned nature of instinct as it further considers the conditions un-der which modern women do intellectual work. Woolf goes to the British

Museum, another department of the cultural "factory" (26), to consult the archive on women.

When one sends in one's slips, requesting books, in all innocence and candor, proposing the question of women to the great factory of theory, one gets a reply consonant with being chased off the turf at Oxbridge: books written by men on women's inferiority.

But that's not all. Woolf is also annoyed by the person seated next to her, a small, scruffy man snorting contentedly every thirty seconds, as he draws in another aperçu out of reading for his notes. If Woolf is maddened by the library, he is contented, fed. When she looks at her notebook, she has only her caricature of Professor von X, a man not attractive to women. "All that I had retrieved from that morning's work had been the one fact of anger" (33). The rest of the chapter is given over to working out this one "fact."

First, Woolf makes a remarkable inquiry into the origin of her own anger, and it is clear that for her, modern human behavior has mimetic, not instinctive origins. Modern behavior is initiated by the behavior of others, not by the commands of nature. She is angry because the Professor is angry. Had he argued his points dispassionately, not wishing women to be found inferior, Woolf would not have reacted in anger. Her anger is a mimetic contamination of his anger.

We should not think that a mimetic hypothesis forfeits the possibility that a woman could initiate a passionate response to the charge of women's inferiority—she could react to the accumulated passion of the archive of such books in general, to which this particular author dispassionately lends his voice. But Woolf presses two principles more important than priority here: that human beings could consider gender issues dispassionately, and that human exchanges are profoundly mimetic.

She will do more with her own mimetic hypothesis, but first she asks why the professors are angry. As she looks at her newspaper, she notes that men produce and reproduce "facts." Men are the proprietors, editors, and subeditors of newspapers, as well as the managers of the events they narrate; if there is a killing, a man will decide whose hair is on the ax. Why are men angry, Woolf asks, if they control everything except the weather?

Woolf begins by working out one facet of a mimetic hypothesis for male anger. Perhaps men are angry in the way the rich are angry at the poor. That is, having created a conspicuous difference between their re-sources and others, having publicly demonstrated that they alone have what everyone else desires to have, the rich suspect the poor, their disciples, of wishing to replace them everywhere (like the fathers in Girard's mimetic rewriting of Freud).

Woolf's exhilarating fictional re-creation of her own research gives us the sense that she is discovering these things as she says them. She proposes suddenly that these mimetic rivalries over things are on the surface, sharing influence with a more metaphysical rivalry which has greater responsibility for making these professors or patriarchs angry. Deeper than the kind of "anger" produced by the dynamics of class (and race), stands the anxiety of gender.

> Possibly they were not "angry" at all; often, indeed, they were admiring, devoted, exemplary in the relations of private life. Possibly when the professor insisted a little too emphatically upon the inferiority of women, he was concerned not with their inferiority, but with his own superiority. That was what he was protecting rather hot-headedly and with too much emphasis, because it was a jewel to him of the rarest price. Life for both sexes—and I looked at them, shouldering their way along the pavement—is arduous, difficult, a perpetual struggle. It calls for gigantic courage and strength. More than anything, perhaps, creatures of illusion as we are, it calls for confidence in oneself. Without self-confidence we are as babes in the cradle. And how can we generate this imponderable quality, which is yet so invaluable, most quickly? By thinking that other people are inferior to oneself. By feeling that one has innate superiority—it may be wealth, or rank, a straight nose, or the portrait of a grandfather by Romney—for there is no end to the pathetic devices of the human imagination—over other people. Hence the enormous importance to a patriarch who has to conquer, who has to rule, of feeling that great numbers of people, half the human race indeed, are by nature inferior to himself. It must indeed be one of the chief sources of his power. (34–35)

The jewel of greatest price is not measured by the resources which make men rich and women poor patrons of Oxbridge colleges, but the imponderable quality of metaphysical distinction between men and women. This ontological difference established at birth also makes global imperialism possible, natural. Male anger is a "fact," a response which proposes itself as an instinct defending sexism's birthright of an imponderable, metaphysical difference in favor of men, against any oppositional thought, attitude, behavior, real or imagined, now or in the future.

Woolf's analysis of anger is so radical that it has never been properly followed up. It is not difficult to see why. Anger is always understood as itself a primary motivation, the hypothesis which explains everything else (and is therefore protected from criticism). Anger is not susceptible to analysis, because it is the sole instinct we have never questioned. Anger is metaphysical, perhaps even our last god. Who among us does not warn others, "Don't get me angry" (which means, Don't provoke the god who guards my integrity, lest he smite you with my hands). Jane Marcus, for example, one of the critics responsible for Woolf's "American Renaissance," censured Woolf repeatedly, for not being angry enough.[14] But for Woolf, being angry was like being mad.

> Women have served all these centuries as looking-glasses possessing the magic and delicious power of reflecting the figure of man at twice its natural size. Without that power probably the earth would still be swamp and jungle. The glories of all our wars would be unknown.
> ... Whatever may be their use in civilised societies, mirrors are essential to all violent and heroic action. (35–36)

In *A Room*, Woolf provocatively values an independent income over suffrage, but it is clear that she comprehends the relation between civil and political society, local issues and reasons of state. Here Woolf names, as coexisting entities, modern civilized societies governed by a transcendent judicial system, and the "heroic" international world which answers to no law.[15] These are the defining circumstances of, respectively, *A Room* and *Three Guineas*. Instead of seeing the modern judicial world develop out of the primitive world of displaced violence, or even the persistence of the primitive for the lack of a world judicial order, Woolf suggests that the global world of heroic conflict depends on the judicial injustice to women.

Woolf here indicates the area of research Conrad worked in *Heart of Darkness*—the connection between racism and sexism. The connection is not produced by Woolf's reading of Conrad, judged by what she wrote of Conrad in essays, diaries, letters. Rather, this convergence is produced by the integrity of their research—two formidable intelligences, with personal experience as various as is possible for two English literary intellectuals living in the same region, see the connection between racism and sexism in imperialism.

Woolf makes a distinction between civilized societies (where the consequences of mirrors and reciprocity are regulated by civil law) and the no-man's land of violent and heroic action, the world of limitless national rivalry and prestige. At the same time, she suggests that a metaphysical conception of the self, where self-confidence and prestige mean more than wealth, governs international affairs as well. As Joyce reminded us, "Nations have their egos, just like individuals."[16] Woolf's immediate contribution to a theory of mimetic conflict is to suggest that the "fact" of anger must be demythologized in international politics as well as gender politics.

Mirrors are not guarantees of splendid narcissistic isolation. In the modern world, the metaphysical self is the guise with which each tries to command the situation of intersubjectivity and interdependence that all face, individuals and nations, by proposing that he-in-the-mirror alone is self-sufficient, autonomous. Mirrors reflect the offer of negative reciprocity to others, of negative feedback which uses others as a glass to confirm the beholder as the model of discipleship and rivalry most worthy of admiration, but in fact most prone to inciting violent behavior.

In 1928, "No force in the world can take from me my five hundred pounds." Problems which are recognizably global can be dealt with by local, educational methods, protected by an overarching judicial system which has belatedly recognized women's property. Mary Beton's inherited income grants her "a new attitude towards the other half of the human race" by releasing her from what bedevils Doris Kilman in *Mrs. Dalloway*, an irrational jealousy of all that everyone else has.

> It was absurd to blame any class or any sex, as a whole. Great bodies of people are never responsible for what they do. They are driven by instincts which are not within their control. They too, the patriarchs, the professors, had endless difficulties, terrible drawbacks to contend with. Their education had been in some ways as faulty as my own. It had bred in them defects as great. True, they had money and power, but only at the cost of harbouring in their breasts an eagle, a vulture, for ever tearing the liver out and plucking at the lungs—the instinct for possessions, the rage for acquisition which drives them to desire other people's fields and goods perpetually; to make frontiers and flags; battleships and poison gas; to offer up their own lives and their children's lives. . . . These are unpleasant instincts to harbour, I reflected. They are bred of the conditions of life; of the lack of civilisation. . . .(38–39)

Woolf enters that great body of postsacrificial thinking which reveals scapegoating, by first refusing the accusation of the accusers against her, then refusing to accuse the accusers, to make them uniquely responsible for scapegoating. "They know not what they do."

What can Woolf contribute to modern writing's development of this postsacrificial modernism? Woolf's abjuring of jargon makes her most high-powered theorizing seem common, ordinary, obvious. (She even denies herself the use of "feminism" in *A Room* and *Three Guineas.*)[17]

We must follow Woolf's inspection of the one fact of anger. Faulty educations breed "instincts" like "the rage for acquisition." Why "rage"? The rage which drives conspicuous consumption must come from the anxiety that others are angrily encroaching upon the self's well-being, represented by its things. The self imagines violent rivalry is behind the accumulations produced by others; only an aggressive program of new acquisitions can regain the lost sense of self-confidence.

Woolf's hypothesis of male anger as the dynamic for civil and political accumulation surveys ground as old as *The Iliad*. The "rage for acquisition" is itself Henry James's remarkable phrase for modern, obsessive accumulation, in a story whose title ("The Beast in the Jungle") renders the mystifications of male self-confidence in imperialistic imagery. It is the repeatable and verifying quality of real intellectual work as research, not deference to her elders or guild proprieties which brings James's phrase or Conrad's work to bear here on Woolf.

> And, as I realised these drawbacks, by degrees fear and bitterness modified themselves into pity and toleration; and then in a year or two, pity and toleration went, and the greatest release of all came, which is freedom to think of things in themselves. That building, for example, do I like it or not? Is that picture beautiful or not? Is that in my opinion a good book or a bad? Indeed my aunt's legacy unveiled the sky to me, and substituted for the large and imposing figure of a gentleman, which Milton recommended for my perpetual adoration, a view of the open sky. (39)

Metaphysical rivalry transforms needs into desires. As long as Mary Beton lacked a room and an independent income, her desires would second the irrationality of barristers who beaver away indoors to make large sums of money, when five hundred pounds a year is enough to live in the sun.[18] Woolf never underestimates the material basis which women's free intellectual work requires, but she values, beyond the accumulation of what others desire, the sane intellectual comprehensiveness achieved when she no longer must emulate any model Milton proposes.

The setting aside of Milton's model does not argue for freedom from influence, the autonomy of intellectual work. Rather, she has been released from envious rivalry, negative reciprocity with men. Woolf everywhere insists on reciprocity. Books are not single; they continue each other. A woman's work is difficult because she needs the books women had it in mind to write (the most likely sources of positive reciprocity for a woman) that were never written. The work of Woolf's fiction is to imagine into visible being a tradition of this anonymous work which made its author possible, the specific historical circumstances, the details of the people who lived to help make a Virginia.

Shakespeare is Woolf's older brother, the sibling who stole what he couldn't borrow, as Stephen Dedalus would have it. Shakespeare's work proposes a model worthy of imitation.

> The reason why perhaps why we know so little of Shakespeare— compared with Donne or Ben Jonson or Milton—is that his grudges and spites and antipathies are hidden from us. We are not held up by some "revelation" which reminds us of the writer. All desire to protest, to preach, to proclaim an injury, to pay off a score, to make the world the witness of some hardship or grievance was fired out of him and consumed. (58)

Girard's cunning formula for what the great novelists know of desire, "it takes a snob to know a snob," applies to Shakespeare. Only someone who felt rivalry deeply could recognize it in others (and recognize it where it lay in the stories others tell). Woolf confesses (for all) that "it is the nature of the artist to mind excessively what is said about him" (58). For Woolf, Shakespeare's work becomes the place where he set his own rivalries aside. Woolf sees past the endless conflicts and querulous desires in Shakespeare's plays to the position from which they are comprehended. Shakespeare's borrowings and adaptations are rewritings of what his antecedents partially discovered, as they prepared for *his* discovery: the mediation of all desire. For Woolf, for Girard, Shakespeare's theatre becomes a grand exposé of envy.[19]

We may see Woolf's fiction accordingly: Woolf tells stories about the antecedents who made her possible, against the odds, as they struggle against a tyranny they can't even name with skills they didn't know they had. If Woolf knows to call such ancient tyranny a patriarchy, she learns how not to exercise this privilege snobbishly, inviting us to complacently watch her antecedents struggle to achieve what we already know. Woolf affirms her solidarity with them.

In making what she knows possible, they make *her* possible. Woolf's anonymous history records their sacrifices so that they need not be repeated. By recognizing how the best part of the past wished to give birth to the future, she no longer rivals it, enviously and obsessively, like the false modernisms which crucify their model-rivals as romantics, Victorians, high moderns, "the" patriarchy, seen from some later modernization. Woolf develops modern writing and modern feminism into progressive, positive traditions by representing its hidden historical and structural origins within the patriarchy, within the intimate and complex conditions of gender.

Mary Beton comes into her own after the war: ten-shilling notes, a room of her own, and the vote. Woolf inherited her independent income before the war, but her dating of Mary Beton confirms what most readers believe of Woolf, that her work came into its own at about the same time, as she writes to better please herself.

Woolf began her career as a novelist with The Voyage Out (1915), writing as if nobody else thought the way she did. To let others see the way she really thought and felt would be to expose oneself as a monstrosity. The narrator of The Voyage Out masquerades as a modernist snob, ironic towards characters and the narrative conventions available, like the narrator of Madame Bovary and Dubliners.[20] Like Joyce, Woolf gradually resolves the problem of modernism, beginning with Jacob's Room, for the same reason: the exclusivist solidarity between author and audience produced by ironically regarding all these "others" must leave all others out, ultimately: the artist, having mocked others, turns on herself for believing she is self-born, autonomous.

Woolf turns towards a common writing that needn't exclude anyone. Over the development of Woolf's novels a certainty grows that others share, or can learn how to share, what she feels. Even, that others would learn from what she knows. "Communication is health." If Night and Day (1919) is, as Katherine Mansfield thought,[21] an anachronistic attempt to seize a prefab audience by avoiding modernist difficulty, Jacob's Room (1921) is openly confident that readers can comprehend the idiosyncratic, different, even oppositional representation of what women know about boys (and the resources they command) who go off to university, then off to war.

Mrs. Dalloway (1925) reprises two characters, Clarissa and Richard, portrayed as upper-class snobs in A Voyage Out. The Dalloways are no longer her whipping boys. Unlike Doris Kilman, Woolf now, in Mrs. Dalloway, admires without envy the élan of the Dalloways' upper middle class social custom. Clarissa now adumbrates Woolf's most advanced and positive ideas of human reciprocity. Revision, according to Woolf's preface to the novel, took suicide away from Clarissa and gave it to Septimus. Clarissa achieves the greater clarity of comprehending Septimus and his suicide, without ever meeting him, hearing of him only through the uncomprehending and unsympathetic Bradshaw at her party.

Septimus feels the extreme alienation that the narrator feels in Jacob's Room. Yet Septimus is unable to communicate any of it, even though he knows that communication is health. Septimus telling Rezia to tell the Prime Minister is not communication.

In general, Woolf's characters anticipate, prepare for the consciousness able to compose the novel. Woolf imagines characters who are the anonymous but necessary antecedents of her own thinking, yet who lack, in some crucial way, her own superior comprehensiveness. She has taught herself how to tell the Prime Minister.

The beginning of Mrs. Dalloway represents London as the mature setting for Clarissa's long-cherished theory about the reciprocity of human consciousness with everything alive or made by living things. Yet Clarissa seems unconscious of the antecedent women who braved the scandal of walking London unaccompanied by brother, husband, servant, who make such recent peripatetic theorizing conceivable for women. Woolf does not undercut Clarissa ironically by what she knows about these antecedents. But she makes Mrs. Dalloway a public alternative to Ulysses, which had reprised in 1921 an exclusively masculine capital.

Clarissa's parties are the commitment of her theory. The aspiration to social influence embedded in her wish to make parties, (like Mrs. Ramsay's charities) is disparaged by her intimates. Peter and Richard each say, with one dismissive voice, "her parties." It is Clarissa's resistance to the tone she hears in both Peter and Richard which helps her to come to a greater consciousness of her theory.

"The Dalloways" (Peter's ironic phrase for Clarissa's future without him) represent the reciprocity of male and female for better or for worse at a particular historical moment, for these two members of a particular class. Richard's return to "his Clarissa" from Millicent Bruton's luncheon measures the intimate circumstances of gender.

> They all smiled. Peter Walsh! And Mr. Dalloway was genuinely glad, Milly Brush thought; and Mr. Whitbread thought only of his chicken.
>   Peter Walsh! All three, Lady Bruton, Hugh Whitbread, and Richard Dalloway, remembered the same thing—how passionately Peter had been in love; been rejected; gone to India; come a cropper; made a mess of things; and Richard Dalloway had a very great liking for the dear old fellow too. Milly Brush saw that; saw a depth in the brown of his eyes; saw him hesitate; consider; which interested her, as Mr. Dalloway always interested her, for what was he thinking, she wondered, about Peter Walsh?
>   That Peter Walsh had been in love with Clarissa; that he would go back directly after lunch and find Clarissa; that he would tell her, in so many words, that he loved her. Yes, he would say that. (*Mrs. Dalloway* 161–62)

Woolf gives Richard a place practically unique in the literature of mediated desire: he learns how to love his wife better by modeling himself on his rival, unresentfully. If Gabriel Conroy is inspired to fail, Richard is inspired to succeed with his wife. This example of positive reciprocity with Peter is viewed and understood by Milly Brush, who is credited by the narrator (who says what everybody is remembering) with knowing what Richard is thinking, at this moment.

Further, Woolf writes to make it impossible to declare whose thoughts we are hearing spoken, Richard's thoughts, or Milly thinking Richard's thoughts. "Yes, he would say that" might be Milly's conclusion as well as Richard's, but the most comprehensive explanation is that it is both of them, interdividually.

Only someone as gifted in common, anonymous English as Woolf could forecast by listening to what Richard thinks that "in so many words" he could not say he loves his Clarissa.

> (But he could not bring himself to say he loved her; not in so many words.)
>   But how lovely, she said, taking his flowers. She understood; she understood without his speaking; his Clarissa. (179)

We may hear these sentences as thought by either, or, more likely, by both. In any version, they must be heard as speaking for Richard. She is his Clarissa. Woolf believes that Clarissa knows that real power and real affection are at stake for women in acutely intimate, particularized circumstances.

> And there is a dignity in people; a solitude; even between husband and wife a gulf; and that one must respect, thought Clarissa, watching him open the door; for one would not part with it oneself, or take it, against his will, from one's husband, without losing one's independence, one's self-respect—something, after all, priceless. (181)

Richard wanted to arrive with something in his hand (Clarissa also likes to bring gifts, and criticizes herself for it). Richard doesn't decide to honor the dignity of independence from the beginning, by thinking that flowers make it unnecessary to say to his wife that he loves her. He wants to, but he is unable; he couldn't tell her. We know the clinical vocabulary for the assistance Richard seeks in flowers. Nothing points up Woolf's theoretical power better than our shame before terms like "displacement" and "compensation" should we use them to short-circuit the superior analytic of Woolf's fictional representation of gender relations.

Clarissa could marry Richard, not Peter. Why? Both love her, but if Richard's mild attentions make her "his Clarissa," it is likely that she would have disappeared into Mrs. Walsh altogether. (Like the Mrs. into Bradshaw.) Like Mrs. Ramsay and Lily, who also face domestic tyrannies, she "couldn't" do it. As we shall see more fully in *To the Lighthouse*, "couldn't" is the first line of anonymous feminism, where a woman, without being able to explain why, cannot submit to what some male needs.

What Richard regrets in himself as diffidence allows Clarissa a measure of independence in a form she can use. Emotions, however universal and timeless they seem, consort with particular social histories. Any man's wish for mutuality with a woman, in a culture which deifies the rage for acquisition, can take on an aggressively possessive coloring. Even Richard's wish to care for Clarissa can become patronizing, especially when it agrees with Peter's disparagement of "her parties."

Woolf demonstrates how the most effective ideological control is concealed, so that its subjects feel vaguely dissatisfied, without knowing why. After Richard leaves, Clarissa knows only at first that she feels desperately unhappy. She reviews the day's disappointments. The expected sources of dissatisfaction, such as the companionship of Elizabeth and Doris Kilman, are rejected, because they are "facts." We would not be wrong to invoke Woolf's sense of "fact" from *A Room* here. Elizabeth and Kilman are not some internal threat that can be thought away; that relation is likely to continue, no matter what Clarissa thinks of it. Clarissa's thinking has a courage and integrity of its own, to face facts, but also to challenge what seems remedial. She feels brought down by some unnecessary, unfair internalized attack fed by her own thinking that can be opposed if it can be recognized.

> It was a feeling, some unpleasant feeling, earlier in the day perhaps; something that Peter had said, combined with some depression of her own, in her bedroom, taking off her hat; and what Richard had said had added to it, but what had he said? There were his roses. Her parties! That was it! Her parties! Both of them criticised her very unfairly, laughed at her unjustly, for her parties. That was it! That was it! (183)

Clarissa begins to answer the voices she knows that would speak against her parties by addressing the very circumstance Woolf represents in *A Room*. Clarissa knows that the mildly dismissive tone of Peter and Richard touches an "instinct" of male authority (internalized in both men and women) to criticize Clarissa or any woman as superficial. Clarissa is one of the humble but necessary antecedents whose local and anonymous resistance make Woolf's public critique of male privilege possible in *A Room*.

She still remembers Peter's criticisms after all these years. She has learned them by heart. She can do them in her head; at times, they seem to do themselves. They "depress" her. She begins to answer the objections she knows they have, one by one, by which she articulates in opposition to them her feeling for giving parties. She knows that Peter thinks she is a snob, and Richard thinks she is foolish to risk her health for "her parties." Her answer, provoked by their dismissiveness, is that "what she liked is simply life" (183).

Having brought herself to answer them, she overreaches herself by using the strength of their privileged voices for criticizing her, in her own favor. She asks herself (in their name) to answer them yet again by explaining what such a phrase means.

> But to go deeper, beneath what people said (and these judgements, how superficial, how fragmentary they are!) in her own mind now,

what did it mean to her, this thing she called life? Oh, it was very
queer. Here was So-and-so in South Kensington; some one up in
Bayswater; and somebody else, say, in Mayfair. And she felt quite
continuously a sense of their existence; and she felt what a waste;
and she felt what a pity; and she felt if only they could be brought
together; so she did it. And it was an offering; to combine, to create;
but to whom? (184–85)

Clarissa knows the value of her thinking, that her answers are deeper,
better than the criticisms she is answering. She insists that her parties are
properly understood as the reallocation of social forces now wasted by
alienation from each other, improvements waiting to happen.

Clarissa demonstrates the most elementary exercise of critical thinking. We speak, then listen to ourselves; we hear how we might sound to
another.[22] Having made herself explain herself, she asks herself from a
place in her thinking that she has never reached before, who are these
parties offered to?

An offering for the sake of offering, perhaps. Anyhow, it was her
gift. Nothing else had she of the slightest importance; could not
think, write, even play the piano. She muddled Armenians and
Turks; loved success; hated discomfort; must be liked; talked oceans
of nonsense: and to this day, ask her what the Equator was, and she
did not know.

All the same, that one day should follow another; Wednesday,
Thursday, Friday, Saturday; that one should wake up in the morning;
see the sky; walk in the park; meet Hugh Whitbread; then suddenly
in came Peter; then these roses; it was enough. After that, how unbe-
lievable death was!—that it must end; and no one in the whole world
would know how she had loved it all; how, every instant . . .

The door opened. (185)

Clarissa knows that her offering is finer than any being she can name as
its recipient. Having reached this new extent, "anyhow" introduces the
devils of self-disparagement which frustrate further thinking. The second
paragraph above shows her going back to her sense of loving life, attempting to relocate her thinking to push it forward again, but Elizabeth opens
the door.

Mr. Ramsay would likely say that his thinking has also suffered from
domestic interruption, but Clarissa is unlikely to share Ramsay's sense of
virtue for heroically suffering it. Clarissa will steal some time at her party

to think about the woman next door, but her own self-disparagement en-sures that she will never write for others what she knows.

Clarissa must work through "her parties." In the end, because of her party, Richard tells "his Elizabeth" how beautiful she is, even though he had not meant to, and both Sally and Peter acknowledge the force of Clarissa ("For there she is") in spite of themselves.

Educated men's daughters, like Clarissa, Mrs. Ramsay, and Lily, are the ordinary intellectuals of Woolf's fiction who become capable of theorizing at least part of their circumstances. Woolf reenacts their thinking, to show how common thoughts accumulate valuable research in human behavior anonymously. Woolf writes up their results, as their beneficiary, as their daughter.

The kinship of Woolf to her characters is most intimate in *To the Light-house*, as its two earliest commentators attest: her sister Vanessa and Vir-ginia herself. On May 11, 1927, Vanessa wrote to Virginia that

> it seemed to me that in the first part of the book you have given a portrait of mother which is more like her to me than anything I could ever have conceived of as possible. It is almost painful to have her so raised from the dead. You have made one feel the extraordi-nary beauty of her character, which must be the most difficult thing in the world to do. It was like meeting her again with oneself grown up and on equal terms and it seems to me the most astonishing feat of creation to have been able to see her in such a way. You have given father too I think as clearly but perhaps, I may be wrong, that isn't quite so difficult. There is more to catch hold of. Still it seems to me to be the only thing about him which ever gave a true idea. So you see as far as portrait painting goes you seem to me to be a supreme artist and it is so shattering to find oneself face to face with those two again that I can hardly consider anything else. In fact for the last two days I have hardly been able to attend to daily life.[23]

The full text of Vanessa's letter is crossed throughout by touches of re-serve, sibling sparring; their sisterhood was marked by lifelong rivalries which they couldn't forgo.[24] Yet Vanessa confesses without reserve that Virginia has radically changed the way that she thinks of their parents now. Two fundamental elements of this change (corroborated by Virginia's own reading of the book) are that Vanessa feels that her parents have been raised from the dead, and that now she meets them on equal terms. In her diary for 28 November 1928 (a little after giving the Newnham and Girton lectures) Virginia wrote that

> His life would have entirely ended mine. What would have hap-
> pened? No writing, no books;—inconceivable. I used to think of him
> & mother daily; but writing The Lighthouse, laid them in my mind.
> And now he comes back sometimes, but differently. (I believe this to
> be true—that I was obsessed by them both, unhealthily; & writing of
> them was a necessary act.) He comes back now more as a contempo-
> rary. I must read him some day. I wonder if I can feel again, I hear his
> voice, I know this by heart?[25]

Woolf is not sentimental about the influence of her father; had his life continued, it would have ended hers. Writing the novel buries them, prop-erly, in her mind.[26] The novel has invited him to return to her mind as an equal, a contemporary, someone Virginia must read. Then she imagines what it will be like to remember this father's voice sounding behind the prose on the page, as he paced back and forth on the terrace outside the drawing room window at St. Ives, perhaps.

Before the writing of the novel, her parents are the baleful influence who make the living obsessed with death. Woolf represents the principal discovery of the great modern writers (one thinks immediately of the family romance according to Joyce and Lawrence), that parents wish their children to live, not die. The structural realignment from rivalry to peace-ful equality Woolf's writing achieves is the redefining moment of mod-ernism. Moderns initially pretend a self-born integrity, to protect them-selves from *les feux de l'envie*, the rivalrous psychology of their antecedents, whose lives as lived would end theirs. Woolf returns to the deck this last, futile hand of modernization in favor of the recognition that somehow she was made possible by this mother, this father. How? And if her mother could make her possible, why wasn't she herself a Virginia?

The opening of *To the Lighthouse* makes it clear that both mother and child anticipate Mr. Ramsay.

> "Yes, of course if it's fine tomorrow," said Mrs. Ramsay. "But
> you'll have to be up with the lark," she added. (*To the Lighthouse* 9)

Mrs. Ramsay's "of course," suggests that James has just asked a condi-tional question, if good weather is enough to ensure a trip to the light-house.[27] Why? Somehow, fine weather is not a "fact" sufficient to guarantee the trip. There must be other circumstances, as mercurial as the weather, which make them both apprehensive. Mrs. Ramsay heads off James's anxiety by invoking their special relationship, their special language: he must be "up with the lark."

We see what they fear soon enough; Mr. Ramsay douses water on their hopes of a fine day, in a way that exceeds fidelity to meteorological fact.[28]

> Had there been an axe handy, or a poker, any weapon that would have gashed a hole in his father's breast and killed him, there and then, James would have seized it. Such were the extremes of emotion that Mr. Ramsay excited in his children's breasts by his mere presence; standing, as now, lean as a knife, narrow as the blade of one, grinning sarcastically, not only with the pleasure of disillusioning his son and casting ridicule upon his wife, who was ten thousand times better in every way than he was (James thought), but also with some secret conceit at his own accuracy of judgement. What he said was true. It was always true. He was incapable of untruth; never tampered with a fact; never altered a disagreeable word to suit the pleasure or convenience of any mortal being, least of all his own children, who, sprung from his loins, should be aware from childhood that life is difficult; facts uncompromising; and the passage to that fabled land where our brightest hopes are extinguished, our frail barks founder in darkness (here Mr. Ramsay would straighten his back and narrow his little blue eyes upon the horizon), one that needs, above all, courage, truth, and the power to endure. (10–11)

James knows that his father uses "facts" to humiliate mother and child. The situation is melodramatically (and pointedly) Freudian. The exaggerated and stagey violence of male emotions displayed here is yet another instance of Woolf's comic deployment of Freudian psychology. Woolf's fiction consistently offers common alternatives to rigidly Freudian interpretation of motive.[29]

James's violent reciprocity with his father is futile, but the reciprocity which follows the parenthesis "(James thought)" is not. Mr. Ramsay's conceit is a secret to himself, not James, for James seems to know the conceit better than his father. The voice we hear as we read is what James can bring to mind of his father's voice, at first coming to consciousness by the same "instinct" that puts the angry Beadle's voice in Mary Beton's mind.

Initially, it is hard to tell whether we are hearing what James says to himself, or what Mr. Ramsay says to himself. As always in Woolf's fiction, this is not mere fetishizing of stream-of-consciousness technique as up-to-date modernism, but a measuring of the mixed consequences of intersubjectivity or interdividuality. What follows from the fact that we are often on each other's minds? How can we improve the restorative power of communication, when communication is health? What can we do about it, when unhealthy "communication" damages us?

The voice James does is "almost" the same as his father's. The difference which develops, like the difference between Woolf only griping that a Beadle yelled at her and what she later demonstrates to an audience as happening to Mary Beton, or the difference between what privileges daughters ask their brothers for, across successive generations, is the foundation of critical consciousness, when coerced imitative discipleship becomes mimickry. Even if we decide that the parenthetical stage direction of "(here Mr. Ramsay would straighten his back and narrow his little blue eyes upon the horizon)" means that Mr. Ramsay has become such an emotional charlatan that he reminds himself to straighten his back at the same moment of each performance, it is impossible to believe that a secret conceit could survive seeing his own eyes as "little blue eyes." The hilarious image of his children springing full-blown from his loins is more likely another send-up of the patriarchy, than anything even Mr. Ramsay could say to his children without being laughed off the terrace.

Part 3, "The Lighthouse," shows how James expands this growing comprehension of his father's secret conceit, to struggle with the instinct which possesses his father. The novel knows better than James why we must first consider James's antecedents in struggling against Mr. Ramsay's tyranny, how others have made his struggle possible.

The extraordinary irrationality of her remark, the folly of women's minds enraged him. He had ridden through the valley of death, been shattered and shivered; and now, she flew in the face of facts, made his children hope what was utterly out of the question, in effect, told lies. He stamped his foot on the stone step. "Damn you," he said. But what had she said? Simply that it might be fine tomorrow. So it might.

Not with the barometer falling and the wind due west.

To pursue truth with such astonishing lack of consideration for other people's feelings, to rend the thin veils of civilisation so wantonly, so brutally, was to her so horrible an outrage of human decency that, without replying, dazed and blinded, she bent her head as

if to let the pelt of jagged hail, the drench of dirty water, bespatter her
unrebuked. There was nothing to be said.

He stood by her in silence. Very humbly, at length, he said he
would step over and ask the Coastguards if she liked.

There was nobody whom she reverenced as she reverenced him.
(50–51)

We have again before us the "fact" of male anger, stronger than the facts
of nature. Where does male anger come from? Ramsay's being is obsessed
with the instability of prestige granted or withheld to intellectual work
judged by (competitive) academic standards. Like the narrator of *Madame
Bovary*, he believes disappointment is the truth of human desire. James
already knows by heart his father's set speech, that man must endure
reaching the fabled land where his brightest hopes founder. Mr. Ramsay
protects angrily a very particular metaphysical truth; he wants James to
reconfirm his own sense of failure, to "learn" that meteorological science
proves it will rain on the very day he wants to go to the lighthouse.

Mrs. Ramsay does not disagree with Mr. Ramsay's "truth." As he himself knows, she is more thoroughly pessimistic than he is. She resembles
Conrad's Marlow, believing that civilization is a thin veneer that keeps us,
luckily, from the truth. Mrs. Ramsay cannot tell him, but she bends her
head before his outburst, to show him what he has done. "There was nothing to be said" speaks for what her gesture says.

Woolf shows us at once how personal relations are moderated by social
forms functioning as "instincts," but how personal will can modify, however slightly, their brute force. The novel identifies with the great love the
Ramsays have for each other as it must work itself through a social discourse we recognize as disfiguring. As in *Mrs. Dalloway*, Woolf has found
a way to represent without idolatry her gratitude to those she recognizes
as her antecedents, and to show their limits without condescension. We
"could not" now feel the rapture of subservience through which Mrs.
Ramsay loves Mr. Ramsay ("She was not good enough to tie his shoe
strings, she felt" [51]), but their own vague dissatisfaction, perhaps articulated for others, only subconsciously, is the origin of our more effective
will to resistance.

At the end of Part 1, "The Window," we see an important intertextual
variation on Richard Dalloway's inability to tell his wife "in so many
words" that he loves "his Clarissa." At the end of the day, Mr. and Mrs.

Ramsay each want something from each other; each answers the other's
desire in a manner which compromises between personal will and internalized social forms or "instincts." Mrs. Ramsay wants the force of her
own pessimism, and her wish for tomorrow's voyage to the Lighthouse,
handed over to her husband's authority. "That was what she wanted—the
asperity in his voice reproving her," which means to them both, roughly,
no going to the Lighthouse tomorrow, but the marriage of the Rayleys
she arranged will turn out all right.

Mr. Ramsay wants his wife to tell him (before he asks) that she loves
him. Other characters in the novel believe that what is wrong with the
Ramsays is that Mrs. Ramsay gives Mr. Ramsay everything he wants.
What could be wrong with telling him that she loves him? Why can't she?

> He could say things—she never could. So naturally it was always he
> that said the things, and then for some reason he would mind this
> suddenly, and would reproach her. A heartless woman he called her;
> she never told him that she loved him. But it was not so—it was not
> so. It was only that she could never say what she felt. Was there no
> crumb on his coat? Nothing she could do for him? (185)

"Things" designates the black hole of ordinary English, standing for all
that speakers cannot bear to represent. As in Flaubert, modern desire produces subjects who learn that whatever they don't have must be too good
for them, and is therefore the only thing worth having. In a patriarchal
world where men determine everything (here, even the weather, the last
frontier designated by *A Room*, is appropriated, if not controlled), there is
no free space where a woman can tell a man who wants to hear, of her own
will, that she loves him. For Mr. Ramsay, this becomes the only thing
worth having, but his desire inevitably rhymes with all the coercive commands uttered by men in general. It would be easier to indicate her love
by serving him.

> Will you not tell me just for once that you love me? He was thinking
> that, for he was roused, what with Minta and his book, and its being
> the end of the day and their having quarreled about going to the
> Lighthouse. But she could not do it; she could not say it. Then, know-
> ing that he was watching her, instead of saying anything she turned,
> holding her stocking, and looked at him. And as she looked at him
> she began to smile, for though she had not said a word, he knew, of

course he knew, that she loved him. He could not deny it. And smiling she looked out of the window and said (thinking to herself, Nothing on earth can equal this happiness)—

"Yes, you were right. It's going to be wet tomorrow. You won't be able to go." And she looked at him smiling. For she had triumphed again. She had not said it: yet he knew. (185–86)

We see the intimate mixture of conditions that gender relations inhabit. Mr. Ramsay's desire to hear that his wife loves him is "roused" by Minta, his book, their quarrel, the end of the day. Mrs. Ramsay's fundamental act of resistance to patriarchal tyranny is inextricably wound round the great love the Ramsays have for each other. Both her continuing love and resistance are expressed by means of Woolf's private challenge to herself, to make the novel convey its most passionate moments by the most ordinary conversational topic in the world: the weather.

Woolf's ordinary English is careful: Mrs. Ramsay "could not" tell him. Before she could ever will herself not to consent further to Mr. Ramsay's demands, she must find the place where she is unable to consent. Consciousness emerges out of primary resistance, when being is at stake. Mrs. Ramsay would disappear, like Mrs. Bradshaw, if she gave in here.

The novel picks up no dissenting thoughts from Mr. Ramsay. Mrs. Ramsay wills with such force that she speaks for them both, interdividually. We are hearing Mrs. Ramsay's mental assertions completely silence his doubts, his desire. That she "triumphed again" suggests the limits of her triumph and the limits of any resulting oppositional consciousness: does every triumph depend on her verbal obeisance, as when she accepts his weather forecast here? And why doesn't Mr. Ramsay really know she loved him, dating back to her last triumph? Why does he keep asking? Or is his request really a plea for sympathy, that he pretends to feel unloved by her unless assured otherwise?

Part of Woolf's faithfulness to human experience is to show the provisional and temporary value of all situations of reciprocity. Mr. Ramsay's belated response to her triumph in loving him beyond their limits is to gather those who are left ten years later to force them to go to the Lighthouse the next day. Lily, James, Cam inherit the responsibility for opposing Mr. Ramsay's tyranny. By the end of the novel, each has made their peace with the Ramsays, in a way that anticipates the peace Vanessa and Virginia receive from *To the Lighthouse:* coexisting with their parents as equals, not rivals.

It is not in coexistence that James sits, at the rudder, waiting for his father to make him personally accountable for the lack of a wind to sail to the Lighthouse.

> He had always kept this old symbol of taking a knife and striking his father to the heart. Only now, as he grew older, and sat staring at his father in an impotent rage, it was not him, that old man reading, whom he wanted to kill, but it was the thing that descended on him—without his knowing it, perhaps: that fierce sudden black-winged harpy, with its talons and its beak all cold and hard, that struck and struck at you (he could feel the beak on his bare legs, where it had struck when he was a child) and then made off, and there he was again, an old man, very sad, reading his book. That he would kill, that he would strike to the heart. . . . tyranny, despotism, he called it—making people do what they did not want to do, cutting off their right to speak. How could any of them say, But I won't, when he said, Come to the Lighthouse. Do this. Fetch me that. The black wings spread, and the hard beak tore. And then the next moment, there he sat reading his book; and he might look up—one never knew—quite reasonably. (273–74)

Because anger is always allowed to explain itself as a self-sufficient psychological motive, every expression of male opinion, of whatever force, always bears the potential threat of sudden, inexplicable violence. Violence is sacred. The father's violence provokes the child's reciprocal violence; the surprise of a peaceful father's sudden anger makes the child's memory exaggerate in mythical fashion the foundational violence as well as his imagined response: beaks, scimitars, stand for homelier twigs and scissors. Woolf's deceptively common version of the double bind created in the child by the father's alternating anger and love grasps Girard's connection of interdividual psychology to foundational anthropology and *l'écriture judéo-chrétienne* in a way not accessible through a mimetic re-reading of Freud. Woolf knows that the father's affection, not hatred, operates the tyranny over Mrs. Ramsay, and now Cam, James, even Lily.

For James his father is the *tyrannos* whose violent traditions must be fought everywhere they occur. This would be, of course, the ideological battle against "the patriarchy," every theorist's whipping boy. If we learn how to struggle as Woolf does, then, correspondingly, what we might win is another kind of internalized father, the living memory of a loving father, also (potentially) everywhere. If the father's violence is a foundational cultural influence because it comes necessarily before the child's, so did the father's love.

James makes a good beginning, by trying to think past the futile reciprocity of an imaginary patricide. He realizes that his resistance must be to the "thing" that need not be his father, that "instinct" which rages to dominate another's being. Yet he has not found the way.

> There he sat with his hand on the tiller in the sun, staring at the Lighthouse, powerless to move, powerless to flick off these grains of misery which settled on his mind one after another. A rope seemed to bind him there, and his father had knotted it and he could only escape by taking a knife and plunging it . . . But at that moment the sail swung slowly round, filled slowly out, the boat seemed to shake herself, and then to move off half-conscious in her sleep, and then she woke and shot through the waves. The relief was extraordinary. They all seemed to fall away from each other again and to be at their ease and the fishing-lines slanted taut across the side of the boat. But his father did not rouse himself. He only raised his right hand mysteriously high in the air, and let it fall upon his knee again as if he were conducting some secret symphony. (278–79)

Jane Marcus has argued for Woolf as a socialist writer bent on dissolving the patriarchal family,[30] but Woolf did not mean children to do without fathers and mothers. "You cannot, it seems, let children run about the streets. People who have seen them running wild in Russia say that the sight is not a pleasant one" (22). For James, Cam, and Lily, something fortuitous happens, as they think about this father, beyond what they know how to do for themselves, which redefines, at least for a moment, their relation to Mr. Ramsay: how they might live with the father in peace, not conflict. They see what Woolf saw that enabled her to write this book, what contemporary criticism would dare not let us see, a patriarch mysteriously reconfigured to bless them, not tyrannize them.

As I have argued, Woolf already knew how to blame the patriarchy for oppressing women. It *does*, but she came to recognize how it can also (to a much lesser extent) sponsor them. If she had accepted the scapegoat version of patriarchs proposed by contemporary feminist theory, she herself was impossible to explain. Woolf wants to recover the great wish all fathers have for all children, that they live in peace, as a cultural resource too precious to be discarded.

Cam has warm, vivid memories of the scents and sensations of the nurturing masculine study. She knows that sometimes, when the fathers ask you if there is anything you want, they mean to help. Cam finds herself accepting her father's voice, and his love, as she repeats her father's words, "how we perished, each alone."

When they reach the Lighthouse, James and Cam see this other father together.

> He rose and stood in the bow of the boat, very straight and tall, for all the world, James thought, as if he were saying, "There is no God," and Cam thought, as if he were leaping into space, and they both rose to follow him as he sprang, lightly like a young man, holding his parcel, on to the rock. (308)

The novel leaves the ultimate struggles, the last word, to Lily. When Mr. Ramsay asked Lily if he could get her anything, one must see that he was thinking of himself.

> Instantly, with the force of some primeval gust (for really he could not restrain himself any longer), there issued from him such a groan that any other woman in the whole world would have done something, said something—all except myself, thought Lily, girding at herself bitterly, who am not a woman, but a peevish, ill-tempered, dried-up old maid, presumably. (226)

Ramsay brandishes no arid scimitar; Lily girds at herself. We have just heard what this Beadle thinks: "She looked a little skimpy, wispy; but not unattractive. He liked her" (225). Lily thinks herself worse than he does, as she takes responsibility for his dissatisfaction. The most significant word comes last, "presumably." Lily "almost" accepts as given what Mr. Ramsay "must" think, until she has heard it out to the end. Her last word identifies these criticisms as belonging to some observer's presumptions (perhaps his).

In *Three Guineas* Woolf recommends that women join a society of outsiders who refuse to participate in the mirror mechanisms of the patriarchy. Lily is their necessary and anonymous predecessor. Lily "could not" give Mr. Ramsay the sympathy he wanted. She fails to serve as a mirror to Mr. Ramsay's raging desire. How does Lily save them from degradation? By exclaiming (helplessly) on Mr. Ramsay's boots. She has fortuitously hit upon ground that she shares equally with him. (Mr. Bankes has always admired Lily's sensible footwear.) Mr. Ramsay kneels down to tie Lily's shoes, twice; readers cannot help remembering Mrs. Ramsay ("she was not good enough to tie his shoes, she thought"). As Mr. Ramsay leaves for the lighthouse, Lily's sympathy for him is released when he no longer needs it.

> And then, she recalled, there was that sudden revivification, that sudden flare (when she praised his boots), that sudden recovery of vitality and interest in ordinary human things, which too passed and changed (for he was always changing, and hid nothing) into that other final phase which was new to her and had, she owned, made herself ashamed of her own irritability, when it seemed as if he had shed worries and ambitions, and the hope of sympathy and desire for praise, had entered some other region, was drawn on, as if by curiosity, in dumb colloquy, whether with himself or another, at the head of that little procession out of one's range. (233)

Lily recognizes in Mr. Ramsay the good father her resistance has helped to recover. This father, who leads the others, blesses her work at the end.

The circumstances of their return make it inevitable that they all are to miss Mrs. Ramsay. Yet Lily, like any modernist, relishes coming out from under her influence.

> But the dead, thought Lily, encountering some obstacle in her design which made her pause and ponder, stepping back a foot or so, oh, the dead! she murmured, one pitied them, one brushed them aside, one had even a little contempt for them. They are at our mercy. Mrs. Ramsay has faded and gone, she thought. We can over-ride her wishes, improve away her limited, old-fashioned ideas. (260)

This might be called ordinary modernization, a laicized version of dominant theory. But her outmoding of Mrs. Ramsay is only temporary, perhaps a reflex of transferred annoyance at the obstacle in her design. By the end of this chapter, Lily is distraught because she cannot invoke Mrs. Ramsay's spirit to return to her.

Lily achieves a provisional accommodation of both Ramsays in her painting, when she thinks that Mr. Ramsay has reached the Lighthouse. She has found a way to represent the force of the Ramsays at the center of her painting, the line for both of them standing where stood the (mimetic) triangle, formulaic of Mother and Child. The past perfect tense ("I have had my vision") indicates that the vision is already over. Like Woolf's novels, the "triumph" of any one painting is provisional, because she must face again the white space of the canvas, which for Woolf is the blank page of the next work.

We know that Lily has another painting of Mrs. Ramsay in her mind for the future, which comes closer to the resuscitation Woolf performs:

> She let her flowers fall from her basket, scattered and tumbled them on to the grass and, reluctantly and hesitatingly, but without question or complaint—had she not the faculty of obedience to perfection?—went too. Down fields, across valleys, white, flower-strewn—that was how she would have painted it. The hills were austere. It was rocky; it was steep. The waves sounded hoarse on the stones beneath. They went, the three of them together, Mrs. Ramsay walked rather fast in front, as if she expected to meet some one round the corner. (299)

Mrs. Ramsay is also at the head of a little group, perhaps Lily and Charles Tansley, perhaps Prue and Andrew. This is the active Mrs. Ramsay with a social conscience, who wanted to be something more than an admired Madonna.

If Lily's explanation to Bankes rings true to him, that Mrs. Ramsay can be represented without diminishment as a dark triangle,[31] there has also been an element of escapism in Lily's allegiance to abstract form. When she felt excluded from the passion of "The Rayleys," she told herself that "she need not undergo that degradation. She was saved from that dilution. She would move the tree rather more to the middle" (154). But Lily's suffering of Mrs. Ramsay's loss means that she cannot be held up as an example of the inhumanness of modern formal abstraction. She has moved closer to Woolf's great gifts of identification, and admitted more of what she feels for Mrs. Ramsay into her work.

The manner of Lily's coordination of the completion of her work with Mr. Ramsay's, with the end of the novel itself, strongly suggests the identification of her work with Woolf's own. She is the kind of anonymous antecedent that makes Woolf's recuperation of her father's curse into a blessing possible. But that does not explain to us why Woolf, of all writers, has reinvested these patriarchal figures with mystery, against the grain of modern critical demystification. The novel even arranges for Mr. Carmichael to lumber his comforting maleness up at the end, blowing seawater like Proteus.

In the early Judeo-Christian writings, a father's care for his children was proverbial, and could be used to explain near-incomprehensible revisions of the conception of an angry and jealous divinity. "If your son asks you for bread, will you give him a stone?" allowed, apparently, only one answer, that of the loving father.

Why is the modern world different? It is no "simple fact" for Stephen Dedalus (despite being told so) that God the Father had loved his soul before he was born. Nor is he moved to identify with his own father, when Simon, thinking to bring himself closer to his son, tells him how much he and his father cared for each other.

Feminism is often read in alliance with other contemporary forms of interpretation: the interests of women are considered by Marxist, psychological, or other theories against oppression. Less often feminism is seen as a form of cultural modernization. Feminism, like other modern interpretive systems, is deconstructive in method, always telling the analysand what s/he doesn't know about their own behavior. *Madame Bovary* and *Dubliners* show us how modern interpretation works: the worst construction put on a person's intentions is the one most likely to be seen as true, lest one seem sentimental, romantic, unsophisticated. The great deconstructive move of feminism is to ferret out complicity with the patriarchy, to expose the bad faith of the fathers everywhere.

Jane Marcus has written convincingly that it is mothering, not fathering, that made Woolf possible as a literary intellectual. Marcus downgrades the positive effects of Woolf's regular family. The women who help Woolf become a writer are outsiders to the patriarchal family. Clara Pater, Janet Case, Violet Dickinson, Caroline Stephen, Margaret Llewelyn Davies are some of the "spinsters and nuns" who make Woolf possible.[32]

As enlightening as Marcus's writing is, there are two problems that indicate we cannot leave this explanation as it stands. First, where did all these wonderful women come from, if the feminist analysis of the soul-killing patriarchy suggests that it took (at least) these five women to make a Virginia? Next, what do we do about *To the Lighthouse*, and its sentimental regard for the family? If Jane Marcus is right, where are the maiden aunts in the novel who mother a Virginia?

What could be more challenging for a feminist like Woolf than to admit those elements of positive reciprocity between herself and her father, in the face of the dominant critical consciousness, which deconstructs every motive to its base? Without admitting the fathers, feminists propose themselves as self-born, the disease of modernism. Woolf proposes to us a new feminism and a new modernism without rivalry and without violence.

Conclusion

Violence and Modernism: Ibsen, Joyce, and Woolf amalgamates two of our most comprehensive theorists in literary studies: Northrop Frye and René Girard. Frye's greatest period of influence was the fifties and sixties—*Anatomy of Criticism* (1957) dominated literary studies because his idea of "literature as a whole" *worked*. Frye's patterns or archetypes showed the resemblance in structure of all literary works of whatever period. Further, he showed that these patterns could be set in a historical sequence by classifying them according to the hero's power of action. In the earliest periods, where we might call our literary texts myths, heroes are nearly gods if not gods, able to do extraordinary things. As we move to the modern period, they become more like us—ironic heroes, in fact.

If Frye initially kept his commitment to the Judeo-Christian scriptures separate, his hypothesis of literature as a whole was never unmotivated.[1] Literature presented "fables of identity." The motive for metaphor was humankind's perennial dream of identity between the human and natural world, golden cities and green gardens giving a common shape to human culture. Although there were many opportunities to link up his thinking with other developments, Frye's influence waned as following him became mere anatomy, finding the same patterns in literature over and over again. Frye's ascendancy and decline are perhaps the perfect example of cultural leadership determined by modernization.

René Girard has suggested that primitive cultures resemble each other in myth and ritual because they have all resorted to the same mechanism for controlling human violence: the scapegoat mechanism, which gets everyone to agree that they have the same enemy. Girard's version of the development from the ancient to the modern world is the deconstruction of scapegoat practices, a growing concern for victims unanimously accused. Ritual accuses one person for everything that goes wrong, but we become increasingly concerned for those whom everyone accuses. Girard reminds us that ours is the only period in human history where victims have rights.

First of all, there are important similarities. Both are grounded in Judeo-Christian writing, both see a concern for weaker subjects growing across literary history as we move to the modern period.[2] Ibsen, Joyce, and Woolf corroborate but also add to this hypothesis generated from Frye and Girard.

Ibsen is interested in a remarkable deformation of this concern for victims: the way that public leaders qualify themselves for public concern and approval through apparent and staged acts of self-sacrifice. He shows us the primitive ritual pattern of sacrifice still operative in the modern world, exploited by politicians and leaders who seek the "concern" and support of the crowd.

"The Dead" finishes off the sorry human episodes of *Dubliners* and prepares the ground for Joyce's greatest writing by focusing on a woman who regrets her young man who, *not at her bidding,* sacrificed himself. Gretta wants a man to live with her, not die for her. Joyce realizes that Ireland also requires self-sacrifice from its leaders and pointedly explains in his fiction why his hero refuses to sacrifice himself, choosing to live rather than die for his country, and to reserve himself even at the end of *Ulysses* because he has not met a woman like Gretta Conroy or Nora Barnacle on 16 June.

Woolf explores yet another part of the problems caused by caring for victims, another way in which a comprehension which ought to compel us to end violence forever is hijacked by violence. Woolf inherits from the feminism of her time the recognition that men make it impossible for women to write and think—they are the victims of patriarchy. She is always willing to bring men to justice for what they have done, but she realizes as well that such a hypothesis can not account for her own power—how did a patriarchy make a Virginia? And even if it was primarily women who mothered Virginia, how were they possible in even worse social conditions?

Further, she struggles with perhaps the last vestigial form of scapegoating—endlessly accusing others of scapegoating. She recognizes the primary difficulty of feminism, which must employ this accusatory mode to achieve justice in a judicial system, but which also imprisons the mind in resentment, keeps it away from the freedom to think of things in themselves. The finest moment in *A Room of One's Own* is when Woolf releases herself from retributive anger.

Woolf's fictions make public the kinds of ordinary women who made her possible. Thus her position is at once prefeminist, to show how feminism became a possibility, and postfeminist, demonstrating what free thinking would look like, beyond the necessary securing of rights in a judicial system, where one must accuse the accusers. *To the Lighthouse* is the supreme achievement, showing as well how a Virginia could descend from the father as well as the mothers. "The time has come for us to forgive one another. If we wait any longer there will not be time enough" (Girard, *The Scapegoat* 212). Forgiveness as we normally understand it requires a prior arraignment, but Woolf magnificently gives us (somehow) the place beyond forgiveness.[3]

We have used the term *Judeo-Christian texts* throughout, to show the parallel scriptures of secular and sacred merging in the modern period. It is more than time to reread this tradition as Abrahamic, another term that has been hijacked away from its originary sense of ending human sacrifice. If we wait any longer, there will not be time enough.

Notes

Preface

1. In *Je vois Satan tomber comme l'éclair*, Girard redraws the mimetic hypothesis heading out from rather than to the Bible. In a chapter entitled "Théorie mimétique et théologie," in *Celui par qui le scandale arrive*, Girard moderates his thirty-year opposition between sacrificial and non- or postsacrificial readings of the Passion.

2. Tobin Siebers has usefully described this moment of "nuclear criticism" in *The Ethics of Criticism*, 220–40.

3. See also Johnsen, "The Treacherous Years of Postmodern Poetry in English"; "Textual/Sexual Politics in 'Leda and the Swan'"; "The Moment of *The American* in l'Écriture Judéo-Chrétienne"; "Madame Bovary: Romanticism, Modernism, and Bourgeois Style."

4. The most impressive example of attributing to a single source (Hegel) the modern interest in the primitive remains Johnston, *The Ibsen Cycle.*

Chapter 1. Myth, Ritual, and Modern Literature after Girard

1. See Frazer, *The Golden Bough.* Most pertinent to this discussion is *The Scapegoat* (1913). For Jane Harrison, see *Prolegomena to the Study of Greek Religion.* The second edition contains essays by Gilbert Murray and F. M. Cornford.

2. See "The Structural Study of Myth" in *Structural Anthropology.*

3. *Les structures élémentaires de la parenté.*

4. *Le totémisme aujourd'hui*, translated with symptomatic finality as simply *Totemism*, tr. Rodney Needham (Boston: Beacon Press, 1963).

5. See *The Origins and History of Consciousness* and *The Great Mother.*

6. See Edward Said, "The Totalitarianism of Mind."

7. Girard, *Mensonge romantique et vérité romanesque; Deceit, Desire, and the Novel* adds a few paragraphs in the beginning which use a structuralist idiom. But see his comment in the introduction, *To Double Business Bound* (p. xiv) on what Kenneth Burke called "terministic traces" in one's writing; these traces are the evidence of the author's and the targeted audience's reading, not necessarily their final commitments.

8. Girard, *La violence et le sacré; Violence and the Sacred.*

9. See Girard, "Interdividual Psychology," *Things Hidden since the Foundation of the World,* 283–431, but also *Job: The Victim of His People,* 111–23.

10. This book takes the position that one must follow the most comprehensive theory of the relation between myth, ritual, and literature. For an alternative approach that maps all mythographers without choosing between them, see Doty, *Mythography.* The choice being argued in this book isn't who (not) to read, but how to read them all. One ought to read *everything* by Freud, Gernet, Lévi-Strauss, Frye, Vernant, and Burkert *again,* from a mimetic hypothesis.

11. For Girard on Lévi-Strauss, see especially *Violence and the Sacred,* ch. 9. Pages 328–32 of *La violence et le sacré* were cut from what is now the first paragraph on p. 240 of *Violence and the Sacred.* See also chs. 8 and 9 in *To Double Business Bound.*

12. Freud, *Massenpsychologie und Ich-Analyse; The Standard Edition of the Complete Psychological Works of Sigmund Freud,* 19: 66.

13. Kofman, "The Narcissistic Woman: Freud and Girard"; Moi, "The Missing Mother: The Oedipal Rivalries of René Girard"; Jacobus, "Is There a Woman in This Text?" The reading of Girard in these essays is sacrificial: Girard is personally blamed for excluding women, instead of being credited for analyzing a system which excludes women. Girard is accused, as is Freud, of resenting the self-sufficiency of women. Further, Kofman even argues that Girard fears the female genitalia, which he will only refer to in Freud's German. Can the patriarchy be unmanned by a few demonstrative women clad in trenchcoats, lurking in the bushes of Lake Lagunita? A *real* dialogue between Girardian and feminist theory might take up the following issues: (1) Girard's theory comprehends the patriarchal dynamics that exclude (sacralize) women; (2) the mimetic theory denies patriarchal as well as matriarchal "essentialism," the autonomy of narcissism as well as coquetry; (3) Girard's commitment to the quasi-theoretical potential of literary texts might challenge the emerging orthodoxy of diagnosing as masochistic Virginia Woolf's unilateral renunciation of masculine violence, competition, even anger. *A Room of One's Own* (1929) insists (in ways that keep company with Girard step by step) that masculine violence is mimetic, metaphysical, contagious. Men dominate the world by crediting themselves with twice the being of women. Resentment alternates with veneration (see Girard's discussion of "cyclothymia" in *Violence and the Sacred*), which can provoke women's writing into doubling male competitive "hysteria," blocking the possibility of seeing things nonviolently, in themselves. See Rich, "When We Dead Awaken: Writing as Revision"; Showalter, *A Literature of Their Own: British Women Novelists from Brontë to Lessing;* Marcus, "Art and Anger." Despite playing an important part in the American renaissance of Woolf studies, these essays add themselves to the depressing tradition of diagnosticians who know better than Woolf herself the cause and cure of her illness. Each feels certain that it is unnatural to choke off the expression of women's anger, but perhaps we could finally try out Woolf's own hypothesis (seconded by Girard's): that being angry was like being

mad. In Hermione Lee's biography of Woolf (1996) we see the welcome returning of authority to Woolf herself.

14. For a careful approach to Girard following Kristeva's own acknowledged debt, see Reineke, *Sacrificing Lives,* esp. pp. 142–46.

15. See Graves, *Greek Myths.*

16. See especially Neumann, *The Origins and History of Consciousness* and *The Great Mother.* Neumann explains the sacred ambivalence of the feminine as "dynamic reversal," the point when a "good" feminine archetype mercurially turns against (the always masculine) consciousness. That is, in Neumann's scheme archetypes of the feminine are graded solely on how they serve or resist men.

17. See Said, *The World, the Text, and the Critic,* esp. ch. 8.

18. The work of Jean Michel Ourghourlian; see *Un mime nommé desir.* More recently, see the work of Henri Grivois in "Adolescence, Indifferentiation, and the Onset of Psychosis."

19. Burkert, *Homo Necans;* also see *Structure and History in Greek Mythology and Ritual; Greek Religion.*

20. See the papers from a 1983 conference in which both Girard and Burkert participated, in Hamerton-Kelly, ed., *Violent Origins.* For the first mimeticization of Burkert's hunting hypothesis, see McKenna, "Introduction," 5–6. McKenna's essay gives one an effective way of connecting the Girardian model to the work of Eric Gans. See Gans's alternative model of the mimetic hypothesis, beginning in *The Origin of Language,* 1981; *Originary Thinking,* 1993.

21. See Gernet, *The Anthropology of Ancient Greece;* Vernant and Vidal-Naquet, *Myth et tragédie en Grèce ancienne; Myth et tragédie en Grèce ancienne,* vol. 2; Detienne and Vernant, *Les ruses de l'intelligence.*

22. See Vernant, "Ambiguité et renversement," in *Mythe et tragédie en Grèce ancienne,* by Vernant and Vidal-Naquet (1972), 101–31.

23. See Girard, *Violence and the Sacred,* 234–36; *Things Hidden since the Foundation of the World,* 99–104.

24. See McKenna, *Violent Difference,* for a thorough reading of Derridean and Girardian difference.

25. See Lévi-Strauss, *Structural Anthropology,* 206–31.

26. See Goodhart, "Lēstas Ephaske," 13–41.

27. He introduced this term in interviews in the seventies. The fullest treatment is in *Things Hidden* and *The Scapegoat.*

28. See Dumouchel and Dupuy, *L'enfer des choses;* Livingston, ed., *Disorder and Order;* Dumouchel, ed., *Violence and Truth.* For a full bibliography of primary and secondary sources up to the moment of publication, see *Stanford French Review* 10:1–3 (1986). More recently, see the electronic archive on mimetic theory maintained by the Faculty of Catholic Theology, University of Innsbruck/Austria (http://theol.uibk.ac.at/mimdok/suche/index-en.html).

29. See Frye, *Anatomy of Criticism.*

30. See Lentricchia, *After the New Criticism,* 3–26.

31. To read the extensive community of all those who still read Frye, consult Robert Denham's fine *Northrop Frye: An Annotated Bibliography of Primary and Secondary Sources*, and two important collections of essays: Cook, Hošek, Macpherson, Parker, and Patrick, eds., *Centre and Labyrinth*, and Lee and Denham, eds., *The Legacy of Northrop Frye*.

32. See Frye, *The Educated Imagination*.

33. I have discussed this aspect of Frye's work in "The Sparagmos of Myth Is the Naked Lunch of Mode: Modern Literature as the Age of Frye and Borges."

34. See Williams, *The Long Revolution*.

35. See Derrida, *Dissemination*, 132.

36. For a discussion of the issue of Zeus's desire, see my "Textual/Sexual Politics in Yeats's 'Leda and the Swan.'"

37. Girard, "Introduction" to *To Double Business Bound*, vii–xvi.

38. If Girard has never written separately on *Nineteen Eighty-Four*, his comments on the modern totalitarian state in *Job* remain extremely useful. Girard has published on Shakespeare almost continuously over the seventies and eighties. These essays were ultimately incorporated into *Theatre of Envy*, which also contains new work on *King Lear* (pp. 179–83). For previous Girardian readings of *King Lear*, see Schehr, "King Lear: Monstrous Mimesis"; Hinchliffe, "The Error of King Lear."

39. Such a reading would of course be impossible without the mothering of feminist analysis: I have found the following essays particularly useful: Fischer-Homberger, "Hysterie und Misogynie—ein Aspekt der Hysteriegeschichte"; Gohlke, "'I Wooed Thee with My Sword': Shakespeare's Tragic Paradigms"; Kahn, "Excavating 'Those Dim Minoan Regions': Maternal Subtexts in Patriarchal Literature."

40. See Said, *The World, the Text, and the Critic*, 290–92.

41. Said, *Orientalism*, 23, 41; Said and Hitchens, eds., *Blaming the Victims*, 178. In *Culture and Imperialism* Said extended his attention to include the resistance to orientalism/imperialism in a new map of overlapping histories.

42. In a brilliant "note" on modernism in *Culture and Imperialism* (pp. 225–29), Said recuperates the limits he sets on Western literature (Jane Austen, Conrad) for criticizing imperialism in the first part of the book. After discussing the great texts of liberation in postcolonial cultures, he returns to metropolitan culture to suggest that liberationist groups within that culture take strength from the postcolonial cultures of resistance. Further, he suggests that irony in modern writing (and here Conrad is crucial) is the sign of the dislocation of commitment to imperialism. It will take a separate book to do Said justice, but irony towards imperialism in Conrad is the sign of the pressure of Judeo-Christian writing—sympathizing, however reluctantly, with the victim.

43. Orwell, *Nineteen Eighty-Four*, 45–46. Subsequent page references are to this edition, following the text in parentheses.

44. See especially Dumouchel and Dupuy, *L'enfer des choses*.

45. See my forthcoming article which plots out Girard's sharing of this term with Michel Serres: "*Freres amis,* Not Enemies: Serres between Prigogine and Girard."

46. Frye's admirably forthright term for the betrayal of the secular scripture.

Chapter 2. Pillars of a Self-Sacrificial Society

1. *Ibsen: Letters and Speeches,* 145.

2. Johnsen, "The Moment of *The American* in L'Écriture Judéo-Chrétienne."

3. At its best we have Fredric Jameson's prodigious converting of insights from one symbolic system to another, as in his conversion of Frye into St. Augustine in *The Political Unconscious* (1981). At its worst the usual translation of literature into theory.

4. Facing p. 445 in Meyer, *Ibsen.*

5. Daniel Haakonsen notes a beautiful example of Ibsen's awareness of expiation in the sagas in "Svanhild," an early draft for *Love's Comedy.* Falk mischievously reminds Svanhild that in the time of the *Volsungasaga,* "a victim [Svanhild] must suffer in order to appease the wrath of the gods" ("The Function of Sacrifice in Ibsen's Realistic Drama," 28). See also Byock, *Feud in the Icelandic Saga,* who reads the sagas as built of "feudemes," an idea which opens the sagas to Girard's model of conflictual mimesis. For a suggestive Girardian reading of the sagas, see Livingston, *Models of Desire,* 135–69. For a remarkable Girardian reading of Ibsen, see Mishler, "Sacrificial Nationalism in Henrik Ibsen's *The Pretenders.*"

6. As we see in the following chapter, Ibsen explores the press's role further in *En Folkefiende (An Enemy of the People),* a play closely related to this one. In our time, the site is television.

7. Rolf Fjelde's widely used translation, for example, gives "for the betterment of society." Fjelde, trans., *The Complete Major Prose Plays,* 16. *Støtte* means to support, and is the verbal form of the plural noun in the play's title, *Samfundets støtter.*

8. Clearly, Ibsen's mind is accumulating substance for his next play, *A Doll House.* There is an undercurrent of watching how women are the scapegoats of society in this play, from draft to the final version.

9. Ibsen, *Nutidsdramaer.* All quotations from Ibsen are from this edition. Page references will follow the quote in parentheses.

10. Ibsen, *The Collected Works of Henrik Ibsen,* vol. 6. All subsequent quotations in English are to this edition (unless noted otherwise); page references appear in parentheses at the end of the quote.

11. Bernick explains to Lona how the stories about Johan seem to have a life of their own:

Du kan vel forestille deg hvorledes alskens rykter sattes i omløp da han og du var borte. Dette var ikke hans første lettsindighet, ble der fortalt. Dorf hadde fått en stor sum penge av ham for å tie og reise sin vei, het det; andre påsto at *hun* hadde fått dem. På samme tid ble det ikke skjult at vårt hus hadde vanskelig for å oppfylle sine forpliktelser. Hva var rimeligere enn at

sladderhankene satte disse to rykter i forbindelse med hinannen? Da hun ble
her og levet i tarvelighet, så påsto man at han hadde tatt pengene med seg til
Amerika, og ryktet gjorde summen bestandig større og større. (43)

You can easily imagine that there were all sorts of rumours in the air after
you two had left. It was said that this was not his first misdemeanor. Some
said Dorf had received a large sum of money from him to hold his tongue and
keep out of the way; others declared she had got the money. At the same time
it got abroad that our house had difficulty in meeting its engagements. What
more natural than that the scandal-mongerers should put these two rumours
together? Then, as Madam Dorf remained here in unmistakable poverty,
people began to say that he had taken the money to America; and rumour
made the sum larger and larger every day. (337)

We have here a complementary pattern to the capacity for sagas to travel and combine, in the ease with which stories of dishonor seem to spawn themselves and consolidate around their victim. The sagas raise the hero up in admiration, while rumor
pulls him down in resentment. No one knows the vertiginous position of society's
"sacred" pillars better than Karsten Bernick.

12. Bjørnson's plays *The Editor* and *The Bankrupt* are often seen as provoking
this play. Bjørnson clearly must also have seen a relation between commerce and the
press; the composition date of the plays is very close. More importantly, we note
with greater understanding and appreciation the habit remarked on by Ibsen's biographers, that Ibsen's only reading seemed to be the newspapers and the Bible.

13. James Joyce quoted Lona's reply to Rørlund in order to raise the fur of the
school authorities in his drama essay.

14. There are several critics who discuss *Kindermord* as a romantic motif in Ibsen.
For a good overview, see Terry Otten, "Ibsen's Paradoxical Attitudes toward *Kindermord.*" See also Tobin Siebers's shrewd characterization of romanticism as inaugu-
rating the modern identification with victims in "Language, Violence, and the Sacred: A Polemical Survey of Critical Theories."

15. See James Joyce, *The Critical Writings of James Joyce,* 46.

16. In earlier drafts, it is clear that Bernick's business partners control influence
over private and public funds. See Ibsen, *The Oxford Ibsen,* 141.

17. Interestingly, Mrs. Holt told Mrs. Rummel that the whole community was in
an uproar over Johan ("hele byen naturligvis var oprørt over ham"). Both are aston-
ished that Lona Hessel joins her fate to Johan at just this moment, when the crowd
is unified against him.

18. Literally, rumor-mongering journalists, full of malice or spite. "Ond" is the
biblical word for evil: deliver us from evil, husbands and wives must share good and
evil alike. It seems to designate evil's reciprocity, its capacity to spread.

19. In *Violence and the Sacred,* Girard points to the relations outside national
boundaries, which also succumb to primitive reciprocity.

20. The words "svulmende feststemning" (52) literally mean surging or over-

flowing festival atmosphere. Rummel has a practical grasp of the immemorial technique of mobilization.

21. In an earlier draft, Bernick asks the crowd "Let him who is without sin cast the first stone" (*The Oxford Ibsen*, 193). The draft shows that Ibsen knows of the "things hidden since the foundation of the world." Perhaps he withdrew the allusion to keep Bernick's ability to defuse the mob modern, secular, and hypocritical. Yet it is also possible that Bernick knows better than Tomas Stockmann in *An Enemy of the People*, who infuriates the crowd by applying the example of Christ to his own case.

Chapter 3. Folkevenner og Folkefiender: Ibsen's Research in Modern Behavior

1. See Johnsen, "Madame Bovary: Romanticism, Modernism, and Bourgeois Style."

2. This project would begin with *Pharmacopoea Danica* (Hafniae, 1805), Ibsen's apothecary reference book in Grimstad.

3. Peter Watts, trans., *"Ghosts" and Other Plays*, by Henrik Ibsen (Harmondsworth: Penguin, 1964), 160.

4. Ibsen carefully prepares for this stage business by giving Tomas (solely in this episode) a hat and stick to put down as he enters the editor's office. It also adds to the appearance of symmetry/rivalry between the brothers.

5. Captain Horster, who allows Tomas to use his house to give the lecture when all other public venues are closed to him, is confronted by the owner of his ship at the end of the meeting. Described only as a fat man, who does not properly greet the women standing with the captain, he suavely asks him if he lends his house for the use of public enemies. When Captain Horster says that it is his own property to use as he wishes, the man says that he will do likewise. Afterwards Horster identifies him as Mr. Vik (the suffix which indicates village in Norwegian). But the next morning Horster reports that Mr. Vik is a nice man, who told him he would have liked to keep Horster, if he dared ("hvis bare torde"—208). Mr. Vik encapsulates the public behavior of the modern crowd that obeys both scapegoating and the imperative against scapegoating.

6. Ibsen described for Henrik Jaeger (his first biographer) his memories of the pillory which stood unused in the town square in Skien. Jaeger, *The Life of Henrik Ibsen*, 10.

7. The best example of rivalry calling the tune is Tomas's idea that Peter won't like it that he didn't make the discovery of pollution himself.

8. Watts, trans., *"Ghosts" and Other Plays*, 143.

9. At one point, they even descend to that signature of mimetic rivalry, mirroring the very language of each other's accusations:

THE MAYOR. . . . As Chairman of the Board of Management of the Baths, I should have thought that I. . . .

DR. STOCKMANN. And I should have thought that I. . . . (113)

10. For an early conjoining of the mimetic hypothesis with thermodynamics, see Michel Serres, *La naissance de la physique dans le texte de Lucrèce.*

11. See Chapter 2, note 21, above.

12. Like Ibsen, Joyce studied medicine but never completed the program. "General paralysis of the insane" is the turn of the century medical term for the tertiary stage of syphilis.

Chapter 4. Joyce's Sisters

The epigraphs for this chapter are from (1) *Selected Letters of James Joyce,* 22; (2) *Ulysses,* ed. Gabler, 521, 523; and (3) Woolf, *A Room of One's Own,* 49.

1. Staley, "A Beginning."

2. Kenner, *Dublin's Joyce;* Magalaner, *Time of Apprenticeship;* Fischer, "From Reliable to Unreliable Narrator," and *Bewusstseindarstellung im Werk von James Joyce,* 29–65; Walzl, "Joyce's 'The Sisters': A Development." For an extensive elaboration of the readings of Magalaner, Walzl, Scholes, and Staley on the revision of "The Sisters," recoded into Roland Barthes's scriptible/lisible distinction, see Morrissey, "Joyce's Revision of 'The Sisters.'"

3. O'Brien, *Ancestral Voices.*

4. According to Hans Walter Gabler's dating of the "Cornell" manuscript for the *James Joyce Archive (JJA* 4: xxix). Thus Gabler's dating requires the adjustment of all previous commentary relating "The Sisters" to "The Dead." "The Sisters" still magnificently anticipates "The Dead," but in the way it anticipates, as Fritz Senn has insisted, *Finnegans Wake:* as a portal of discovery. See Senn, "'He Was Too Scrupulous Always': Joyce's 'The Sisters.'"

5. Stanislaus Joyce, *My Brother's Keeper,* 90.

6. *Ibid.,* 124.

7. See James Joyce, *Dubliners,* 254.

8. *JJA* 7: 83 and 84, 104.

9. The image almost certainly comes from Tomas Stockmann. Even two early examples of Joyce's schoolboy prose seem to bait their sponsors. Joyce must have derived ironic satisfaction by paying back the pandybatting episode later described in *Portrait,* when in "Trust Not Appearances" he concluded that the eye betrays the character of a person ("See it in your eye"—*Ulysses* 561). "Force (the futility of)" was perhaps the matriculation-essay assigned to Joyce, but by the evidence of the surviving fragment, its working title ought to be "Subjugation," by which Joyce subversively affiliates the common discipline and consequences of being "subject" to priest and king.

10. Denson, *Printed Writings by George W. Russell (A.E.): A Bibliography,* makes it clear that Æ's *New Songs,* the anthology "Stephen" is excluded from, was published in March 1904, and selections finalized perhaps as early as the date of Russell's preface, December 1903. Denson also notes that *New Songs* was reviewed by Gogarty in *Dana's* first issue; a reading of Gogarty's review suggests an uncertain compromise between puffery and satire, the Yeats and the Joyce touch.

11. In any case, Declan Kiberd's note in his edition of *Ulysses,* that "The young Joyce was so ashamed of the fact that his first story was published in 'the pig's paper' *The Irish Homestead* that he adopted the pen-name 'Stephen Dædalus' to conceal the embarrassing connection" (956) cannot account for Joyce's insistence on associating himself in manuscript and letters with this pseudonym.

12. *Dubliners* 2. On an ACLS Travel Grant in 1984 I discovered the "Berkeley Campbell" story for myself, reading the *Irish Homestead* in the Newspaper Library of the British Library on Colindale Road. I made the identification of "The Old Watchman" in a paper given at the Tenth International Joyce Symposium in Copenhagen, 1986, and included it in "Joyce's Many Sisters and the Demodernisation of *Dubliners,*" in *New Perspectives on Dubliners,* ed. Mary Power and Ulrich Schneider (Amsterdam: Rodopi, 1997). My essay was submitted in 1993, before I saw Gabler's edition, but it is a welcome corroboration by an exemplary specialist in the genetic approach to Joyce.

13. Atkinson's *Dictionary of Literary Pseudonyms* (173) lists "Berkeley Campbell" as the pseudonym of Charles Lionel Duddington, but Duddington's dates make this impossible.

14. See Walzl and Weisbrun, "Paresis and the Priest." There are also the "investigations" of J. B. Lyons, *Thrust Syphilis Down to Hell and Other Rejoyceana,* esp. 21–96, and Kathleen Ferris, *James Joyce and the Burden of Disease.*

15. See Bowen, "Joyce's Prophylactic Paralysis." Also Carens, "Some Points on Poynts and Related Matters."

16. Epstein, "Hidden Imagery in James Joyce's 'Two Gallants,'" 369–70.

17. See Walzl and Weisbrun, "Paresis and the Priest."

18. James Joyce, "Oscar Wilde: Il poeta di «Salomè», *Il Piccolo della Sera,* 24 marzo 1909; rpt. in *Scritti italiani/James Joyce,* by Joyce, 60–66.

19. The translation in *The Critical Writings of James Joyce,* ed. Ellsworth Mason and Richard Ellmann, omits "infedeli" (unfaithful) and mistranslates "incapaci di aderirvi" as "unable to yield to it" (173). The difference is, of course, that they yield often enough, but can't "stick it." *Critical Writings* elsewhere translates "aderire" literally as "adhere": "non aver potuto aderire scrupolosamente" (*SI* 132) is rendered "not having been able to adhere scrupulously" (*Critical Writings* 180). These mistakes have been set aright in the new Oxford edition of the critical writings.

Chapter 5. To Live, Not Die, for His Country: Stephen D(a)edalus and Ireland's Future

The epigraphs for this chapter are from Bakounine 67; Joyce, *Stephen Hero,* 250; Joyce, *A Portrait of the Artist as a Young Man,* 220; Girard, *Things Hidden,* 183; and a statement by Tom Paulin made at Leeds University in 1982.

1. For a full discussion of Joyce's reflection on *Dubliners* as satire, see my "Joyce's *Dubliners* and the Futility of Modernism."

2. See Brandabur, *A Scrupulous Meanness.*

3. Manganiello, *Joyce's Politics;* Reynolds, "Torn by Conflicting Doubts."

4. Now corrected in the new Oxford edition of Joyce's critical writings: *Occasional, Critical, and Political Writing*, ed. Kevin Barry.

5. See Gabler, "The Seven Lost Years."

6. Hans Walter Gabler, preface to *JJA* 4: xxvii.

7. Renan, *The Life of Jesus*, 257.

8. "Aspersion," the closest word in English for "spargimento," is impossible because of the condemnatory and secular connotations which have developed alongside the ritual ones: "casting aspersions." Joyce's manuscripts contain several callow references to ritual aspersion, but mockery suggests the ulterior suspicion of a malevolent reality to be feared. Joyce adds to the end of chapter 20 of *Stephen Hero*: "If I told them there is no water in the font to symoblise that when Christ has washed us in blood we have no need of other aspersions" (*JJA* 8: 395). Fragment B, the brief episode once planned for the end of *Portrait* which contains Doherty, who is to become Mulligan in *Ulysses*, begins: "shed his blood for all men they have no need of other aspersion" (*JJA* 10: 1219).

But the most remarkable and revealing use of *aspergere* occurs in the Trieste Notebook in an early entry under the heading "Giorgino" (his only son, named after his brother who died): "I held him in the sea at the bath of Fontana and felt with humble love the trembling of his frail shoulders: *Asperge[s] me, Domine, hyssopo et mundabor: lavabis me et super nivem dealbalor.* Before he was born I had no fear of fortune" (*The Workshop of Dædalus*, 99). This touching entry expresses the spirit of *Portrait* and anticipates my conclusion, that the Abrahamic tradition assures us that our Father does not wish our children to be sacrificed.

9. In the phantasmagoria of the Circe chapter of *Ulysses*, it seems that Spenser is to blame for this all-too-Irish history.

It rains dragon's teeth. Armed heroes spring up from furrows. They exchange in amity the pass of knights of the red cross and fight duels with cavalry sabres: Wolfe Tone against Henry Grattan, Smith O'Brien against Daniel O'Connell, Michael Davitt against Isaac Butt, Justin McCarthy against Parnell, Arthur Griffith against John Redmond, John O'Leary against Lear O'Johnny, Lord Edward Fitzgerald against Gerald Fitzedward, The O'Donoghue of the Glens against The Glens of The Donoghue. (*Ulysses* 695)

Irish history becomes farce as it moves from potential allies who find themselves locked in mimetic rivalry, to beings who seem exclusively born of and for rivalry.

10. See *Stephen Hero*: "In spite of his surroundings Stephen continued his labours of research and all the more ardently since he imagined they had been put under ban" (39). In the manuscript, "put under ban" is underlined in crayon (*JJA* 8: 105).

11. Girard, *Violence and the Sacred*, 188–89.

12. See *JJA* 8: 497, where this sentence is marked in the margin by a perpendicular line in crayon.

13. Henke and Unkeless, eds., *Women in Joyce*.

14. "[I]n order to further identify himself with his hero, he announced his inten-

tion of appending to the end of the novel the signature, *Stephanus Dædalus Pinxit.*" Stanislaus Joyce, *My Brother's Keeper*, 244.

15. Bradley, *James Joyce's Schooldays*, 129.

16. *The Complete Dublin Diary*, 12.

17. *Life of Jesus*, 82.

18. In "Ecce Puer," we can see the tears in Joyce's eyes. Stephen Joyce read the ending of "The Dead" in 1986 at Copenhagen with tears in his eyes.

19. I owe this insight to Edward Brandabur.

20. inter opus monitusque genae maduere seniles
et patriae tremuere manus; dedit oscula nato
non iterum repetenda. (*Metamorphoses*, VIII, 210–12)

21. "The Seven Lost Years," 26–28.

22. *Dublin's Joyce*, 131.

23. *The Rhetoric of Fiction*, 323–36; see also Scholes, "Stephen Dedalus, Poet or Esthete?"; Peterson, "Stephen and the Narrative of *A Portrait of the Artist as a Young Man.*"

24. J. F. Byrne sent Joyce a letter in bog Latin dated 19 August 1904, in which he said he couldn't lend Joyce the pound he had requested.

Miro cur habes satirizatum amicos vestros, num pecunia eorum defuit? . . .
Fleo quod non habeo pecuniam, sed impossibile est ex petro trahere lactam,
aut ab ille qui summis in locis terrae nudus vivet, arripere quod non habet
super crures ejus. Sum, sicut dicunt populi, vester S. S. Joannes. (*Letters* 2: 47)

Ellmann identifies the satire as "The Holy Office," but it is particularly interesting that Byrne blames the "populace" for naming him Joyce's precursor, suggesting that this symbolism is public mockery.

Chapter 6. Finding the Father: Virginia Woolf, Feminism, and Modernism

1. Caramagno, *Flight of the Mind*, 140.

2. Bell, *Virginia Woolf*, 55.

3. Woolf's earliest writing, according to Quentin Bell, was for the *Hyde Park Gazette*, a handwritten newspaper which dealt with family events at 22 Hyde Park Gate. One can also derive Woolf's understanding of class from the changing intimacy of a family with its servants, over her lifetime.

4. *Three Guineas*, 66.

5. For an interesting conjunction of a theoretical and a literary text, see Scholes, *In Search of James Joyce*, 174–77.

6. For Woolf, fiction is the exemplary means for understanding how someone like Clarissa Dalloway, across class and gender lines, understands Septimus Smith.

7. This is what the collected essays are good for, beyond annotating what Woolf read, while she was writing other things.

8. Andrew McNeillie, in his useful notes for *The Essays of Virginia Woolf*, vol. 3 (1919–1924), p. xv, has identified this phrase as recalling G. E. Moore's *Principia Ethica*, but I don't think Moore or his apostles could have made it common.

9. See Watkins, *Worktime*. Watkins's argument for the possibility of oppositional criticism in English departments, despite what global analyses of institutional behavior like Foucault's imagine as possible, is all the more likely in fiction-making itself.

10. In particular, see the work of Jane Marcus: *Virginia Woolf and the Languages of Patriarchy* and *Art and Anger*.

11. See Strachey, *The Cause*, which Woolf refers to, where Strachey notes that women planning a meeting in a public hall didn't have the experience to estimate the carrying power of a woman's voice.

12. "When you asked me to speak about women and fiction I sat down on the banks of a river and began to wonder what the words meant. They might mean simply a few remarks about Fanny Burney; a few more about Jane Austen; a tribute to the Brontës and a sketch of Haworth Parsonage under snow; some witticisms if possible about Miss Mitford; a respectful allusion to George Eliot; a reference to Mrs. Gaskell and one would have done" (3).

13. Hogarth Press published James Strachey's definitive English edition of Freud; it is not impossible that Woolf read it letter by letter, setting type as a distraction from her own work. Also, Adrian Stephen by this time was already steeped in psychological theory.

14. Marcus, *Art and Anger*.

15. There is no reason for believing that Clarissa Dalloway's confusion about Armenians or Albanians represents what Virginia Woolf knew about *her* husband's work. For the distinction between judicial and international, see *Violence and the Sacred*.

16. Joyce's beautiful deadpan comment on relations between England and Ireland, rhyming here with both Woolf and Conrad, appears, as noted in Chapter 5, in "Ireland, Island of Saints and Sages" (*CW* 154).

17. It occurs only as a man's accusation against Rebecca West as an "arrant feminist" (*A Room* 35).

18. Woolf respected George Gissing for what this recognition cost him. See "The Private Papers of Henry Ryecroft," in *Essays of Virginia Woolf*, vol. 1, p. 133.

19. See Girard, *Theatre of Envy*.

20. See especially the way she mocks narrative privileges by characterizing them as the movements of a peeping tom.

21. Quoted in Bell, *Virginia Woolf*, vol. 2, 69.

22. See Watkins, *Critical Act*.

23. *Letters of Virginia Woolf*, 572.

24. "When in late October [1928] Virginia went to Cambridge and gave her lectures at Newnham and Girton there was, as Vanessa remembered, an atmosphere of triumph—a kind of ovation; Maynard Keynes came up with what seemed to her unnecessary *empressement*, saying, 'Well there can be no doubt who is the famous sister now.'" Bell, *Virginia Woolf*, 140.

25. *Diary of Virginia Woolf*, 208.

26. Similarly, at the ending of *Sons and Lovers* Paul finally recognizes that Gertrude Morel is dead, and her son, Paul, is alive.

27. "Yes, of course" was added after the "Original Holograph Draft," perhaps to point one's attention to what James must have asked his mother; see *To the Lighthouse: The Original Holograph Draft*, p. 37 (manuscript page 4).

28. The French translation is unable to deliver this excited chatter of mother and child: "Il faudra levrait avec . . ." *La promenade au phare*, 15.

29. James brandishes a blade threateningly in opposition to his father's; later, he is seen sitting "impotently" between his mother's knees, holding a pair of scissors, his blades bracketed like Oedipus's feet. Finally, in a gem of literary deadpan, James looks at the lighthouse (which has received endless Freudian interpretation, as Woolf knew it would) in Part 3 and realizes that the lighthouse need not mean one thing only. Freud offers the appropriate background music to the flawed relations between Mr. Ramsay and his family. If Woolf could have provided a soundtrack to the novel, she would no doubt have chosen Wagner.

30. Marcus, *Virginia Woolf and the Languages of Patriarchy*.

31. It *is* a great accomplishment, for Mrs. Ramsay thinks that her private image of her consciousness, a wedge-shaped core of darkness, is invisible to others.

32. Marcus, *Virginia Woolf and the Languages of Patriarchy*.

Conclusion

1. "And, as some of those who write about me are still asserting that I ignore the social reference of literary criticism, the sub-title calls the attention of those who read me to the fact that I have written about practically nothing else." Frye, *Stubborn Structure*, x.

2. Their work remarkably anticipates Gianni Vattimo's analysis of the weakening in Being according to Heidegger as *pensiero debole*; see especially Vattimo, *Belief* (1999), and Derrida and Vattimo, eds., *Religion* (1998).

3. See Derrida, *On Cosmopolitanism and Forgiveness* (2001).

Works Cited

Anderson, C. G. "The Sacrificial Butter." *Accent* 12 (winter 1952): 3–13.

Atkinson, Frank. *Dictionary of Literary Pseudonyms.* London: Clive Bingley, 1982.

Bakounine, Michel. *Dieu et l'État.* Geneva: Imprimerie Jurassienne, 1882.

Bell, Quentin. *Virginia Woolf.* New York: Harcourt Brace Jovanovich, 1972.

Bly, Robert. *Selected Poems.* New York: Harper and Row, 1986.

Booth, Wayne. *The Rhetoric of Fiction.* Chicago: University of Chicago Press, 1961.

Bowen, Zack. "Joyce's Prophylactic Paralysis: Exposure in *Dubliners.*" *James Joyce Quarterly* 19, no. 3 (spring 1982): 257–73.

Bradley, Bruce. *James Joyce's Schooldays.* New York: St. Martin's Press, 1982.

Brandabur, Edward. *A Scrupulous Meanness.* Urbana: University of Illinois Press, 1971.

Burkert, Walter. *Greek Religion.* Cambridge: Harvard University Press, 1985.

———. *Homo Necans.* Berkeley: University of California Press, 1983.

———. *Structure and History in Greek Mythology and Ritual.* Berkeley: University of California Press, 1979.

Byock, Jesse. *Feud in the Icelandic Saga.* Berkeley: University of California Press, 1982.

Campbell, Berkeley. "The Old Watchman." *Irish Homestead* 10 (July 2, 1904): 554–57.

Caramagno, Thomas C. *The Flight of the Mind.* Berkeley: University of California Press, 1992.

Carens, James F. "Some Points on Poynts and Related Matters." *James Joyce Quarterly* 16 (spring 1979): 344–46.

Cook, Eleanor, Chaviva Hošek, Jay Macpherson, Patricia Parker, and Julian Patrick, eds. *Centre and Labyrinth.* Toronto: University of Toronto Press, 1983.

Denham, Robert. *Northrop Frye: An Annotated Bibliography of Primary and Secondary Sources.* Toronto: University of Toronto Press, 1987.

Denson, Alan. *Printed Writings by George W. Russell (A.E.): A Bibliography.* Evanston: Northwestern University Press, 1961.

Derrida, Jacques. *Dissemination.* Trans. Barbara Johnson. Chicago: University of Chicago Press, 1981.

————. *On Cosmopolitanism and Forgiveness*. Trans. Mark Dooley and Michael Hughes. New York: Routledge, 2001.

Derrida, Jacques, and Gianni Vattimo, eds. *Religion*. Stanford: Stanford University Press, 1998.

Detienne, Marcel, and Jean-Pierre Vernant. *Les ruses de l'intelligence*. Paris: Flammarion, 1974.

Doty, William G. *Mythography*. University: University of Alabama Press, 1986.

Dumouchel, Paul, ed. *Violence and Truth: On the Work of René Girard*. Stanford: Stanford University Press, 1988.

Dumouchel, Paul, and Jean Pierre Dupuy. *L'enfer des choses: René Girard et la logique de l'economie*. Paris: Grasset, 1982.

Ellmann, Richard. *James Joyce*. New and rev. ed. New York: Oxford University Press, 1982.

Epstein, Edmund L. "Hidden Imagery in James Joyce's 'Two Gallants.'" *James Joyce Quarterly* 7 (summer 1970): 369–70.

Ferris, Kathleen. *James Joyce and the Burden of Disease*. Lexington: University of Kentucky Press, 1995.

Fischer, Therese. *Bewusstseindarstellung im Werk von James Joyce von Dubliners zu Ulysses*. Frankfurt: Athenäum Verlag, 1973.

————. "From Reliable to Unreliable Narrator: Rhetorical Changes in Joyce's 'The Sisters.'" *James Joyce Quarterly* 9 (fall 1971): 85–92.

Fischer-Homberger, Esther. "Hysterie und Misogynie—ein Aspekt der Hysteriegeschichte." *Gesnerus* 26, nos. 1–2 (1969): 117–27.

Fjelde, Rolf, trans. *The Complete Major Prose Plays*, by Henrik Ibsen. New York: Farrar Straus Giroux, 1978.

Frazer, James George. *The Golden Bough*. 12 vols. London: Macmillan, 1911–15.

Freud, Sigmund. *Das Ich und das Es*. Leipzig: Internationaler Psychoanalytischer Verlag, 1923.

————. *Massenpsychologie und Ich-Analyse*. Leipzig: Internationaler Psychoanalytischer Verlag, 1921.

————. *The Standard Edition of the Complete Psychological Works of Sigmund Freud*. Trans. James Strachey. Vol. 19. London: Hogarth Press, 1961.

Frye, Northrop. *Anatomy of Criticism*. Princeton: Princeton University Press, 1957.

————. *The Educated Imagination*. Bloomington: Indiana University Press, 1964.

————. *The Stubborn Structure: Essays on Criticism and Society*. Ithaca, N.Y.: Cornell University Press, 1970.

Gabler, Hans Walter. "The Seven Lost Years of *A Portrait of the Artist as a Young Man*." In *Approaches to Joyce's Portrait*, ed. Thomas F. Staley and Bernard Benstock, 25–60. Pittsburgh: University of Pittsburgh Press, 1976.

Gans, Eric. *The Origin of Language: A Formal Theory of Representation*. Berkeley: University of California Press, 1981.

————. *Originary Thinking: Elements of Generative Anthropology*. Stanford: Stanford University Press, 1993.

Gernet, Louis. *The Anthropology of Ancient Greece*. Trans. John Hamilton and Blaine Nagy. Baltimore: Johns Hopkins University Press, 1981.

Girard, René. *Celui par qui le scandale arrive*. Paris: Desclée de Brouwer, 2001.

————. *Deceit, Desire, and the Novel*. Baltimore: Johns Hopkins University Press, 1965.

————. *Je vois Satan tomber comme l'éclair*. Paris: Grasset, 1999.

————. *Job: The Victim of His People*. Stanford: Stanford University Press, 1988.

————. *La violence et le sacré*. Paris: Bernard Grasset, 1972.

————. *Le bouc émissaire* [The scapegoat]. Paris: Bernard Grasset, 1982.

————. *Mensonge romantique et vérité romanesque*. Paris: Bernard Grasset, 1961.

————. *Theatre of Envy*. Stanford: Stanford University Press, 1992.

————. *Things Hidden since the Foundation of the World*. Stanford: Stanford University Press, 1987.

————. *To Double Business Bound*. Baltimore: Johns Hopkins University Press, 1978.

————. *Violence and the Sacred*. Trans. Yvonne Freccero. Baltimore: Johns Hopkins University Press, 1977.

Gohlke, Madelon. "'I Wooed Thee with My Sword': Shakespeare's Tragic Paradigms." In *Representing Shakespeare: New Psychoanalytic Essays*, ed. Murray M. Schwartz and Coppélia Kahn, 170–87. Baltimore: Johns Hopkins University Press, 1980.

Goodhart, Sandor. "Lēstas Ephaske: Oedipus and Laius's Many Murderers." In *Sacrificing Commentary: Reading the End of Literature*, 13–41. Baltimore: Johns Hopkins University Press, 1996.

Graves, Robert. *Greek Myths*. Harmondsworth, England: Penguin Books, 1972.

Grivois, Henri. "Adolescence, Indifferentiation, and the Onset of Psychosis." Trans. William A. Johnsen. *Contagion* 6 (spring 1999): 104–21.

Haakonsen, Donald. "The Function of Sacrifice in Ibsen's Realistic Drama." *Ibsen Yearbook* 8 (1965–66): 20–40.

Hamerton-Kelly, Robert, ed. *Violent Origins*. Stanford: Stanford University Press, 1987.

Harrison, Jane. *Prolegomena to the Study of Greek Religion*. London: Cambridge University Press, 1927.

Henke, Suzette, and Elaine Unkeless, eds. *Women in Joyce*. Urbana: University of Illinois Press, 1982.

Hinchliffe, Michael. "The Error of King Lear." In *Actes du centre aixois de Recherches Anglaises*. Aix: Université de Provence, 1980.

Ibsen, Henrik. *The Collected Works of Henrik Ibsen*. Vol. 6. Ed. and trans. William Archer. New York: Charles Scribner's Sons, 1906.

————. *Ibsen: Letters and Speeches*. Ed. Evert Sprinchorn. New York: Hill and Wang, 1964.

———. *Nutidsdramaer*. Oslo: Gyldendal Norsk Forlag, 1989.

———. *The Oxford Ibsen*. Vol. 5. Ed. and trans. James Walter McFarlane. London: Oxford University Press, 1961.

Jacobus, Mary. "Is There a Woman in This Text?" *New Literary History* 14 (autumn 1982): 117–41.

Jaeger, Henrik. *The Life of Henrik Ibsen*. Trans. Clara Bell. London: William Heineman, 1890.

Johnsen, William A. "*Freres amis*, Not Enemies: Serres between Prigogine and Girard." In *Mapping Michel Serres*, ed. Steven Connor and Niran Abbas. Ann Arbor: University of Michigan Press, 2004.

———. "Joyce's *Dubliners* and the Futility of Modernism." In *James Joyce and Modern Literature*, ed. W. J. McCormack and Alistair Stead, 5–22. London: Routledge and Kegan Paul, 1982.

———. "Madame Bovary: Romanticism, Modernism, and Bourgeois Style," *MLN* 94 (1979): 843–49.

———. "The Moment of *The American* in l'Écriture Judéo-Chrétienne." *Henry James Review* 10, no. 3 (spring 1984): 216–20.

———. "The Sparagmos of Myth Is the Naked Lunch of Mode: Modern Literature as the Age of Frye and Borges." *boundary 2*, 8 (fall 1980): 297–311.

———. "Textual/Sexual Politics in 'Leda and the Swan.'" In *Yeats and Postmodernism: Contemporary Essays in Criticism*, ed. Leonard Orr, 80–89. Syracuse, N.Y.: Syracuse University Press, 1991.

———. "The Treacherous Years of Postmodern Poetry in English." In *Forked Tongues: Comparing Twentieth-Century British and American Literature*, ed. Anna Massa and Alistair Stead, 75–91. London: Longman, 1994.

Johnston, Brian. *The Ibsen Cycle*. University Park: Pennsylvania State University Press, 1992.

Joyce, James. *The Critical Writings of James Joyce*. Ed. Ellsworth Mason and Richard Ellmann. New York: Viking, 1959.

———. *The James Joyce Archive*. Ed. Michael Groden et al. 63 vols. New York: Garland Publishing, 1977–79.

———. *Dubliners*. Ed. Robert Scholes and A. Walton Litz. New York: Viking, 1969.

———. *Letters of James Joyce*. Ed. Stuart Gilbert. New York: Viking, 1957.

———. *Letters of James Joyce, II*. Ed. Richard Ellmann. New York: Viking, 1966.

———. *Occasional, Critical and Political Writing*. Ed. Kevin Barry. Oxford: Oxford University Press, 2000.

———. *A Portrait of the Artist as a Young Man: Text, Criticism, and Notes*. Ed. Chester G. Anderson. New York: Viking, 1968.

———. *Scritti italiani/James Joyce*. Ed. Gianfranco Corsini and Giorgio Melchiori. Milan: Arnoldo Mondadori, 1979.

———. *Selected Letters of James Joyce*. Ed. Richard Ellmann. New York: Viking, 1975.

———. *Stephen Hero*. New York: New Directions, 1963.

————. *Ulysses: A Critical and Synoptic Edition.* Ed. Hans Walter Gabler. New York: Garland, 1984.

————. *Ulysses.* Ed. Declan Kiberd. London: Penguin Books, 1992.

Joyce, Stanislaus. *The Complete Dublin Diary of Stanislaus Joyce.* Dún Laoghaire, Ireland: Anna Livia Press, 1994.

————. *My Brother's Keeper.* New York: Viking, 1958.

Kahn, Coppélia. "Excavating 'Those Dim Minoan Regions': Maternal Subtexts in Patriarchal Literature." *Diacritics* 12 (1982): 32–41.

Kenner, Hugh. *Dublin's Joyce.* Bloomington: Indiana University Press, 1956.

Kofman, Sarah. "The Narcissistic Woman: Freud and Girard." *Diacritics* 10 (September 1980): 36–45.

Lee, Alvin A., and Robert D. Denham, eds. *The Legacy of Northrop Frye.* Toronto: University of Toronto Press, 1994.

Lentricchia, Frank. *After the New Criticism.* Chicago: University of Chicago Press, 1980.

Lévi-Strauss, Claude. *Le totémisme aujourd'hui.* Paris: Presses universitaires de France, 1962.

————. *Les structures élémentaires de la parenté.* Paris: Presses universitaires de France, 1949.

————. *Structural Anthropology.* Trans. Claire Jacobson and Brooks Grundfest Schoepf. New York: Basic Books, 1963.

Livingston, Paisley, ed. *Disorder and Order: Proceedings of the Stanford International Symposium (Sept. 14–16, 1981).* Stanford Literature Studies (vol. 1). Saratoga, Calif.: Anma Libri, 1984.

————. *Models of Desire.* Baltimore: Johns Hopkins University Press, 1991.

Lyons, J. B. "Paresis and the Priest." *Annals of Internal Medicine* 80, no. 6 (1974): 758–62.

————. *Thrust Syphilis Down to Hell and Other Rejoyceana.* Dublin: Glendale Press, 1988.

Magalaner, Marvin. *Time of Apprenticeship: The Fiction of Young James Joyce.* New York: Abelard Schuman, 1959.

Manganiello, Dominic. *Joyce's Politics.* London: Routledge and Kegan Paul, 1980.

Marcus, Jane. "Art and Anger." *Feminist Studies* 4 (1978): 66–69.

————. *Art and Anger.* Columbus: Ohio State University Press, 1988.

————. *Virginia Woolf and the Languages of Patriarchy.* Bloomington: Indiana University Press, 1987.

Meyer, Michael. *Ibsen.* Garden City, N.Y.: Doubleday, 1971.

McKenna, Andrew. Introduction to *René Girard and Biblical Studies (Semeia 33),* 5–6. Decatur, Ga.: Scholars Press, 1985.

————. *Violent Difference.* Urbana: University of Illinois Press, 1992.

Mishler, William. "Sacrificial Nationalism in Henrik Ibsen's *The Pretenders.*" *Contagion* 1 (spring 1994): 127–38.

Moi, Toril. "The Missing Mother: The Oedipal Rivalries of René Girard." *Diacritics* 12 (summer 1982): 21–31.

Morrissey, L. J. "Joyce's Revision of 'The Sisters': From Epicleti to Modern Fiction." *James Joyce Quarterly* 24, no. 1 (fall 1986): 33–54.

Neumann, Erich. *The Great Mother.* Trans. Ralph Manheim. Princeton: Princeton University Press, 1972.

———. *The Origins and History of Consciousness.* Trans. Ralph Manheim. Princeton: Princeton University Press, 1970.

O'Brien, Conor Cruise. *Ancestral Voices.* Dublin: Poolbeg, 1994.

Orwell, George. *Nineteen Eighty-Four.* New York: New American Library, 1982.

Otten, Terry. "Ibsen's Paradoxical Attitudes toward *Kindermord.*" *Mosaic* 22/23 (summer 1989): 117–31.

Ourghourlian, Jean Michel. *Un mime nommé desir.* Paris: Bernard Grasset, 1982.

Peterson, Richard F. "Stephen and the Narrative of *A Portrait of the Artist as a Young Man.*" In *Work in Progress: Joyce Centenary Essays,* ed. Richard F. Peterson, Alan M. Cohn, and Edmund L. Epstein, 15–29. Carbondale: Southern Illinois University Press, 1983.

Reineke, Martha. *Sacrificing Lives.* Bloomington: Indiana University Press, 1997.

Renan, Ernst. *The Life of Jesus.* New York: Modern Library, 1927

Reynolds, Mary. "Torn by Conflicting Doubts: Joyce and Renan." *Renascence* 35, no. 2 (winter 1983): 96–118.

Rich, Adrienne. "When We Dead Awaken: Writing as Revision." *On Lies, Secrets, and Silence: Selected Prose, 1966–78.* New York: Norton, 1979.

Said, Edward W. *Culture and Imperialism.* London: Chatto and Windus, 1993.

———. *Orientalism.* New York: Pantheon, 1978.

———. "The Totalitarianism of Mind." *Kenyon Review* 29 (March 1967). 256–68.

———. *The World, the Text, and the Critic.* Cambridge: Harvard University Press, 1983.

Said, Edward W., and Christopher Hitchens, eds. *Blaming the Victims: Spurious Scholarship and the Palestinian Question.* London: Verso Books, 1988.

Schehr, Lawrence R. "King Lear: Monstrous Mimesis." *SubStance* 11, no. 3 (1982): 51–63.

Scholes, Robert. *In Search of James Joyce.* Urbana: University of Illinois Press, 1992.

———. "Stephen Dedalus, Poet or Esthete?" *PMLA* 89 (September 1964): 484–89.

Senn, Fritz. "'He Was Too Scrupulous Always': Joyce's 'The Sisters.'" *James Joyce Quarterly* 2, no. 2 (winter 1965): 66–72.

Serres, Michel. *La naissance de la physique dans le texte de Lucrèce: Fleuves et turbulence.* Paris: Les Éditions de Minuit, 1977.

Showalter, Elaine. *A Literature of Their Own: British Women Novelists from Brontë to Lessing.* Princeton: Princeton University Press, 1977.

Siebers, Tobin. *The Ethics of Criticism.* Ithaca, N.Y.: Cornell University Press, 1988.

———. "Language, Violence, and the Sacred: A Polemical Survey of Critical Theories." *Stanford French Review* 10, no. 3 (1986): 203–19.

Staley, Thomas. "A Beginning: Signification, Story, and Discourse in Joyce's 'The Sisters.'" *Genre* 12 (winter 1979): 533–49.

Strachey, Ray. *The Cause: A Short History of the Women's Movement in Great Britain.* London: Virago, 1978.

Vattimo, Gianni. *Belief.* Stanford: Stanford University Press, 1999.

Vernant, Jean-Pierre, and Pierre Vidal-Naquet. *Mythe et tragédie en Grèce ancienne.* Paris: François Maspero, 1972.

———. *Mythe et tragédie en Grèce ancienne.* Vol. 2. Paris: Éditions La Découverte, 1986.

Waisbrun, Burton A., and Florence L.Walzl. "Paresis and the Priest: James Joyce's Symbolic Use of Syphilis in 'The Sisters.'" *Annals of Internal Medicine 80* (June 1974), 756-62.

Walzl, Florence. "Joyce's 'The Sisters': A Development." *James Joyce Quarterly* 10, no. 4 (summer 1973): 375–421.

Watkins, Evan. *The Critical Act: Criticism and Community.* New Haven: Yale University Press, 1978.

———. *Work Time: English Departments and the Circulation of Cultural Value.* Stanford: Stanford University Press, 1989.

Williams, Raymond. *The Long Revolution.* London: Pelican Books, 1961.

Woolf, Virginia. *The Diary of Virginia Woolf.* Vol. 3 (1925–1930). Ed. Anne Olivier Bell. New York: Harcourt Brace Jovanovich, 1980.

———. *The Essays of Virginia Woolf.* Vol. 1 (1904–1912). Ed. Andrew McNeillie. San Diego: Harcourt Brace Jovanovich, 1986.

———. *The Essays of Virginia Woolf.* Vol. 3 (1919–1924). Ed. Andrew McNeillie. New York: Harcourt Brace Jovanovich, 1988.

———. *The Letters of Virginia Woolf.* Vol. 3 (1923–1928). Ed. Nigel Nicholson and Joanne Trautmann. New York: Harcourt Brace Jovanovich, 1978.

———. *La promenade au phare.* Trans. M. Lanoire. Paris: Editions Stock, 1968.

———. *Mrs. Dalloway.* New York: Harcourt, Brace, and World, 1955.

———. *A Room of One's Own.* New York: Harcourt, Brace, and World, 1957.

———. *Three Guineas.* New York: Harcourt, Brace, and World, 1966.

———. *To the Lighthouse.* New York: Harcourt, Brace, and World, 1955.

———. *To the Lighthouse: The Original Holograph Draft.* Ed. Susan Dick. London: Hogarth Press, 1983.

Index

Anathema, 11
Anderson, C.G., 107
Anthropology, 14
Archetype, 16
Aristotle, 12, 14

Bakounine, Michel, 84
Bell, Quentin, 109, 153n3, 154n4
Bell, Vanessa, 126. *See also* Woolf, Virginia (sister)
Benveniste, Emile, 13
Bible, vii–viii, 5, 17, 67; Gospels of, 81, 88, 103. *See also* scripture, secular
Bjørnson, Bjørnsterne, 148n12
Bly, Robert, "Finding the Father," 108
Booth, Wayne, 105
Bradley, Bruce J., 153n15
Brandabur, Edward, 153n19
Burkert, Walter, 5, 10, 14, 145
Byock, Jesse, 147n5

Cambridge Ritualists, 1
Campbell, Berkeley, "The Old Watchman," 73–74
Case, Janet, 138
Cornford, F.M. 1, 4
Caramagno, Thomas 109
Conrad, Joseph, *Heart of Darkness*, 116, 130
Cultic female figures, 9
Curran, C.P., 85

Dana, 72, 85
Davies, Margaret Llewelyn, 138
Deane, Conor, 94
Denson, Alan, 150n10

Detienne, Marcel, 8,11
Derrida, Jacques, 11, 13, 155n3
Dickinson, Violet 138
Dionysus, 17

Eglinton, John, 72
Ellmann, Richard, 85–87, 104

Feminism, 7, 109–12, 123, 138, 140
Ferris, Kathleen, 151n14
Fischer, Therese, 70
Fischer-Homberger, Esther, 146n39
Fjelde, Rolf, 147n7
Flaubert, Gustave, 41, 54, 131; *Madame Bovary*, 80, 98, 109, 128, 133
Frazer, Sir James, x, 1, 57, 143n1
Freud, Sigmund, 1, 6, 7–10, 12, 15, 80, 98, 109, 128, 133; father-identification, 7; identification, 6; incest, 8; Oedipus complex, 6; *Das Ich und das Es*, 7–10; *Massenpsychologie und Ich-Analyse*, 7–10, 15; *Totem and Taboo*, 10
Frye, Northrop, vii, viii, xii, 2, 5, 14–15, 59, 66, 139, 147n46; archetype, viii, 2; displacement, 15; fables of identity, 14, 139; identification, xii, 15; literature as a whole, vii–viii, xii, 18, 32, 139; mode, xii, 15–16; monomyth, 14; motive for metaphor, 15, 139; myth, xii, 14–15, 139; pharmakos, 14–16; secular scripture, 15; sparagmos, 14, 17; *Anatomy of Criticism*, vii–viii, 14–15, 139; *The Educated Imagination*, 15; *Fearful Symmetry*, viii; *The Great Code*, vii; *The Secular Scripture*, vii–viii; *Words with Power*, vii

Gabler, Hans Walter, 73, 75, 105, 150n4, 151n12
Gernet, Louis, 11, 13, 145n21
Girard, René, vii–33 passim, 34, 77, 81, 84, 88, 97, 105, 119, 139–140, 143n7, 144n9, 144n11, 145n27, 146n38; difference, 4–5, 10, 54; Freudian father, 6–9; hominiza-tion, 3, 5; Judeo-Christian writing, 5, 12, 17, 24, 32, 36, 133; judicial mechanism, ix–xi, 55, 92; kingship, ix; mimetic hy-pothesis, vii–viii, xii, 9, 18, 20, 24, 35–36, 46–48; model, 3, 9, 30, 77, 97, 100; myth, 3, 12, 139; narcissism, 3, 77, 97–98; onto-logical sickness, 16; pharmakos, 6; prohi-bition, 4, 6, 8–9, 11, 22; psychoanalysis, 9; reading of Freud, 6–10; reciprocity, 36, 81, 90–91; resentment, 35, 42; ritual, ix, xii, 3, 4, 6, 54, 139; rivalry, 4, 6–8, 22, 42, 54, 71, 77, 97; romantic/romanesque, 4; sa-cred, 22; sacrificial crisis, x, 54–55, 59, 92; sadism, 3; scapegoat, ix, xi, 6, 16, 18, 54, 139; scapegoat mechanism, xiii, 26, 31–32; stereotypes of persecution, xi, 19; texts of persecution, 13, 16; thematiza-tion, 18; unmediated desire, 2; victims, xi, xiii, 11, 17, 26, 139; *Celui par qui la scandale arrive*, vii–viii, 143n1; *Deceit, Desire and the Novel*, viii, 3, 16, 34, 42, 54, 77, 97, 98; *Je vois Satan tomber comme l'éclair*, vii–viii, 143n1; *The Scapegoat*, 145n27; *Theatre of Envy*, 55–56, 154n19; *Things Hidden Since the Foundation of the World*, 23–24, 81, 84; *Violence and the Sacred*, viii, 4–5, 8, 9–13, 54, 81, 98, 148n19, 154n15
Gohlke, Madeleine, 146n39
Goodhart, Sandor, 12
Gospels. *See* Bible
Graves, Robert, 8
Grivois, Henri, 145n18

Haakonsen, Daniel, 147n5
Harrison, Jane, 1, 143n1
Hinchliffe, Michael, 146n38

Ibsen, Henrik, x, xiii, 18, 34–67, 140–41; Lona Hessel, 78; media, 36–37, 44, 58;

sacrifice, 37, 47; sagas, 36; self-sacrifice, 37, 47–49, 53, 55; Nora Helmer, 78; *A Doll House*, 53; *Enemy of the People*, xiii, 55–67, 149n5, 150n9; *Pillars of Society*, xiii, 35–53, 147n1, 148n11, 149n11, 149n21; *The Wild Duck*, 53
Irish Homestead, The, 70, 76, 80, 100

Jacobus, Mary, 144n13
James, Henry, 41; Christopher Newman, 98; *The American*, 42; *Portrait of A Lady*, 78; "The Beast in the Jungle," 118
Jaeger, Henrik, 67, 149n6
Jameson, Fredric, 147n3
Johnsen, William, 143n3, 146n36
Johnston, Brian, 143n4
Joyce, James, x, xiii, 41, 42, 67–107, 117, 127, 140; betrayal in, 85–91; 94, 106–107; Stephen Dedalus, x, xiv, 100–7; "Araby," 77; "The Dead," 70, 77–83, 97; "Epiphanies," 71; *Finnegans Wake*, 86; "Ireland: Island of Saints and Sages," 89–91; "James Clarence Mangan," 92–96; "A Painful Case," 89; *A Portrait of the Artist As A Young Man*, 83, 84, 85, 100–7; *Scritti Italiani*, 89, 92; "Silhou-ettes," 70–71; "The Sisters," 70–77, 87;"The Shade of Parnell," 106; *Stephen Hero*, 72, 73, 83, 84, 98, 109, 152n8; *Ulysses*, 69, 72, 101, 107, 121, 152n9
Joyce, Stanislaus, 70–72, 76, 88; *Dublin Di-ary*, 72, 88; *My Brother's Keeper*, 152n14, 153n14
Jung, Carl, 14

Kenner, Hugh, 70, 104, 105, 107
Kenny, Louise, 73
Kiberd, Declan, 151n11
Kofman, Sarah, 144n13

Lawrence, D. H., 33, 127, 155n26
Lee, Hermione, 145n13
Lentricchia, Frank, *After the New Criticism*, 14
Lévi-Strauss, Claude, 1–2, 5–6, 12, 14, 143n4; *The Savage Mind*, 2
Livingston, Paisley, 147n5

Lukács, Gyorgi, 110
Lyons, J.B., 151n14

Magalaner, Marvin, 70
Manganiello, Dominic, 87
Mansfield, Katherine, 120
Marcus, Jane, 116, 134, 138, 144n13, 154n10
McKenna, Andrew, 145n20, 145n24
McNeillie, Andrew, 153n8
Mishler, William, 147n5
Milligan, Alice, 73
Modernism, vii–33, 35–36, 41, 54, 58, 70, 75, 93, 106, 118, 129, 138
Modernization, xii–xiii, 27, 34, 76–78, 106, 136, 138, 139
Moore, G. E., 153n8
Morrissey, L. J., 150n2
Murray, Gilbert, 1
Myth, vii–33, 56

Neumann, Erich, 1, 8, 143n5, 145n16
Norman, H. F., 73

O'Brien, Conor Cruise, Ancestral Voices, 70
Oedipus, 42
Orwell, George, xii, 14, 18, 24–31; double-think, 30; Nineteen Eighty-Four, 18
Otten, Terry, 148n14
Ourghourlian, Jean Michel, 145n18

Parnell, Charles Stewart, xiii, 67, 88, 100, 102, 106–7
Passion, The, 67, 80, 82, 86
Pater, Clara, 138
Patriarchy, 7, 109, 120, 133–34, 138, 140
Paulin, Tom, 83, 85, 151n
Persecution, 41, 53, 60–61, 64–65, 91, 105
Peterson, Richard, 153n23
Pharmakos, 8–14, 16; See also Frye, Northrop: pharmakos; Girard, René: pharmakos; scapegoat
Postmodernism, xii, 25, 93
Pound, Ezra, 104
Purgation, 56

Reineke, Martha, 145n14
Renan, Ernest, 87–89, 99

Reynolds, Mary, 87–88
Rich, Adrienne, 144n13
Richards, Grant, 75, 76, 86, 88
Rivalry, 38, 60, 62–63, 65, 77–78, 80, 82, 86, 90, 93, 95, 118, 119, 122, 126, 132, 138
Russell, George W. (AE), 72–73, 85, 150n10

Sacred, 29, 57, 90, 103, 133
Sacrifice, xiii, 37, 44–45, 47, 81, 89, 91, 107
Said, Edward, 2, 5, 9, 24–25, 146n42; critical elaboration, 29; secular criticism, 24; totalitarianism of mind, 2, worldliness, 28–29; Orientalism, 24
Sartre, Jean Paul, 2
Scapegoat, x, xiii, 12–18, 29, 39, 41, 55–56, 58, 82, 88, 94, 96, 117, 134; See also pharmakos; Frye, Northrop: pharmakos; Girard, René: pharmakos; scapegoat
Schehr, Lawrence, 146n38
Scholes, Robert, 153n5
Schmitz, Ettore (Italo Svevo), 104
Secular scripture, 15, 67. See also Bible
Self-sacrifice, 37, 57, 78, 80, 81, 91, 98
Senn, Fritz, 150n4
Serres, Michel, 147n45, 150n10
Shakespeare, William, xii, 18, 119; King Lear, 18–23, 49
Showalter, Elaine, 144n13
Siebers, Tobin, 143n2
Sophocles, 11–13
Staley, Thomas, 150n1
Stephen, Caroline, 138
Strachey, Ray, 154n11
Structural anthropology, 1
Structural linguistics, 1

Totemism, 1
Tragedy, 12
Tyrannos, 8, 11, 133
Vattimo, Gianni, 155n2
Vernant, Jean Pierre, 5, 11, 12, 145n21
Victim, 41, 46–47, 55–56, 64, 66, 81–82, 91, 93, 99–100, 102, 105
Vidal-Naquet, Pierre, 8, 11, 145n21
Violence, viii, xi–xiii, 5, 18, 23, 30, 33, 66, 90, 92, 133

Walzl, Florence, 70, 151n17
Watkins, Evan, 154n9
Wilde, Oscar, 67, 82, 96, 99, 105
Williams, Raymond, 16
Woolf, Virginia, x, xiv, 7, 41, 79, 108–138, 140; anger, 113–19, 130, 133, 141; instinct, 113; *Mrs. Dalloway*, 117, 121–26, 130; *Night and Day*, 120; *A Room of One's Own*, 69, 79, 108, 110–19, 131, 154n12; *Three Guineas*, 110, 116, 135; *To the Lighthouse*, 127–38, 155n27; *The Voyage Out*, 120

Yeats, W. B., 72, 75

Zeus, 17

William A. Johnsen, formerly associate chair for graduate studies and coordinator for undergraduate programs, is professor of English at Michigan State University. Since 2000 he has been a member of the Advisory Board of the Colloquium on Violence and Religion.